A BASKET *of* DEPLORABLES

What I Saw Inside the Clinton White House

LINDA TRIPP

with *Dennis Carstens*

Post Hill
PRESS

A POST HILL PRESS BOOK

A Basket of Deplorables:
What I Saw Inside the Clinton White House
© 2020 by Linda Tripp with Dennis Carstens
All Rights Reserved

ISBN: 978-1-64293-772-5
ISBN (eBook): 978-1-64293-773-2

This is a work of nonfiction. All people, locations, events, and situations are portrayed to the best of the author's memory.

Post Hill Press
New York • Nashville
posthillpress.com

Published in the United States of America
1 2 3 4 5 6 7 8 9 10

CONTENTS

Prologue by Linda Tripp. v
Impressions by Dennis Carstens x

Chapter 1: Intro to Linda 1
Chapter 2: The Bush White House 9
Chapter 3: Meet the Real Clintons 24
Chapter 4: The Main Clinton Scandals 45
Chapter 5: Whitewater. 47
Chapter 6: The Travel Office Massacre 51
Chapter 7: Filegate 58
Chapter 8: Hillary Clinton and Vince Foster 62
Chapter 9: Vince Foster's Death 72
Chapter 10: The Main Bill Clinton Sex Scandals. 91
Chapter 11: Kathy Shelton, Gennifer Flowers,
          and Marilyn Jo Jenkins 116
Chapter 12: Introduction to Monica Lewinsky. 121
Chapter 13: Monica in 1996. 129
Chapter 14: Monica and Andy Bleiler. 147
Chapter 15: Michael Isikoff: Part One, March 1997 154
Chapter 16: Isikoff: Part Two. 167
Chapter 17: Norma Asnes and the Attempted
          Seduction of Linda 181
Chapter 18: Office of the Independent Counsel 194

Epilogue by Dennis Carstens. 199
Linda's Last Word 202

In Memoriam

This book is dedicated to the memory of Linda Tripp Rausch. Her sudden, swift, and too-soon passing left a hole in the hearts of many. It was her enormous courage and love of country that led her to tell the truth about two of the most corrupt politicians in our nation's history. Knowing she would be vilified from coast to coast by the protectors and enablers of these two extremely flawed people, she held forth and did America a great service. A book dedication and simple thank-you hardly seem adequate.

Rest in peace, heroic soul.

PROLOGUE

by Linda Tripp

This writing journey began as a personal journal more than ten years ago, eighteen years after I first met Bill and Hillary Clinton and fourteen years after the hurricane that was "The Clinton-Lewinsky Scandal." As the years passed, it also became more difficult to ignore the aging process. As hurtful as the media portrayal of me was, I always thought one day I would have the courage to correct the record. That day was a nebulous "someday" and something I didn't have to think about "now."

But "now" had suddenly arrived, and I began to think I was running out of time to tell the story from the perspective of someone who had been there. Most of what has been told, and specifically what has been written, has been by those whose real agenda was to continue as Clinton loyalists, always providing yet more cover for them. These self-proclaimed journalists were not in the Clinton White House and have universally gotten it wrong.

Some say I am the most notorious woman of all time. I knew that my family, principally my grandchildren, deserved to learn the truth as I had lived it before it was too late. A journal seemed to be the best solution. So, several years ago, I began to write. That journey would be a long one, with twists and turns, starts and stops, but in the end, it resulted in this book.

My comfort zone had always involved burying things I wanted to forget. I was extraordinarily good at compartmentalizing unpleasant memories and putting them in boxes. Out of sight, out of mind. But that is selfish, because this story is not about me. It is not even about Monica Lewinsky. Not really. It is about two of the most corrupt political operatives to ever grace the international stage. It is a story that needs to be told.

Slowly, my reticence began to change. There were instances over time that began to prompt me to take my head out of the sand. There were the countless retrospectives of that time. All seemed superficial; all seemed lacking. It all felt wrong. The continuing shenanigans of the Clintons are reminiscent of that which had come so many years before, notably during Hillary's run for the White House. Twice. Except for a few op-eds, I hadn't warned anyone. Added to that, I found myself feeling guilty that I had never spoken up. But it was not just the civil servant side of me that felt guilty. The personal side was worse.

Several instances happened in quick succession that prompted me to begin writing. There was the time my nephew, then in high school, told me that his Aunt Deed—as he called me—had been a topic of discussion in his social studies class. His confusion about this and his questions bothered me. His father, my brother-in-law, would often joke: "When are you going to write that book so I can finally know what really went on?" And the worst was when my eldest granddaughter came home from school one day many years ago saying, "Omi, I didn't know you were famous. Were you a bad person?" I was at a loss for how to respond to this sweet six-year-old. She is now fourteen and deserves answers. And, not to sound too full of myself, so do the American people. History deserves perspective.

From the beginning, I had always had the full, unquestioned, and unwavering support of my amazing family and my closest friends. Yet during this ordeal, we never fully discussed what had happened, why it had happened, or why I had taken the extraordinary steps that I did. They simply stood by my side, knowing I would have done something so dramatic only for what I considered to be valid reasons. A part of me felt I owed this to them.

No one knew better than me the way I had been depicted in the media. And, as they say, the press drafts history; the books cement it for posterity. Often, truth is the accidental casualty.

And there were so many books—all written from an outsider's point of view, unfailingly from a political perspective, all by bystanders to history who chose to malign me as an avarice-driven political hack with a political agenda. My silence over those many years had allowed all of them—Jeffrey Toobin in *A Vast Conspiracy*, Michael Isikoff in *Uncovering Clinton*, and Sydney Blumenthal in *The Clinton Wars*, to name just a few—to define me. And in doing so, they framed the dialogue from their point of view while I stood silent.

These very same people had loudly and repeatedly accused me on national TV of being motivated by the desire to write a book. In that relatively new twenty-four-hour news cycle, it was a veritable cacophony, all asserting knowledgeably and in lockstep that I did what I had done motivated by greed. If you knew anything about me at that time, you would have thought from the repeated claims derisively alleging "it was all about a book deal" that I chose to turn the world upside down to sell books. Many of these same Clinton loyalists and protectors, within a year, wrote bestsellers. Apparently, the irony and hypocrisy were lost on them.

With all of this in mind, I began the laborious effort of writing a journal. One day, in the distant future, this would provide my family answers to all the questions, asked and unasked. They would finally have a level of understanding I had never provided before.

So, I wrote. And, as I revisited this painful time, I found myself bombarded with memories. Events long buried began to surface, and as I faced them all for the first time in so many years, I slowly began to realize that what I had lived, and what I had to say, was important.

My best friend, who lived this entire ordeal with me, had for decades encouraged me to write a book. It had never been an option. I told her of my decision to write the journal and, despite her urging, I assured her it would remain just that.

Slowly as my journal progressed, as I said, the memories flooded back. And once I found myself back in 1993, I couldn't stop. My journal began to look more and more like a book I would like to read. I did nothing about it, but it was at this point that my journal began to be far more detailed.

A book. Could I do this after all? I had the vague and unarticulated sense that this was meant to be. As always, my trepidation surfaced, knowing that the very facts, as melodramatic as they were, could be construed as unadulterated Clinton bashing. That so many years after the fact, everything would still be seen through a political lens. That what I wrote could be considered questionable or perceived as vindictive or vengeful, inadvertently giving credence to those who said all those years ago that my agenda was political. If so, the obvious question to put to my critics would be: "Why did she wait so long?"

I plodded on, knowing that the incendiary facts would be challenged simply because of who I am, but also knowing there were those who would believe what I had to say.

The actual writing served as a catharsis of sorts, but in the back of my mind I felt myself in the middle of a real-life push-pull. As the journal morphed into something much more, the old fears began to overtake me. Other than my best friend for more than thirty-five years, I told no one. If no one knew, it did not exist.

There was a selfish concern too. My dear husband and I had made a wonderful life for ourselves over the many previous years. We'd been together for twenty years. We cherished our simple lives, treasured our privacy and anonymity, made possible by the slow-paced area in which we chose to live. We were surrounded by our grandkids and our horse farm and the normalcy that a consistent low-profile life afforded us. We were richly blessed and knew it. I didn't want to do anything that might jeopardize our idyllic lives.

As I wrote my journal, now a bona fide manuscript, I was overcome by all the old fears. Fear of the bullying that would surely ensue, and fear for the physical safety of myself and my family. In looking for ways to justify the cowardly decision to abandon the whole thing, I rationalized that as politically radioactive as I had been, it was unlikely that any publishing house would touch me anyway. As is true in most of academia, publishing houses tend to be a part of the liberal establishment. I was the enemy.

As much as I believed mine was an important accounting of events back then, remaining silent seemed the wiser solution. After a great deal of pondering, I made my decision: I shelved the idea. The journal would be there for my family one day. A book would not.

Until now, ten years later. As with many small things in life, a seren- dipitous occurrence triggered a series of events that resulted in what you are reading today.

I had come to know an author whose work I admired greatly. His fast- paced works of fiction enthralled me. I was introduced to him through a dear friend. She convinced him to send me one book in particular. It is titled *Political Justice*, and I was captivated by it. I could not put it down. In fact, my interest was so piqued after reading *Political Justice*, I was prompted to read all the author's excellent legal mystery/courtroom dramas, leaving me much like his thousands of admirers, enthusiastically and eagerly awaiting the next book. The author is the very talented Dennis Carstens, who has written eleven great works of fiction, and he encour- aged me to write this book. He thought it was an important historical work that needed to be told, and he showed me how to do it.

Self-publishing had never occurred to me. But when it did, all at once everything seemed possible. A liberating sense of freedom followed. I would no longer be beholden to those who would silence me. My voice would finally be heard. I would not need the services of publishers whose disinterest I felt was guaranteed. And my lingering fears, while never completely gone, at least took a backseat to the euphoria of being able to share my unique journey with others.

Dennis Carstens would prove to be invaluable, and he worked with me hand in hand to weave what had begun as a journal—all my written memories—into a cohesive story line. Without the input of the immensely talented Dennis, none of this would ever have seen the light of day. I am enormously grateful to him.

I invite you, from the safety of your own lives, to come along on my journey.

IMPRESSIONS

by Dennis Carstens

Please allow for a brief introduction of myself. I am a retired lawyer and the author of a series of ten legal mystery/courtroom dramas available on Amazon. A friend of Linda Tripp's is a fan of my writing and emailed me with a request. She asked me if I remembered who Linda Tripp was, and would I mind sending Linda a specific copy of one of my books, *Political Justice*? Of course, I remembered Linda and gladly sent her a copy. Linda mentions more about this in her introductory chapter in this book. A couple of weeks later I received an email from Linda, and she could not have been more complimentary about the book she had read. In short, this is how we connected and how we came to collaborate on her story.

I remembered Linda's becoming almost a household name during the scandal that led to the impeachment of a president of the United States for only the second time in the nation's history. At the time, being a lawyer, I understood that perjury, subornation of perjury, and obstruction of justice are serious felonies. These charges are "high crimes and misdemeanors" required by the Constitution for impeachment. Also, abuse of power, if bad enough, can be an impeachable offense if the House so decides. The Senate Democrats ignored this rather obvious truth on behalf of one of theirs.

First, an uncomfortable confession. I voted for Bill Clinton twice. First in '92, because I thought it was time for a postwar president and a new generation, my generation, to take over. "Thank you for your service; now go out to pasture, you World War II pols." I voted for him again in '96 because the country was at peace and prospering. Had I known then what so many others have come to know about the sleaze in which the Clintons and their support group wallow, I would have gladly given my parents' generation at least another four years.

Bill Clinton was impeached for committing these crimes and was guilty as charged, but the Senate Democrats voted not to remove him from office. Clinton's defense lawyers, as was their job, were able to convince the Senate Democrats and most of the nation that the case against President Clinton was only about an extramarital affair. "If it is okay with Hillary, why should you care?"

Most of us have seen and heard, over the past twenty years, who Bill and Hillary are and what they are truly about. If you still do not know or refuse to believe it, they are about two things only: power and money, and they are capable of just about anything to obtain both. And that is from the picture of them they have allowed us to see in public. Behind the scenes, they are so very much worse. For starters, to call the Clintons users of people is analogous to saying the ocean has water in it. Users of people are minimally who they are.

Let's be blunt about these two. The Clintons' motto should be: "Why tell the truth when a perfectly good lie will work just fine?" For years I have watched in wonder how so many people refuse to believe this about them, even when they are so obviously, blatantly lying. They look into the cameras and treat us all with absolute contempt. What they are actually saying is, "You idiots are so far beneath us that lying so boldly to you is what you deserve, and we know that enough of you will still believe us."

Then there are those people, many of whom are lawyers—and, as such, officers of the court—who have themselves lied on the Clintons' behalf even under oath, which is perjury. They have lied to cover up crimes and reprehensible behavior, scandals, multiple instances of sexual abuse of women, and on and on. Then these people are tossed aside like a used napkin when they are no longer of use to the Clintons, especially to Hillary. I see some of these people on TV talk shows who still believe that the Clintons are their friends. Cult members who are starry-eyed and talking as if their puppy dog loyalty to the Clintons is reciprocated. I just shake my head in wonder at the naïveté of such people. What do these two have that makes so many people want to throw themselves at their feet, wrap their arms around the Clintons' ankles, and whimper like puppies? I simply do not get it.

Take an objective look at Hillary's behavior during and after the election campaign of 2016. When asked during a debate with Donald Trump if they would both accept the results of the election, Hillary literally laughed at the very idea that she would not accept the results. "Of course I will," she boldly declared. Then when the results were in and Donald Trump had won, Hillary accepted the results with an amazing display of grace, dignity, and class in an effort to help heal the nation and allow us all to move on. Isn't that what she did? Maybe not.

Hillary has spent the entire time since the election allowing the façade to come down and letting everyone get a good look at the real Hillary Rodham Clinton, the behind-closed-doors Hillary. The angry, bitter, mean, vindictive, malicious, nasty, entitled, small, tiny, petty person that she is. No, I did not get carried away with that description. There are any number of worse things to truthfully say about her.

During my time working with Linda Tripp as she told her story, I received an almost horrifying insider's view of whom Bill and Hillary Clinton truly are. The impressions I came away with are of two deeply flawed people who somehow have been able to demand and receive total fealty from so many who should have known better. Here's a question that needs to be answered: how did these two find each other? On an entire planet filled with billions of men and women, how is it that these two managed to run into each other and team up like this? The dark stars must have aligned for this. It is almost too weird for fiction, let alone reality.

In contributing to the writing of this book, I worked with Linda exclusively using a journal she was writing for her family. She had literally hundreds of pages of the behavior of the Clintons that could have and should have gone in here. Most of it would have been disgusting to a rational adult but would have been akin to bombing the rubble. Instead, we decided to go with the highlights to keep the book from being repetitive, long, and possibly a little boring. We decided to stay with the main items that were criminal sexual abuse and that unmasked these two hypocrites.

I fully understand that this is only my layman's opinion, but I find Bill Clinton to be an exceptionally weak man. Charming to women and men alike and an excellent politician (is that a compliment?), but incapable of controlling himself and his basest instincts. A man who became the most powerful person on the planet, yet a man who would cower like a little boy who nervously had to pee while being ripped to shreds by his control-freak wife. And this would occur on an almost-daily basis. He was powerless in front of a woman who would, with a vile, foul mouth, dress him down in front of others with language that could shock a sailor six months at sea.

There is also Bill's political ideology or, more accurately, his lack of any. He has been praised as a president able to compromise for the betterment of the country. To work with Republicans to solve problems. Compromise? How could he not compromise? Without any true political beliefs, there was no reason for him not to compromise. I believe the only reasons Bill is a Democrat were to help win elections in Arkansas and because Hillary is a true-believer Democrat. I do not think running as a Republican would have made one bit of difference to him if being a Republican was what he needed to be to win and obtain power.

Willing to compromise? I found a man so beaten down that he had trouble standing up to almost anyone face-to-face. Bill Clinton would be pitiful if he were not also a sexual predator. But for his political achievements, and if the Clintons were held to the same standards as the great unwashed deplorables they clearly despise, Bill Clinton would be a registered sex offender.

As for Hillary, where to begin? Before I get started, let me be clear about something. I am a lawyer by training and education, and have become a decent writer. I am not a psychiatrist or psychologist, nor have I ever played one on TV. I have never met Hillary Clinton or in any way interviewed and/or counseled her for a mental illness. I am a layman, and any diagnosis of mine is strictly my layman's opinion. Except the evidence is almost beyond a reasonable doubt.

Given all of the behind-the-scenes accounts of her behavior (available more than ever since November 2016), the "us versus them" paranoia, the unreciprocated demand of absolute loyalty, and the public

xiv   *A Basket of Deplorables*

Dr. Jekyll and private Mr. Hyde faces, Hillary Clinton is, I believe, an undiagnosed paranoid schizophrenic. The woman is likely mentally ill. I do not mean that flippantly. I mean it sincerely. I believe she needs serious psychiatric care.

Doubt it? As just one little example—there are an almost endless supply of them—when she habitually claimed there was a "vast right-wing conspiracy" out to get her and Bill, most rational adults chocked this silliness up to be political posturing. It was not. Hillary Clinton believed it in the beginning, and she believes it is still out there preventing her from becoming president. Has she ever taken any real responsibility for the election loss? Or for anything else?

This is, again, an amateur's opinion, but again, the symptoms are clear and obvious. Hillary is also, likely, a pure sociopath. There does not seem to be a single authentic particle in this woman. None. She has no human empathy or concern for anyone but herself and what she wants. You do not have to be a licensed shrink to see it. Hillary wears her unconcern, in most cases absolute disdain, for others almost with pride. This also explains how she can so seamlessly shift from threatening women her husband has sexually abused to proclaiming herself to be the worldwide champion of women. And worst of all, she believes it.

There is also her reckless attitude toward the nation's security. I am a veteran of the U.S. Air Force. During my time in the Air Force, for almost three years of it, I was assigned to the Operations Center of the National Security Agency. The 24/7, 365-days-a-year, "We never sleep" frontline monitor of America's enemies. I held the highest security clearance the nation had. Everything that went on in that room had the highest top secret classification there was. I tell you this so you know I have very real experience dealing with classified material.

There absolutely was a cover-up of Hillary's too-numerous-to-count crimes involving her handling of classified material. No question about it.

Hillary tried to claim that she did not know that material she had disseminated was classified. That is such a blatant lie that it is insulting. Everything a secretary of state does in the capacity of secretary of state is classified, and she knows that. It is basic security. She also tried to make us believe that she did not know it was forbidden for her to use a private server for government business. Nonsense. Another blatant and insulting lie. Another moment when she looked into the camera and lied. If she had a molecule of honesty in her, she would have proclaimed: "I have so much contempt for all of you, I believe I can tell you anything and you will believe it." Sadly, many people did believe her lies and still do. The real Hillary simply does not care. If she had to make a choice between protecting the nation's secrets and facilitating her personal convenience, she would always choose her convenience.

During the campaign of 2016, occasionally she would stoop to allow one of the deplorables to ask her a question. Rarely, but it did happen. I remember one in particular. A young woman had the temerity to ask Hillary if she thought she might be indicted. Hillary literally laughed at the suggestion before confidently proclaiming, "No." I found it interesting she did not declare her innocence. She simply knew she would not be indicted. How did she know? How else could she know? She had been told this by the Obama people—likely Barack Obama himself.

Of course, there was far worse to come. There would be more cover-ups of Hillary's crimes by the Obama administration and deep-state corruption machine. They blatantly covered for her and wrote her exoneration before the investigation was done. Then, once again, she looked at the American people with such obvious contempt and virtually admitted that the law does not apply to the politically connected.

We all remember James Comey in July 2016 on TV going through a partial list of Hillary's crimes regarding her handling of classified material. Almost everyone believed that Comey was going to at least recommend putting the case to a grand jury. Instead, the sanctimonious Comey let her off the hook by claiming she did not have intent. My chin hit the floor. It seems Comey has never bothered to attend a security briefing, and he certainly does not know the law. Or he was scamming us as part of the cover-up conspiracy, which is likely what was going on.

The act of transmitting classified material by means of an unsecured mode of communication is, in and of itself, sufficient to show intent to do so. Allow me to repeat that to be clear. Simply sending classified material by use of an unsecure device is sufficient, by itself, to show the requisite intent to transmit classified material by an unsecure means. Especially when you do it the hundreds of times that we knew of for sure she did. How many tens of thousands more times did she do it and then obstruct justice by scrubbing her server to cover it up? Do it once and it may be an accident. Do it again and you should be gone. Period.

Then there is the security of her basement server itself. Any one of millions of bored teenagers could have hacked their way into Hillary's server. Given Obama's terrible lack of foreign policy success, is it a stretch to think that Russia, China, Iran, and many others tapped Hillary's server and knew our position on any number of issues? And further, that they then used that information to make Obama look like a kid playacting at being a grown-up when he negotiated with them? Think about the Iran nuclear deal. Yes, I understand that Hillary was no longer secretary of state then. But if they were hacking her server, the Iranians would have known Obama's attitude toward foreign policy since day one. The Iranians went into those negotiations knowing that if they pushed long enough, they would get everything they wanted, including a huge payday.

What Hillary did was the equivalent of my taking several boxes of classified material out of the National Security Agency's offices and putting them in the trunk of my car. Except the trunk of my car is more secure than her basement server. The trunk of my car has a lock on it. If I had done 10 percent of what Hillary did, my feet would not have touched the ground on my way to prison. Why? Because that type of "I don't care about anyone else" attitude of hers puts the entire nation, every one of us, in serious jeopardy. And Comey and his merry little band of "we know best" do-gooders covered it up for her.

I've already admitted voting for Bill twice back in the nineties before we knew anything about these two. During the 2016 election, I am proud to say, I made a vow to myself that I would chew my right hand off at the wrist before I would let it mark a ballot on Hillary's behalf. This, of course, at least in Hillary's world, made me part of the ever-present, omnipotent "vast right-wing conspiracy" out to get her. Where do I go to get my membership card?

Finally, a commentary on our judicial system. The selective enforcement of the law, despite the notion that no one is above the law, has always been with us. The wealthy and the politically connected have always been with us to some degree. Selective enforcement is also hardly a failing of the American judiciary. In fact, America's may be the least corrupt system of all time. Having said that, it has never been so blatantly abused as it has become since the advent of the Clintons. No one, let alone two people, has ever gotten away with the long list of crimes and corruption of these two. And it is because of the incestuous and inbred nature that has become the permanent government in Washington.

The left has made it clear that certain groups and individuals are, indeed, above the law. Academia, the billionaires in Silicon Valley, and the Hollywood celebrity propaganda culture, in conjunction with 90 percent of the media, have made those on the political left exempt from it. Why? Because they are the occupants of the moral high ground upon which they have elevated themselves. This is why the inside-the-Beltway culture is aligned with the Democrats who have always believed they know what is best for us. Just ask them.

This is also why those on the left hate President Trump, the unwashed Walmart masses, the frozen rubes, the trailer trash and hillbillies living in flyover country—that place that used to be known as America. These people are not worthy of them and are a threat to their privileged positions. And this attitude started mostly with the Clintons. There has never been a time in the history of this country when the idea to "throw the bums out" has been more important. Good luck to all of us.

Chapter 1
INTRO TO LINDA

It's all about perspective. We all come to make decisions and life choices based on our own personal framework of reference. To understand who I am and why I did what I did, a little of my background will be helpful.

I grew up in the 1950s in a solidly middle-class household. My biological father, a former sergeant in what was then the U.S. Army Air Corps, hadn't left the military far behind. He was a strict, controlling, militant figure. He believed in a regimented household and, more important, in corporal punishment, and he never hesitated to use it. In today's society, he would be considered abusive because he believed right and wrong were black and white, with no shades of gray. At least for everyone but himself. Be that as it may, the point is, I did not grow up a child of politics.

He was a post–World War II veteran. After the war, as part of the initial occupation forces, he found himself, at eighteen, stationed in Eschborn, Germany. The army life, with its strict rules and discipline, seemed to suit him. My mother is a German who was living in Höchst, part of the greater Frankfurt am Main region, and that is where they met in 1945 and married in November 1948. She was eighteen; he was twenty-one. They were kids.

I was born Linda Rose Carotenuto in November 1949. By then, my father had separated from the Army. We landed in Montclair, New Jersey. There, with the help of the Army, he attended Montclair State Teachers College, where we lived on campus. Upon his graduation, we moved to Morristown, New Jersey, for his first teaching job. Ultimately, we moved to a neighboring town and the house I grew up in.

I had a pretty typical middle-class upbringing growing up in New Jersey during the fifties. When compared to the lives of my friends during these years, perhaps the most significant difference was that my mom, my sister, and I frequently traveled to Europe during the summertime to visit our beloved German grandparents. Despite the enormous distance, they became very important in our lives. International air travel during those days was not the routine sort of travel it is today. It was a huge deal for all of us. Our family was a bit different in this regard when compared to the average household in our neighborhood. Life in the fifties wasn't *Ozzie and Harriet*, but the value systems were eerily similar. Mom stayed home. Dad went to work. By this time, I had a younger sister as well, and we did the all-American activities that kids did during the fifties.

We all had chores. There was a sense of responsibility and accountability. Giving back was emphasized, and we quickly learned that for those to whom much has been given, much should be given back. It was for that reason that I spent several years as a volunteer candy striper at the local hospital. It felt good to contribute, and I enjoyed the work. In fact, it made me briefly consider the possibility of a future in nursing.

It was also an innocent time. We climbed trees and caught tadpoles. We ice-skated on the local pond in the dead of winter and raced our sleds down the steep hill following every snowstorm. We swam at the local swim club in the summer. Of course, there was the local Girl Scout Troop 13, of which I was a member for many years. Each year, we went camping and marched as proud patriotic children of the fifties in the Memorial Day parade.

In retrospect, I realize it was all about a solid value system. Life revolved around family, church, and school. We knew nothing else. Our Lady of Mercy Church was the local Catholic church, and there I had my First Communion and Confirmation. I was married there, and my two children were baptized there. We went to Catholic studies (CCD) weekly, confession on Saturday, and mass every Sunday without fail, sick or not.

For the most part, mine was a typical upbringing for the times, and it would be pretty unrecognizable today. My friends and I all shared a quiet patriotism. A love of country was something that had been instilled early on. Most important, between home and church, there was an overriding, no-nonsense grasp of right and wrong.

My biological father's name is Albert Carotenuto. He was a strict authoritarian. In my eyes, this handsome but impenetrable man was a raging bully. I feared him my entire life.

He taught science at Morristown High School and coached the varsity football team. Coaching football was something he dearly loved. At some point, he became the head of the science department. The other teachers affectionately called him "Sarge" due, I'm assuming, to his military background but also to his favored dictatorial demeanor. It seemed to fit.

It is because of my experience with him that I detest bullies and passionately believe they should be held accountable for their actions. It is probably also a good part of the reason that I could not tolerate the behavior of Bill Clinton, the supreme bully, all those years later. Clinton had the strength and might of the United States government behind him as he betrayed his country. So, he has "Big Al" to thank for my contempt for him, for my sense that what he did should be exposed. As bad as he was, Hillary was a lot worse. And that became a part of it as well.

A mediocre student at best, above all in math, I was much more interested in reading, writing, and history and had zero interest or ability, as it would turn out, in math or science. I seemed to have more right-brain traits for subjective, creativity-type thinking. Worse, I knew no one else with this lopsided condition. It made me feel utterly stupid. Everyone else in my college preparatory classes breezed through algebra, geometry, trigonometry, and calculus. I limped through and completed the bare minimum of math requirements. In fact, math is still a challenge, as my elementary school grandchildren can attest.

My father heartily concurred that if I was not stupid, my IQ score was at the very least a misprint—a case of transposed numbers. He too could not understand how math in general and the sciences in particular, subjects that came so easily to him, positively stymied me.

But give me a pen and I could write. And write. And write. Or devour a book. Through books, I could leave my home and be transported anywhere without leaving my room. It was a daily adventure in books. My book-reading journeys through the years rivaled my actual European travels, and all were quite real to me. Still, reading was not math or science. So, as far as Al was concerned, it did not count.

Whose childhood is perfect? Mine was not, but it had plenty of good times, largely because of my mother. She is an incredible woman, a role model, and the reason I survived childhood. Her kindness is legendary, and she is still with us and beloved by all our friends. She made a loving home for us, and she has always been there for us every step of the some-times-rocky way. She is also of the generation that firmly believed that children should be seen and not heard, but her way of enforcing that concept was gentle, never harsh. She went along with the "yes sir/ma'am" and "no sir/ma'am" requirements of our childhood, but she did not punish us if we lapsed. She was the velvet to Al's iron fist, and it would be many years before I could appreciate her inner strength in the face of my father's brute presence. My mother is a remarkable human being, and my sister and I are blessed to still have her.

Through it all, there was a sense of duty, honor, and country. It was never preached, but was always present and infused in both myself and my sister by a sort of osmosis. It was a big deal when, as a little girl, I learned that my mother became a proud naturalized citizen. Having grown up in war-torn Nazi Germany, she had an appreciation for the freedom and liberty of our country; she never took those things for granted. We didn't either.

By the time I married a first lieutenant in the U.S. Army, I was well schooled in complete reverence for the flag and what it stood for. I would come to learn that the members of the armed services were the unsung heroes of my generation and always would be.

During high school, my SAT results came in. As expected, I was off the chart in the verbal portion and borderline moronic on the math. That pretty much ended any hope I might have had for college. By this time, Big Al had fled with another woman, so there was no money for college anyway, and I was not scholarship material. What to do?

The Katharine Gibbs School in Montclair, New Jersey, was the answer. With an impeccable reputation, this school was basically a white-gloved combination of a vocational tech and finishing school for young women. I was determined that I would learn to be the best executive secretary out there. I could commute with friends who had also made this choice, and that is what I did.

Back then, attire was critical, and it had to be professional business garb each day. The school had recently done away with the white-gloves-and-hat requirement for daily attire, but the required garb wasn't much better. I didn't have these business clothes. It was difficult, and I was often called into the director's office for a "come to Jesus" moment about my improper dress. My grades were good though, so I was given chance after chance to nail the attire thing. I never fully succeeded.

I graduated from high school in June 1968. By this time, my world was rapidly changing, as were the lives of my mother and sister. For it was during this time that we first met the man who would later become our real father. A man whose inherent kindness and decency touched the hearts of virtually everyone he met. Until Dr. B, I had no real comprehension of what an actual father was. With him, I learned. We all did. His was a pure and unconditional love; he had an encouraging point of view and an ever-present kindness. He was a U.S. history professor. We adored him but lost him too soon, in 1996. His death was something from which we have never fully recovered. We had him for a short twenty-seven years—years filled with love. He will always remain, to our entire family, not only our father but the most influential person in our lives. The sudden loss of him was enormously difficult, and it has not gotten easier in the ensuing years.

By the time I graduated from high school, I had met Bruce Tripp at the Minuteman restaurant in Florham Park, New Jersey, the family-style restaurant where several of my high school senior friends and I waited tables part-time. Bruce and a few of his friends were seniors at Fairleigh Dickinson University and were the short-order cooks. They were funny, irreverent, and older.

Bruce was funny and fun yet had a serious side too. He was a biology major with a minor in chemistry, was very athletic, and seemed very smart. But he was a party boy too, who decided in 1968 to enlist in the Army and go to Officer Candidate School. This was at the height of the Vietnam War and the time of the draft. Bruce decided that he would prefer to be an officer if he was going to be a solider.

We stayed in close touch, and my friends and I visited Bruce and his new buddies often at various locations: Fort Dix, New Jersey, for basic training; Fort Leonard Wood, Missouri, for advanced infantry training; and Fort Benning, Georgia, for graduation from Officer Candidate School.

By 1970, Bruce, now Lieutenant Bruce Tripp, had orders for Vietnam. It seemed like all the sons, brothers, and nephews of everyone we knew were headed to Vietnam. There were so many destined never to return. The news each night chronicled the number of dead. It was a horrific time, and it was a war that virtually no one could comprehend. Why were our sons dying in that faraway land?

Bruce was stationed in Cam Ranh Bay in a Signal Corps unit, so he was not engaged in daily jungle warfare. During his year in the country, he was given a weeklong R&R. He invited me to join him in Hawaii to share it with him. We stayed at the Hilton Hawaiian Village on Waikiki Beach.

One evening, we had dinner at the top of the Ilikai Hotel, in the Polaris revolving restaurant overlooking Diamond Head, a volcanic cone. It was there that he proposed to me, and of course I accepted. We set the date for October 16, 1971, after his tour in Vietnam was finished. It was when we married that I became Linda Tripp. How little did I know how infamous that name would someday become.

I had made meticulous plans for our wedding, but at twenty-one, I had not spent much time preparing for the actual marriage. Bruce was making a career of the Army, not the most popular thing to do at that time. After a monthlong honeymoon in Europe, we came back to a posting at Fort Monmouth in New Jersey. Bruce earned his master's degree during this time, and I learned quickly that officers' wives were expected to behave in a certain way—reminiscent of the Katharine Gibbs School. One of those expected things was that dreaded attire thing again, and then of course there was the monthly tea or coffee. With silver. On the bright side, there were cakes. Lots of cakes.

Young wives deferred to the wisdom of the much older wives, the deference due not only to their age but also to the rank held by their husbands. I found it all a bit bizarre, but I happily played the role. If it made them happy, why not? Yes, ma'am.

Until I got a job. Horror of horrors. The wives of enlisted men worked. Officers' wives did good works for free and observed the traditions. You simply do not miss officers' wives' events. Ever. I had passed the civil service test and entered the system as a GS-4 employee. You could not start much lower, but it was a foot into the federal system. With an army officer husband and the frequent moves to other Army installations, it was my best bet. I would end up working for the federal government on and off, but mostly on, for the next thirty years, with breaks, of course, to have my children, until I was forced to retire following the Clinton scandal.

Bruce's career took us to many different postings over the next twenty years. Every chance I had, I would find a job in the civilian world in support of the military. Of course, there were occasions when I could not work. One of these reasons was born on April 26, 1975, when Ryan Michael Tripp made his initial appearance. Another would be when his sister, Allison Marie Tripp, came to us on April 25, 1979. Yes, she was born one day before her brother's birthday. Apparently, she could not hold out another day. But then again, neither could I. Our children would quickly become the light of our lives, as they both are today.

An Army life can play hell on a marriage. The demands are great. In late 1981, Bruce was transferred for a twelve-month tour in South Korea. Dependents were not allowed to go along. At the time, we were living in Columbia, Maryland, where the children and I stayed while Bruce went off to Korea.

We had terrific neighbors and friends. I never felt alone. The ladies of the neighborhood asked me to join their Wednesday-morning bowling league, and since kids were invited, I did. It was great fun. I could not bowl to save my life, but it was a nice time with great people. It was also at this time that several of the neighborhood women talked me into learning bridge. I wasn't a very good bridge player, but I enjoyed these women immensely. Many years later, they would be the women with whom I discussed Monica Lewinsky as her tale of Sodom and Gomorrah became too much for me to handle on my own.

During all this time, I continued to work in civil service government jobs. For example, after Korea, Bruce was sent to Allied Forces Central Europe, headquartered in Brunssum in the Netherlands. This is NATO. There, I went to work for a two-star general, the senior military representative for the United States at NATO. I was surrounded by wonderful professionals from all of the NATO countries.

Upon returning to the States, we were transferred to Fort Bragg, North Carolina, the largest military installation in the world. I continued to work for the government without a break in service, first at Special Operations Command at Fort Bragg proper, and later behind the fence for the unit that supported Delta Force. I wish I could say more about that particular assignment; suffice it to say, it was unusual but very interesting.

Life at Bragg was probably our favorite posting, except I came to realize that our normal was not normal enough. Life in general was just too short to remain in a loveless marriage. Ultimately, we would separate briefly but try one more time for the sake of the children. Big mistake. When it's over, it's over. Let me be clear about something: Bruce was and still is a terrific father and grandfather, and for this at least, I still love him.

It was 1990 when we got divorced, after we moved back to the Maryland/D.C. area. I needed a job right away and took one in the Pentagon. To avoid a break in service, I took the very first job I could find. But I knew for the first time in my adult life that this time, the sky was the limit. I was no longer going to be constrained by yet another Army move. What I did with my career from that point forward would be all up to me. Little did I know the strange, twisted journey I was about to embark upon.

Chapter 2
THE BUSH WHITE HOUSE

I began working at the White House in April 1991, midway through the presidency of our forty-first president, George Herbert Walker Bush. I came in as a complete political neophyte, but one with a healthy respect and deep interest in the history of the White House and its early occupants.

I had been hired by the correspondence unit under the saintly Maureen Hudson, who had headed the department for years. While on paper I was to be assigned to this unit, I was specifically hired to be a West Wing "floater." Being a floater simply meant I would fill in where needed in the West Wing in support of the president's senior advisors. It was an honor to be able to serve there in any capacity, and I was grateful for the opportunity.

The correspondence unit occupied a large suite of offices on the ground floor of the Old Executive Office Building (OEOB; now called the Eisenhower Executive Office Building). The old building with its many towering windows overlooked West Executive Avenue and the White House. The OEOB is part of the overall White House grounds. It is across West Executive Avenue Northwest from the West Wing. While the West Wing itself is attached to the White House, the OEOB is also considered part of the West Wing. West Executive Avenue Northwest is a closed street inside the White House compound.

At that time, the correspondence unit was a well-oiled machine, daily turning out thousands upon thousands of perfectly prepared pieces of correspondence and executive orders. Most letters were created to be signed by the autopen, but timeliness and perfection were the standards. Hardworking women, many who had been there for decades, staffed this unit. They were a very professional and impressive crew. I liked them all. More to the point, I was awed by their work product. "Efficient" does not begin to cover their system.

Upon arrival, my first assignment was to start filling out the enormously complex paperwork for yet another security clearance. The adjudication process would take roughly ninety days, so the more quickly the paperwork could be done, the faster the process could begin. At that time, I had held Top Secret clearances for many years in the Pentagon, but the White House requires its own.

In the midst of filling out pages upon pages of security information, I was also being trained on the mystery that was the creation of so many types of correspondence and the various merging programs that magically made the letter match its recipient. I was like a duck out of water and could not make sense of any of it. I think it was then that my admiration for these women began to grow in leaps and bounds.

Maureen was the epitome of patience, however, and since that part was not going so well, and because they didn't expect me to fill out paperwork for eight hours a day, when a call came from the travel office down the hallway for someone to fill in on the phones, Maureen asked me if I'd like a break from paperwork to help out. I agreed it would be nice to get to know some of the offices that supported the West Wing. I did that periodically over the first few weeks, (nothing more than answering phones and the like), and while the work was a bit mundane, I only had to remind myself that it all supported the operations of the White House to realize that anything, however mundane, was a contribution to living history. I got to know the guys in the travel office. All of them were good, decent, hardworking people. Much more on the travel office later.

By the time I submitted the fully completed paperwork for my new security clearance, the kindly Maureen had a new request. By this time, she had given up on my picking up what all the other women assigned to correspondence did so effortlessly. This request, as innocuous as it was at that time, would ultimately be the one that changed my entire trajectory at the White House.

Even though I had been hired to be a West Wing floater, Maureen asked me if I would be amenable to working as a floater in the OEOB until my security clearance came through. She explained that although floaters were exclusive to the West Wing and not meant to support the president's staff, housed in the OEOB, she had received a pressing request from the portion of the president's media relations office located upstairs in the OEOB. She thought that since it would be at least ninety days for my clearance to come through, and since I couldn't float to the West Wing until it did, if I was agreeable, she would make an exception.

To this day, I remain convinced that a good part of that decision was my complete ineptitude in learning the complex merging and computer machinations that spouted out the countless different letters and executive orders each day—the work products so professionally pumped out by the thousands by the very capable women of the correspondence unit. Maureen was just too kind to say so.

I was thrilled. To familiarize myself with the White House office diagram, I had been studying the different departments that made up the president's senior staff. I knew that media relations was headed by the special assistant to the president for media relations. Most, if not all, special assistants and their staffs reside in the OEOB and report to their superiors in the West Wing. In this case, they reported to the assistant to the president for media affairs. But that is all I knew.

To understand how unusual and unprecedented my situation came to be, it is necessary to understand the structure of the White House. In any administration, there are many political appointees who are appointed by the president and whose positions support him in that capacity. Each president brings these people in with him. They are supposed to leave with him.

Then there is also the White House permanent staff, consisting of hundreds of people. These people cover many offices within the complex that support the institution of the presidency as well as the structures making up the White House compound. I fell in this category.

In addition, at any given time there are also government agency staffers in various departments, both military and civilian. These people are temporarily assigned to the White House and are known as "detailees." They remain on their originating agency's rolls for pay purposes but are detailed to the White House for a predetermined amount of time.

All White House employees, regardless of appointment, political or not, temporary detailee or not, serve at the pleasure of the president. There is no job security of any kind at the White House—at least on paper.

Before Bill Clinton, however, while all the foregoing was true, not one of the permanent staff had ever been summarily fired to make room for a political appointee, or for any reason at all. Each incoming president was thankful for the cadre of employees who worked to make the White House function efficiently. This gave members of the permanent staff, with their decades of experience, a sense of job security through any number of administrations of both parties. All that changed in 1993.

Speaking of the White House permanent staff, before I, ostensibly as a West Wing floater, worked in the Bush White House and then again in the Clinton White House, no apolitical employee had ever served in an actual support position in the West Wing. Certainly not in the administrations of two opposing parties at the level in which I found myself in two administrations, those of Bush and Clinton. It had just never happened before.

My situation was different for several reasons. One, I always remained on the floater/correspondence payroll. But I was offered and accepted positions and promotions that technically were political appointments. This happened in both administrations. As I said, it had never happened before, and I seriously doubt it has happened since.

When I was first hired as an apolitical civil servant in the correspondence unit, one of the most compelling points repeatedly imparted to me was that I was being hired to support the institution of the presidency, not the sitting incumbent. It was stressed again as I took the oath of office.

The oath we swore to was: "There are many political appointees to support the sitting president. We are here to support the institution of the presidency, and in addition to this oath, that is our entire loyalty, first, last, and always." In fact, I met several much older women in correspondence who had been there since Nixon, one as far back as Kennedy. They had served several presidents with honor.

Of all the permanent staff I met during my time at the White House, I never knew any of their political affiliations or they mine. It truly was a nonissue. Everyone was honored to be there; we all looked forward to serving each incoming president to the best of our ability. It was almost a feeling of family, a sort of close-knit mom-and-pop approach to supporting the institution.

The White House permanent staff at that time consisted of several hundred hardworking people in offices such as correspondence and travel as well as the electricians, curator, residence staff, housekeeping staff, telephone operators, grounds staff, florist, kitchen staff, gift unit staff, photographer, framer...the list goes on and on, with all of the permanent staff committed to making the White House trains run on time. Faceless, seemingly nameless, often unseen, this army of worker bees took great pride in their work. All were honored to serve in even a small capacity in support of the institution of the presidency.

The Bush White House's media relations office—as with all the White House offices, whether in the OEOB or the West Wing—was filled with young, smart, and enthusiastic people who were overtaxed with work, and the office was understaffed. It was an incredibly fast-paced atmosphere of constant motion, with all work product impacting the schedule of the president. The whole thing seemed to be run by an impressive twenty-something person of amazing ability. Her name was Maggie Minogue. With her unflappable poise and her trademark graciousness, she effort-lessly kept all the balls in the air. For me, it felt as if I would no sooner arrive at work than I would happen to look up and realize lunch had been skipped again and it was time to head home. Time flew by; there were never enough hours in the day.

The people in the media relations office were very grateful for any help at all, and it became instantly clear that I should pitch in wherever I saw a need. I did, and over a period of close to three months, I ended up taking on projects having to do with the president's media events outside of Washington. It is safe to say that this job propelled me to other things in the West Wing that had little to do with floating.

When my security clearance came through, I was able to float in the West Wing. Dorrance Smith, the assistant to the president for media affairs, asked Maureen's office if I could be assigned to his West Wing office "for a while." He, as a senior advisor to the president, qualified for floater support. So off I went to the West Wing and into another world.

I was there for several months and enjoyed it immensely. However, floaters are not meant to stay for months. Generally, the assignment is for a period of hours to days but not months. So, Maureen, to whom I was still officially assigned, finally insisted I float where needed. Dorrance asked me to stay right where I was, but it would have meant accepting a political appointment position. I was not prepared to lose what little security I had as a career civil servant, so I regretfully declined.

After media relations, I floated to several senior staffers as well as to the Office of the First Lady in the East Wing of the White House. Before Hillary Clinton, all first ladies had their offices in the East Wing. I enjoyed all of it and had a healthy respect for the friendly, blunt, yet inherently gracious Barbara Bush.

At some point, I found myself in the Office of Administration, in the basement of the West Wing. As with the rest of the offices, this was a busy, friendly, professional group; this one was headed by Tim McBride. It was during this time that I was asked to float to the office of the chief of staff, when Samuel Skinner, former secretary of transportation, took over. Skinner arrived with a large contingent of his senior staff, and working with the very professional "Skinner people" was one of the highlights of my time at the White House.

I stayed there several months, and again the environment was hectic, fast-paced, and professional. The chief of staff's office is in the Oval Office Corridor, with the Oval Office literally steps away in one direction and the Office of the Vice President steps away in the other direction. Needless to say, it was an honor to be working at this level.

Sam Skinner was removed in the waning days of the 1992 presidential campaign, and Jim Baker, secretary of state, was named chief of staff; he brought an even larger entourage with him. The thought was, in the face of what was looking increasingly like a losing campaign, Jim Baker could save the day. His staff would have much preferred to remain back at the State Department. They were literally counting the days until they could return. I remember thinking they would be wise to remember that there would be nothing to return to if President Bush lost the election.

The newly appointed chief of staff needed someone to support his incoming deputy chief of staff, Robert Zoellick, in the same suite of offices. Zoellick had also come from the State Department. I was tapped once again, and this time I was given the title executive assistant to the deputy chief of staff to the president. With the new title and job came a pay raise. I jumped from being a GS-8 employee to GS-11. The downside was working from 7 a.m. to 11 p.m., and life had turned upside down.

My time in that office is a story all its own. It was during the waning days of the '92 election, and "frenetic" doesn't begin to cover it. There were now factions that the new Baker group had brought over from the State Department and the old guard. A new speechwriter was brought in—from Kentucky Fried Chicken, of all places. A friend of mine, Tony Snow, was still the chief speechwriter on paper, but the work was going to the chicken guy. Tony wrote beautiful and compelling speeches for the president. He asked me to get these speeches in front of Zoellick and Baker, but in the end, they didn't even read them.

We were all well prepared by our superiors for what our roles would be during the changing of the guard—that is, when a new administration would come in; the focus was on making that transition as seamless as possible. The politics of the outgoing president and those of the incoming were irrelevant to the permanent staff, as I mentioned. So, I was prepared when President Bush lost the election. Oh, we are all human. I had a great deal of admiration and respect for him—in fact, for the entire first family. Since I had been working in close proximity to them for so long, I felt a sense of loss when they left. They were good, decent, kind, caring people, so I suppose that was natural.

They had surrounded themselves with the same type of caring individuals, all hard workers. They would all be missed. In the face of a resounding electoral defeat, with a sense of sadness throughout the compound, President Bush did something unexpected. I suppose in an effort to lift spirits, he called for all the West Wing staff to gather. He appeared to take great joy in surprising his staff by having Dana Carvey show up at the White House. Carvey, known for his not-so-flattering *Saturday Night Live* impersonations of President Bush, was the last person we expected to see. As the staff gathered, wondering what was up, Carvey entered to the strains of "Hail to the Chief." It was brilliant, provided some much-needed levity, and simply highlighted for all of us the decency of the man. In the wake of an electoral devastation, he was thinking of others. That is who he was. Somehow, it made the transition even more painful. Still, it was time for the changing of the guard, and it was time to look forward. I could not have imagined the abyss awaiting. No one could have.

Richard "Dick" Darman, head of the Office of Management and Budget, had given me some unsolicited advice days before we all took our leave of one other after the election. The conversation took place in the chief of staff's office. He said, "Linda, go back to correspondence. No president has ever touched the permanent staff."

I would be going back to correspondence after my vacation, and I looked forward, silly me, to floating, really floating this time, the way it is meant to be: moving between different departments, supporting for a few hours or a few days whichever member of the president's most senior staff needed some help. That was the plan. But, as they say, the best-laid plans.... I could never have predicted what followed. So much for the plan.

January 20, 1993, in my opinion, is a date that should live in infamy. It is the date William Jefferson Clinton was sworn in as the forty-second president of the United States. At least, that is what we were led to believe.

When the Clintons arrived in Washington, I was on a long-overdue vacation. I was happy to be able to avoid all the inauguration hoopla, the freezing temperatures, and most of all, the traffic. I needed the time at home to recuperate from the crazily intense hours of the campaign. I was finally able to spend a little time at home with my kids. With the frenetic schedule during the campaign, I hadn't been able to do so for several months, and had to rely on my parents to come stay with us to take up the slack.

My vacation was short lived. After the inauguration, I received a phone call from Maureen Hudson. Sounding as surprised as I felt, she relayed that she had received a phone call from the Immediate Office of the President. This is the long-version name for the office of those who work directly for the Oval Office. I was being asked to come back early from my vacation and work directly with the new president's Oval Office staff. When I suggested she send another floater, she told me that I had been requested by name.

I acquiesced, of course, but did say that I could not return to the sixteen-hour days of the past. In fact, I recall making a specific condition for accepting this assignment: the guarantee that I could work from 8:30 a.m. to 5 p.m. I could no longer be an absentee mom. To my surprise, everyone signed off on it—a near impossibility in any White House.

I knew nothing about the Clintons that would have prevented me from accepting the job anyway, so of course I accepted. By the time they left office, I am fairly certain that they wished I had not accepted. But then, I am not responsible for their behavior.

After the Bush White House, entering the Clinton White House was like stepping through the looking glass. The Clintons should have put a sign at the entrance to the West Wing: "Abandon your conscience, morals, and ethics, all ye who enter here. Loyalty is the only virtue."

I was the only apolitical person in the Clinton West Wing. The jobs of all the White House permanent staff, regardless of area of responsibility, were to make sure that the business of the presidency was able to function smoothly and professionally. I was the lucky one who landed smack dab in the middle of the Oval Office.

When David Gergen came in as a presidential advisor, he was the most senior person to ever have supported presidents in opposing parties. He didn't last long. I was the only support person to have landed in this situation. I know I was the first. I am positive I was the last as well.

With the arrival of the Clintons, it immediately became clear that a bizarre form of absolute loyalty was expected—to the Clintons, plural. In fact, it was clear that nothing else was as critical. Not ability, not work ethic, not dedication to getting the job done. Blind, fall-on-your-sword loyalty. Check-your-conscience-at-the-door loyalty. In fact, considering the clear demarcation between the two "teams," if anything, a sense that we were all working for Hillary Clinton, rather than the president, existed. But that wasn't the only obvious oddity.

The Bush White House had been a well-oiled machine relying heavily on procedure and protocol. It hummed along mightily, if quietly, and through a grueling schedule (a normal White House day begins at 7 a.m. and ends whenever but generally not before 8 p.m. on an average day, and sometimes as late as 10 p.m.). There was a sense of teamwork, optimism, and almost thankfulness that we were all so fortunate to have this incredible opportunity to support the president in the White House.

Schedules were tight and adhered to, and procedures were firmly in place, with offices staffed 100 percent by professionals. There was always a significant emphasis on producing quality work, and there was a system in place for everything. We were required to wear business attire. In this relatively conservative environment, you didn't see many red suits. There was a more conservative, adultlike approach to everything, which included business dress. There was an overall sense of respect for the history of the White House and a feeling of obligation to do it proud. No one forgot where they were sitting; no one forgot where they were. We gave it our all.

Enter the Clintons—and a brave new world. Or so we thought. "Chaos" was the word of the day. This was also the West Wing, but it seemed more like Grand Central Station at rush hour. It was as if these people had never managed anything. Revolving doors, drop-ins, no protocol, no rules...the counterculture had taken over, and people were reveling in their new roles. It was jeans, sweatshirts, and sneakers all the way. Since even pantsuits had been forbidden for women in the West Wing under the previous administration, this was startling.

It came as no surprise, after we heard that their guests jumped on the bed in the Lincoln Bedroom, that Bill and Hillary were peddling overnights there to the tune of millions in fundraising for the privilege. It felt like a different planet. I remember wondering if this transition was indicative of others in the past. I was told that this was new to everyone.

With an ever-present sense of disdain for that which had come before, a new element was now ruling the school. The very air seemed to change. It was as if the radicals of the sixties had finally taken over the school and thrown out everything in their way. It was startling, to be sure. And still, I rationalized that this was a new generation that would grow into a healthy respect for the institution of the presidency and its history. Wishful thinking. It would only get worse.

Where during the previous administration there had been a reverence for the institution of the presidency and a sense of history, during this one those things were notably absent. I used to joke that the only thing about the Clinton West Wing that was remotely similar to the Bush West Wing was the real estate, but even that began to change. I mentioned it to a senior White House staffer in the first few weeks of his first term. The swift answer was, "Linda, you're not in the Bush White House anymore." Truer words were never spoken.

From my very first day in the Clinton West Wing, there seemed to be an overriding sense of optimism on the part of the permanent support staff. They had done this many times before, and they looked forward with anticipation to what this new administration would do. It was a new day. I shared their optimism. No one could have imagined, let alone predicted, what was to follow.

From the very beginning, there was a not-so-subtle difference in the atmosphere in the West Wing—one that I could not readily identify. It was something that transcended the downright casual approach to business. I was working literally steps from my old desk in the outer office of the chief of staff. Now I was sitting a few feet away from there in support of the Oval Office itself. The geography had not changed, but everything else had. There was a bizarre aura of unfathomable secrecy, a sense of something resembling paranoia of everything. It seemed to me, a Clinton outsider, that those closest to the president were constantly looking over their shoulders. It didn't take long for me to realize why.

The reason was Hillary Clinton herself. Her whereabouts were closely monitored, and close attention was paid to the squawk box that constantly relayed her whereabouts in particular, as well as the whereabouts of the president and daughter Chelsea. Much could fall through the cracks, but knowing Hillary's precise whereabouts never did. It was strange and wholly unfamiliar. I wondered why there was so much emphasis on where the first lady always was.

What I couldn't understand at first was why the mere presence of the first lady would cause the paranoia. An oddly ominous sense of foreboding seemed ever present. An inexplicable tension permeated the atmosphere; it was almost palpable. It was an unseen but very real presence that enveloped the entire West Wing. It hovered over everyone and everything. Oddly, it engendered a very nonprofessional, loosey-goosey, no-rules, no-procedure, no-protocol way of running the White House. It was totally different from what I was used to.

I would later learn what this was all about. It revolved around a very undisciplined president with unheard-of predilections, and it was from this that I began to think of those around him as falling into one of three categories: the Protectors, the Facilitators, and last but by no means least, the Graduates. Their areas of responsibility will become clear later, but suffice it to say that these three factions had very different—in fact opposing—goals. The only thing they had in common was their paranoia about Hillary and her precise whereabouts. It all made for chaos. But it was also all beginning to make a strange sort of sense.

Ultimately, as time went on, a more professional workplace was something that they would be forced to adopt, but in the early days it did not exist. Schedules were not ironclad; they were sort of suggestions, and with no one was this more obvious than with the undisciplined president himself. It was clear in the beginning that he chafed at being in "the fishbowl," that he was unused to being confined, that procedures that had been in place for decades were not for him. He was a dichotomy from the beginning, a good ol' boy who loved to spontaneously interact with people yet a person unquestionably accustomed to getting his way, with a hair-trigger volatility if he didn't. Bill Clinton was almost like a coddled, pampered child, a powder keg ready to blow.

It didn't take long for Hillary to show herself. Again, and this cannot be overemphasized, the one thing the Clintons wanted, absolutely demanded, was total loyalty to them and their personal agenda. Not the country, not the presidency. Personal loyalty to them only. Hillary above all others. "Eight years for Bill; eight years for Hill" was the Clinton White House mantra, and getting behind that and what it meant was a good idea for survival.

When the Clintons came in, they made a lot of noise about cutting waste and excess in government spending. They pushed this to the public, who reacted very positively, notably the liberal media. The Clintons claimed they were going to cut staff and spending, ostensibly to set an example for the rest of government as part of deficit reduction. At least that was what they put out to the public.

There were literally hundreds of career civil servants with excepted status, which meant that they had no civil service protection; they all served at the pleasure of the president. No previous president in modern history had fired these professionals to replace them with political hacks. The list, as mentioned previously, included but was not limited to correspondence staff, travel office staff, White House operators, housekeeping staff, maintenance staff, residence staff, florists, cooks, curators, those who assigned furniture and artwork to staff, and IT personnel, just to name a few.

Hillary practically salivated over these slots. To her, they meant nothing more than positions she could use to fill with the ever-important Clinton loyalists. I was hearing rumblings of this in the Oval Office Corridor, but I never imagined what she had in store.

This was where the job cutting would come. She could rid herself of those who, by sole virtue of the fact that they had worked for the Clintons' utter enemies, the Bush family, made them undesirable. Then she could replace them with those who had shown a blind loyalty to the Clintons. The reason centered around the fact that these cuts would save the taxpayers money. Right. In fact, the cuts would ultimately cost the taxpayers more than what was "saved."

In early February 1993, a few short weeks into their term, Hillary summarily dismissed all of the professionals working in the correspondence office. She did not do it personally, of course. She left that to the oldest Graduate of them all, the ubiquitous Marsha Scott. The women in the correspondence office were some of the lowest-paid people in the government. This should have been the last place to cut staff, especially to save money.

To provide perspective, this office handled over eighteen million pieces of mail during the four years of the Bush administration with pride, professionalism, and dedication. And they were sacrificed at the altar of government cost cutting and staff reduction. And Clinton corruption. They were told one day that it would be their last day, that they should clean out their personal belongings and would be escorted to the door. No notice. No thanks for their service. Many had been there for decades. It was callous and unfeeling and unfair. As bad as that was, what was ultimately worse was the damage it did to the presidency.

I was stunned. It was then that I realized a few things. I too had to watch my back. I faced the reality that this was a copresidency with only one Clinton elected but the other having even more influence—our first lady ruled the school. And she was ruthless.

In the end, there was no cost cutting or staff reduction. The Clintons simply brought in loyalists to replace the fired staff—and, in fact, brought in more of them, which ultimately cost the taxpayers more money. So much for cost savings. The previous dedicated professionals were sacrificed to Clinton paranoia.

The decision to axe the entire correspondence office wreaked havoc on the system while causing uncertainty and concern amongst the permanent staff. Pieces of mail piled up by the thousands in overflowing rolling bins that seemed to literally overtake the first floor of the OEOB. Mail spilled onto the floor as it just kept coming and was kicked aside. No one knew what to do with any of it. When it all finally disappeared, I was told it all had simply been discarded.

Hillary brooks no opposition. I am sure many, many more would have lost their jobs had there not been a hue and cry from the press when this happened, rapidly followed by a huge resistance to the travel office decimation. After both Hillary-created situations, plus the sudden explosion by Hillary, I am certain further mass firings were temporarily curtailed. There was only so much political capital she was willing to spend on a bunch of lowly slots. The mass firings came to a temporary end, but the purging of people believed to be nonloyalists of the Clintons was not over. Hillary's paranoia about anyone who might be a member of the totally disloyal "them" was never-ending. In fact, she was just getting started. She just became savvier, more duplicitous, and more careful. No one ever said she wasn't a quick study.

Chapter 3
MEET THE REAL CLINTONS

Hillary and Bill Clinton: two different yet close political peas in a very odd pod. They might be as close as two peas could be but are worlds apart too. I never saw signs of an actual marriage. I saw an undeniable and extraordinary political partnership daily. They each fed off the other's needs, both wholly dependent upon the other for the achievement of their goals. Two enabling peas sharing one pod, with differences as compelling as their similarities and the entire garden as their playground.

Before I go any further introducing you to Bill and Hillary Clinton, there is something you need to know if you don't already. The Clintons you were allowed to see bear no resemblance to what those of us who worked in the White House saw daily behind closed doors when the cameras were off. This is something to keep in mind while reading this account of them. These two had been practicing wearing public masks for years. To a certain degree, all politicians do—but not with at the same level of Jekyll and Hyde perfected by the Clintons.

First and foremost, the Clintons are users. They are easily the least empathetic people I have ever known. If you can bring something for their benefit, something that will help them achieve power and wealth, they will keep you around. When you have been used up, they will discard you with no more thought than tossing a used Kleenex in the trash. If you doubt that, wait for the chapter concerning Vince Foster's death.

What is amazing is how many people they treated like this who still rabidly support them. People who believe that their puppy dog loyalty, adoration, and devotion to the Clintons is reciprocated. So many people are willing to sell their soul and values, and risk their life and livelihood, for them. Perjury was not just a way of life with these two; it was minimally demanded. As I wrote above, keep this in mind. It explains a lot about who they absolutely are and how casually they use people, then toss them aside.

In the beginning, not only did I want to like Bill and Hillary on a personal level, but I truly did like them. The notion that as a member of the permanent support staff I was out to get them is silly and is a sign of Hillary's paranoia. It speaks to their fundamental hatred of all holdovers, the evil "them." I have no doubt that every member of the permanent support staff, at least in the early days of Clinton's first administration, was honored to serve the new president. I was honored to serve. Of course, this was before Hillary started to purge the staff who were "them" in favor of her personal loyalists.

Bill and Hillary appeared in those first few months to be first and foremost policy wonks who had somehow landed at the very epicenter of the universe with unimaginable access to change. It was a heady time for them—or it would have been if everything else had not begun to unravel.

Initially, they seemed to be "big idea" people. Bill seemed to love to hear everyone's opinion. The more opinions, the better. Bill is a people person down to his core. He had time for anyone. I believe it was all genuine. He feeds on people. It is his own personal oxygen. He thrives on personal interaction, and he has an uncanny ability to make every single person he meets feel important. At the end of a long day of meetings, he would emerge from the Oval Office looking exhausted, deflated, strung out, in need of a people fix. His personal interaction style is an amazing thing to witness and is unique to him. I have never seen it before or since.

In this way and in so many others, he is the true antithesis of Hillary. Because of this need for people, his schedule was in a constant state of chaos. People were waiting for him almost throughout each day because he was always late for meetings. It was not intentional; it was simply who he was. At the same time, his lateness seemed to be an endearing trait. Bill Clinton was impossible not to like.

Hillary was on the opposite end from Bill on the gregariousness spectrum. She was all business all the time. A chill seemed to accompany her wherever she went, but only when there were no cameras around. Whenever I see someone on TV talking about how pleasant and personable she is, I have to laugh. These are people who know only the public Hillary, the one she allows people to see. Behind the scenes, away from cameras and donors, is where you will find the real Hillary. While Bill looked for opportunities to engage with people and seemed to so enjoy it, she was distant and remote. Hillary was less interested in human interaction and much more comfortable simply issuing orders for the staff to snap to attention to and carry out. She seemed to have no interest in anyone else's opinion or any sort of response from anyone, including—maybe even specifically—Bill. Remember, this is what was going on behind the scenes. Hillary was always very cognizant of her public persona. Eight years for Bill, eight years for Hill.

Hillary was somewhat of a pontificator and was interested only in getting her way on any given subject. But he was the president, the elected one. There were times that she seemed almost irked that he was the one who had been elected. Bill seemed to genuinely want to learn from others; she seemed to want to stifle them so she could be heard. Again, behind the scenes, Hillary also clearly showed utter disdain for Bill himself. It would not take long to figure out where that was coming from, but early on it was simply puzzling.

On the inside, away from the public, all of this was hard to miss, as was the unusual dynamic between them. All I had seen of the Clintons in the previous year was what everyone else had been allowed to see on the campaign trail: countless images of huge ear-to-ear smiles and lots of hand-holding. It all seemed so genuine. They were a very attractive and capable couple.

The behind-the-scenes-reality that I saw was something different. Still, it would be a while before I fully understood the critical importance of the public masks they wore. The Clintons lived in a parallel universe that included smoke and mirrors, bimbo eruptions, pay for play, sleazy land deals, private investigators, Graduates, Protectors, and Facilitators, just to name a few elements. Most important, above all else, was the role of Hillary's "politics of personal destruction" that would play in the never-ending cover-ups.

It was a partnership of sorts. Their shared ambition was on display for all to see, and it had been wildly successful so far. But it was a lopsided partnership and a power struggle between them right from the beginning. The entire time I was at the White House, whether working in the Oval Office Corridor or upstairs in the counsel's office directly next to Hillary's West Wing office, I never saw signs of a marriage. That was reserved for the public. The hand-holding took place when the cameras were present. They could be going at each other tooth and nail one minute, then the next walk out to Marine One on the South Lawn holding hands, smiling, and waving to the cameras—for all the world the very image of a committed and content couple.

This power struggle had an unusual dynamic. It had to do with influence and who would call the shots on any given day. The image of these two working together for the good of the nation was laughable. When Bill was up, Hillary was down. But when he was down, she was not just up, she was the de facto president. Of course, Bill was in the doghouse virtually all the time for his sexcapades, which she condoned. They were also not the least bit discreet about their screaming matches.

Oddly, their favorite phrase of endearment between them was a loud and venomous "You fucking Jew bastard!" And they saw no incongruity in it! Hillary was particularly fond of the expression, but they both used it frequently when screaming at each other and in a very watched setting—the White House.

There were frequent screaming matches with the f-bomb used creatively in every form of speech...but notably with such hate. I was told that you could bet on whatever the blowup of the day was; nine times out of ten it would be about one of Bill's women. Nothing enraged Hillary more because she believed 100 percent that they would not survive his out-of-control sexual addiction's getting out into the public domain. This was a constant. As a result, he was always in the doghouse, and it empowered her. I saw it as a pretty weird dynamic for a marriage.

Both the Clintons used foul language quite liberally, and not just in private. In the halls of the White House, it was a constant occurrence. Not only was Hillary never outraged when Bill assaulted and abused women, but she was never outraged by coarse language concerning women. Both Hillary and Bill, when referring to women, preferred the c-word as opposed to the p-word and used it liberally—he used it toward Hillary constantly. He also told Monica Lewinsky that he needed "pussy" nonstop. Yet Hillary was outraged by Donald Trump's coarse language regarding women? The notion that there is some reason for her to be outraged about it is just ridiculous.

I recall a specific instance early on. In 1993, Bill hosted his twenty-fifth Georgetown University class reunion at the White House. Hillary caught him getting too chummy with an old flame, and she went ballistic. The fallout lasted for days. Amazing, especially when you remember that Hillary knew all about his extramarital activities. She had spies in the White House everywhere watching us all for loyalty. They were also to report back regarding Bill's behavior. Not only did she know, but she condoned it, enabled it, and threatened any number of these women to keep their mouths shut. Not because she cared. It was to protect her image and her political ambitions. Never forget: eight years for Bill, eight years for Hill.

Hillary never missed an opportunity to take advantage of Bill's behavior to get her way. This is likely why she put up with it. She would rather have the power than a marriage that was a partnership. When she ran twice for the presidency on her own, Hillary could legitimately take credit for having experience as a presidential candidate. All aboard the Hillary train. But early on, I had no idea where this would lead us. I would soon learn.

Clinton advisor Paul Begala once said, of his buddy's taking office, "Stroke of the pen, law of the land. Kinda cool." This blatant statement summed up the attitude of those early days: "Whatever we want to do, we can do." Except right away, undercurrents began to move beneath the surface. Those could not be missed either, and they erupted sometimes one at a time, sometimes all at once. In a rapid-fire way, the mirage simply cracked and came crashing down around us.

No one else seemed bothered by it. Early on, it became clear that this was the standard Clinton MO. The "I feel your pain" candidate and his very smart wife morphed into scary human beings right before my eyes in the White House. It was difficult to reconcile the reality with the image so carefully packaged and presented to the public. Bill and Hillary Clinton are the consummate politicians. There is not a genuine particle in either one of them. It is as if they were programmed since birth to be this way. The amazing part of this is how did these two manage to find each other?

If I had known then what I know now, I would have fastened my seat belt, because the roller coaster to beat all roller coasters was just beginning. And the charade grew day by day.

Very early on in his first term, President Clinton announced the formation of a new task force on national health care reform. This would be the widely anticipated launch of one of the centerpieces of his presidential campaign. For public consumption, it was Bill who named Hillary to head it up. The way most decisions in this administration were made, however, it is far more likely—and it was believed within the West Wing—that Hillary had named herself, then begrudgingly allowed the elected one to make the announcement.

The other pea in the Clinton pod now had a bona fide job. Hillary was unelected and unconfirmed, but the campaign promise of two for one was finally unfolding. The copresidency had officially begun, even if she had been forced to take an office other than the Oval or Al Gore's vice president's quarters in the West Wing. It was a temporary setback at most.

In any case, Bill further announced that the health care plan would be submitted to Congress within the first one hundred days. He was obviously ambitious but delusional as well. No matter, this was an incalculably valuable sound bite. They were going to save the world! Promises of the campaign were bearing fruit. That it was rotten fruit would soon become apparent, but it was fruit of a sort nevertheless.

By this time, even fawning journalists had noticed Hillary's use of the royal "we" whenever she spoke. It may have given them pause and should have raised concern. But the media then, as now, were not likely to question a Democratic administration. Besides, two for one was what the Clintons had promised the nation during the campaign, and now they were simply delivering. I am not sure the nation had any idea what this meant. It was noteworthy to me because from my vantage point, it was the only true promise they had made. And the most frightening.

Of course, when the two for one became a political liability, Hillary reinvented herself as a bastion of domesticity. She was not orchestrating domestic U.S. planning and policy, and she certainly was not ruling the White House. No, Hillary was majoring in *domesticity*. No policy-making there. She was busily decorating and redecorating the residence, planning intimate dinners and intricate state functions, and even considering adopting a child. She really did leak that out. That all of this was a hoot to those who knew better remained a state secret. Hillary is what Hillary says she is. No questions asked. Period. It was comical when much later she reinvented herself as a New Yorker gunning for the Senate, magically morphing back into the copresident she had always been. Domesticity? Puh-leeze!

Hillary's appointment to head the health care task force was nepotism at its best, but it was not a groundbreaking event. Nepotism had existed in the executive branch well before this. Previously, though, these critical appointments had been confirmed by the Senate and had been actual existing positions for which the recipient was paid. There was no gray area.

The official and nonofficial nature of Hillary's public employment belied the actual power she exerted over every issue of significance in the White House. Her power permeated the compound, and she ruled with an iron fist. There was not even a hint of a velvet glove. While health care was her official cause, her influence and reach were equal to Bill's. With the elected pea routinely trembling in her presence, it made for a bizarre arrangement to be sure. It could not have been too cozy in that pod for Bill most of the time.

What followed was weird on its face. The health care task force took on a somewhat dark persona that baffled most of us. Secrecy worthy of a Delta Force mission quickly ensued. Names of the hundreds who made up the task force were treated similarly to classified information. This was noteworthy since, to put it mildly, real classified-document control was at best loosely handled in the Clinton West Wing.

Those pesky military people with their annoying rules and regulations were considered a necessary evil, but the entire security thing was a joke—it did not happen except in the National Security Council offices and the Situation Room. Routinely, the rest of the offices had classified documents unconcealed and lying out in the open. That was a foretaste of Hillary's attitude toward the nation's security when she set up a personal, unsecured server in her home. If there was a choice between her convenience and guarding the nation's secrets, the choice was obvious.

With the health care task force, however, strict secrecy was the watchword. Meetings were secretly held; the content of and attendees at these meetings were state secrets. There was a sense of paranoia, but I suppose that did not mean someone was not out to get them.

I was puzzled, but what did I know? It smacked of a covert operation, but why? I did not know then that Hillary was hell-bent on creating a gargantuan and quite radical monster of untold proportions, that this clandestine operation was, at its core, a design centered around her lofty master plan. Eventually its sheer enormity and convoluted solutions would sink the Hillary ship. Not then. Initially, if I wondered anything, it was if this first lady would ever do things in a straightforward way, or if these cloak-and-dagger methods would become a pattern. I need not have wondered. It became crystal clear within a matter of days.

In a remarkable burst of secret activity, the task force put together a colossal, almost fourteen-hundred-page tome of monstrous big government. A bureaucratic nightmare, it became the issue from which to run from for most members of Congress.

In a frenzy of activity, Hillary finally briefed Congress on her personal baby in early fall and faced an underwhelming reaction, to say the least, and with good reason. Politicians from both parties saw her plan as an enormous, unwieldy, and monumentally expensive dose of big government. She was stunned. This would be the last time Hillary allowed herself to lose anything during Bill's presidency.

Despite the clandestine nature of the task force, there had been plenty of buzz about alternative strategies concerning health care reform. The secrecy guaranteed we didn't hear much, but we knew it was going to be a ginormous package of staggering weight and cost. We also knew that it was Hillary who was insisting on this mammoth effort. It was Hillary who dismissed the voices who strongly touted the advantage of incremental reforms, rather than the whole cumbersome and unwieldy package. Her all-or-nothing approach was challenged. The thought was that the attainment of some reform would be better than the downfall of the entire package. But no dice. She was a full, round pea residing in the most powerful pod of them all. She was not a split pea.

The final dagger in the heart of Hillarycare, as the health care reform plan was dubbed, was the mistake the health care task force made by letting the public find out the true cost. During the campaign, the Clintons had sold it to the public as a cost-free way to provide health insurance to millions of people who did not have it. How any adult bought into the idea that the government could insure thirty million people and it would not cost anything is anyone's guess. They learned their lesson though. When Obamacare was forced on us, instead of telling the public the real cost, the Obama administration simply lied about it. Over and over.

In September 1994, Hillary's albatross of a health care reform plan gave its last gasp. In its demise, Hillary could take sole credit for leading one of the single most important campaign promises to its inevitable conclusion. The task force itself had cost the taxpayers literally millions upon millions of dollars. All this for a fanciful program that never stood a chance except in the mind of Hillary.

Nothing at the White House occurs in a vacuum, and Hillary's health care debacle did not either. She was blamed for the resounding defeat. The earth began to slowly shift, well before the official health care death knell sounded. But while there were signs of the seismic shift away from all things Hillary, it was also apparent to those inside the White House walls that the Clintons had a lot more in common than it appeared. Still, the public's perception of their personalities bore no resemblance to what I observed. The theater was not even remotely akin to reality.

During this time, Hillary's star began to dim. She had singlehand-edly handed the administration its biggest defeat to date, and there was a not-so-subtle symbolism here too. She had exposed her hand. She was now clearly seen as the big-government guru she was down to her core. And her resolve that a defeat such as this would never happen again was clear. She simply would not let it.

Early on, as health care stumbled and then stumbled again, one could sense the ever-so-slight shift of power. This would be short lived. Much like a child's seesaw, as I mentioned previously, when she was up, he was down. And vice versa. Rather than a team, they came across as power mongers fighting for the upper hand. There did not seem to be much concern over who had been elected. That seemed to be a detail better left alone. The stakes were high. He seemed to derive power from her failure. And although ostensibly it was his failure too, the onus was on Hillary. Later, I would come to know that she derived her power from his ludi-crous pattern of personal behavior, something that had been ongoing, I was told, during their entire marriage.

In a bizarre way, she benefited from his misdeeds and took full advan-tage of the resultant power shift. Since his infidelities put him in the doghouse so regularly, the power inured to the benefit of the unelected Hillary more and more. Years later, when Bill was literally caught with his pants down, the power struggle came to an abrupt end. She had won. Permanently. He had lost. For always. The pea pod was now pea soup. From that moment on, the fact that his reckless behavior had threatened not only his presidency but also her future political viability made Hillary the unquestioned boss. The balance of power had finally shifted inalter-ably in her favor. She is still the boss.

These two shared a condescending and quite superior fundamental premise: they really believed they were the only two people capable of decision-making for the great unwashed. Of far more significance, they were bound to no rules. Within this no-boundaries zone, they happily operated in a state of what appeared to be self-entitled arrogance, with the predominant belief that for them, the ends justified the means. Always. It would take a while, but the entire nation finally came to learn that ethics, morality, and even the laws were for the "little people" and not for those named Clinton. It was clearly apparent inside the Clinton White House.

They both seemed to hide behind facades, hers different in some ways from his. Bill was the gregarious, "I feel your pain" kind of everyman thriving on people contact. Hillary was the polished brainiac with little time or patience for people. Adoring throngs of people were Bill's oxygen; acquiring power and wealth were Hillary's—at any cost. Both people were equally compelling. Both were able to successfully hide behind a veil of accomplishment, professionalism, and seemingly good intentions. What was seen publicly was a mask of the highest order; they allowed the public to see only the desirable traits and shielded the more significant ones, the real ones, from public view. It worked.

While Bill Clinton's temper was legendary and his volatility a force of nature, he did not affect people the way Hillary did. People were intimidated by his outbursts, and no one looked forward to his rages, but it was different. Everyone in the White House was simply afraid of her all the time. Even loyalists who had dedicated their careers to the Clintons were among those who shook in her presence. The only ones immune to this fear seemed to be her cadre of extremely close advisors. And I do mean extremely close. For everyone else, there was simply an intimidation of the grandest sort, and it was all an enigma to me. Why would anyone be afraid of a first lady? Why would the president appear to fall into this category? What an unusual dynamic this was.

It would not take me long to understand that this first lady saw enemies around every corner, and no one was exempt from possible exposure. With the travel office scandal, I learned that where no enemies lurked, she would create them to suit her needs. It mattered not a whit that she was destroying the lives of actual people as she plowed forward. People in general were not her concern. They were voters, of course. But she did not see them as living, breathing, feeling people. They were simply disposable in the furtherance of the "common good"—that is, the common good of Hillary.

I honestly wondered how I had come to be in the West Wing at all with this pervading atmosphere of paranoia. If anyone was going to be perceived as an enemy, it was going to be someone who had worked in the office of the former president's chief of staff. To the Clintons' credit, they gave me a break—until my own sense of disgust was pretty much openly revealed during events to come.

There also was an unusual dynamic between Hillary and Vice President Al Gore. On the surface, they were chillingly cordial. He seemed to try to be friendlier than she was willing to accept. It was an odd dynamic to be sure.

From an outsider's perspective and simply judging by the reported news during the campaign and then the election, the Clintons and the Gores had all appeared to be good friends. They were the new generation heading hand in hand to Washington, forging ahead with a bridge to the future. They would reverse untold damage. There was a sense of togetherness, of shared commitment. The reality was somewhat different. The relationship was strained. Al and Tipper Gore seemed a necessary evil but not necessarily a desirable addition to the administration. I wondered why. They seemed like such a nice, authentic couple with an actually authentic family. They did not seem to require props to appear this way.

In an odd sort of way, at times it seemed that Hillary and Gore quietly battled to retain the number-two slot on the ticket. There was nothing overt about this; it was an under-the-surface kind of simmering. He had come perilously close at Hillary's hand to losing his coveted West Wing real estate. But it was most telling in the way their staffs interacted. Hillary's staff had a special disdain for the Gore group. It was as if an intense rivalry had begun, and it would be a fight to the finish to determine who would be anointed the second-most-influential person in this administration—and, by association, which staff held the most clout. Few who observed this doubted that it had always been Hillary, and that, in fact, she was second to none. In the end, Gore seemed to be relegated to the most senior of staff members with a deceptively important title but with emphatically no more influence than Hillary. Or her staff. Gore was effectively neutralized, even though he retained the more coveted office.

Jumbos, which were blown-up photos of the president, would come to play a pivotal role in the Monica Lewinsky situation. But back then, they could be seen displayed prominently in the West Wing of the White House as well as in the OEOB. Jumbos came courtesy of the White House official photographer, who provided candid shots of the president and the first lady, and were hung on available wall space.

After Clinton was inaugurated, during the early days of the administration, we expected the new head shots of him and Al Gore to appear as replacements for the dual head shots of President Bush and his vice president, Dan Quayle. These are the traditional and official photos and, of course, the head shots that hang side by side of the president and vice president in just about every federal office in the land. But in the beginning days of this White House, Al Gore's head shot was nowhere to be seen. He had been unceremoniously replaced by Hillary's grinning countenance right next to hubby Bill. Everyone was instructed repeatedly that this was Hillary Rodham Clinton and to not forget it. Emphasis on the Rodham. When people were asked where the vice president's picture was, the answer was a series of shrugged shoulders. Eventually this changed, and Gore managed to get his face up next to Bill's.

As a newly minted vice president, Gore seemed to struggle to establish his own credible presence. I believe this is not new for vice presidents in general. Most of them have to find their own productive niche in a job that officially requires little more than waiting for what is akin to a doctor's putting down his stethoscope and saying "next"—and most often waiting in vain. I am certain though that the dilemma Gore faced was far more problematic than that of previous vice presidents. This vice president would be the first who would actively have to compete head-to-head for number-two status within the administration. Somehow, it was the first lady who created all the obstacles. It was all so odd to me.

In one way, Gore was successful. He was able to forge an agreement whereby, without fail, he and Clinton would lunch together once a week. Alone, with no aides. This effectively circumvented Hillary and kept him somewhat in the loop. I used to hear mutterings when the schedule was tight, as it usually was, over the "requirement" to keep the lunch on the books. But the president seemed to enjoy the lunches, and it was clear Gore did too. In the end, I believe Gore was marginally more altruistic than either of the Clintons, and I also believe his forays into the murky world of questionable fundraising were done at the behest of his political bosses. While he seemed to become a willing lackey, I don't think he was a natural at the shady Clinton dealings.

Still, Hillary's vision of a deputy presidency was somehow thwarted by the very existence of this pretender, a vice president in name. Gore was pretty much marginalized, kept to vice presidential issues of no great significance, which allowed Hillary to maintain her unofficial role as the "goddess of domestic policy."

In the end, as with all the vice presidents who had come before him, Gore's job description consisted of one sentence. It was the most important sentence a job description could contain. He simply had to remain alive, with the ability to immediately step in as president in the case of a presidential catastrophe. I often wondered what Hillary thought of that. In one fell swoop, everything would be gone, and the pretender would accede to the throne. Where would that leave her?

It was not only Al Gore who earned Hillary's disdain. It was clear she was unimpressed by not only George Stephanopoulos, Bill's communications director, but also Dee Dee Myers, Bill's first press secretary. I was surprised that each lasted as long as they did, having seen the way Hillary and her staff marginalized their accomplishments. She had a palpable disdain for all the president's West Wing political advisors. These were people other than Hillary who were too influential, people who did not always share her point of view. They didn't see enemies lurking around every single corner. Many of them would soon be gone.

Her natural suspicion concerning perceived political enemies was far more intense than that of the president. She questioned everyone's methods and motives; a constant swearing of allegiance to the team was a requirement in her eyes. Everyone who was an outsider was on Hillary's list of "Our Enemies"—a term she constantly used and meant. Since even insiders made that list, there were so very few loyalists she would ever trust. It made for a Nixonian-type siege mentality, with the rest of us wondering why.

I would later learn that it was Hillary who orchestrated the politics of utter annihilation and opposition destruction. This was always followed in the spirit of "the best defense is a good offense." Upon unleashing devastation on her perceived enemies, she then publicly bemoaned the "politics of personal destruction," metaphorically wringing her thick hands. The irony was lost on most. And while Hillary was the orchestrator, Bill was a complicit player in all her schemes. He simply could ill afford not to be, but more than that, he had no real objection to any of it anyway. Neither one was ever constrained by conscience. They simply had no moral compass and saw no need for one. Remember: ethics, morals, the laws—these were for the "little people." The Clintons' quest for wealth and power, things they felt they so richly deserved, was the righteous end that justified any means.

As I write this, I realize how all of it must sound. I suppose it does seem as if I indeed did have it in for them from the onset. That is simply not true. My perspective these days reflects all of what came before, and as I document my personal journey, I find it difficult to put into words the horror I experienced during my time in the Clinton White House. The disenchantment came so quickly. There was nary a minute to enjoy the history being made, to even enjoy the honor of working for two presidents of opposing parties in the West Wing, because the disillusionment came right away.

My agenda was always to work to the very best of my ability in support of the institution of the presidency regardless of the incumbent, regardless of party affiliation. My personal fissure began when it quickly became apparent that supporting the presidency and supporting this incumbent were at diametrically opposed odds. What should have been two parts of a whole became two distinct parts having nothing to do with each other. I could not support the institution of the presidency while sitting idly by as the incumbent and his wife tore away at the very fabric of that same institution. I believed in being a team player. The question became, whose team? For me, the choice became very clear.

There is no doubt that I believed the campaign had been unnecessarily nasty. But since my experience with campaigns had been limited, I didn't even know if this was worse than the norm. I harbored no ill will; it was more a sense of anticipation as to what the Clintons would be like. In the beginning, I chalked up some of the minor weirdness to a generational thing. These two were generational peers of mine and acted like it. The behavior and comportment of the previous administration were possibly the work of an older generation. I tried to rationalize all of it. In the end, I simply could not justify any of it in my mind.

This was not a generational difference; this was an ethics difference, a values difference, and what increasingly seemed to be an actual hoax perpetrated on the American people. Since what was publicly disseminated bore no resemblance to the truth, my experience became akin to having a backstage pass at a macabre play. Only those behind the drawn curtain could see the reality; the audience was simply regaled by the heavily rehearsed theatrics. Only it was not theater. It was the White House. The audience was the American people; the theatrics were a massive cover of lies, mistruths, and subterfuge—in the White House. I had not signed up for this. No one should have to sign up for this.

For virtually all of those in the West Wing who had happily come in with the Clintons, this was simply business as usual. There were a few odd exceptions. George Stephanopoulos, the impressive young Turk of the '92 campaign, was an enigma to me. I knew only what I had observed during the campaign: a bright and very youthful-looking spokesperson with a laser focus, effectively making his points. Again and again. If anything, I found him somewhat intimidating. The reality was somewhat different. Smart, dashing, pleasant, and dedicated, this son of a priest was both the Clinton right arm and a subtle voice of reason. His youthful appearance belied his true worth and his extraordinary abilities. He seemed to be ideologically in sync with the president. He was loyalty personified, yet it was clear he had a conscience, and it was also clear he had a good sense of right and wrong. There was a goodness, a decency to Stephanopoulos. All in all, to me he seemed a poor fit. I would later wonder if his abrupt departure from the White House was at least in part a decision to take a higher road.

The rest of the staff was unflappably accustomed to the shenanigans on all levels. This applied to the two opposing camps equally. If there was any sort of commonality between the two, this was it. Those in both Hillary's camp and Bill's were mindlessly oblivious to the darker undertones of the West Wing activity. Most had spent considerable time in the Clinton periphery, and no one even seemed to notice the disingenuousness. It simply did not exist as anything other than part of the Clinton playbook. No one even raised an eyebrow. Had the disingenuousness been only an insincerity or even a political coloring of events, that would have been one thing. When it became downright nefarious, when black was white and white was black, is when it became overwhelming to me.

It was clear from early on that a permanent career staffer had no business in the Clinton White House. We had not sworn the necessary blood oath of personal fealty. I certainly had not. Nor should we have. It would take a bona fide Clinton Kool-Aid-drinking appointee to look the other way, and in retrospect, the Clintons were right to distrust "them." Not because "they" were disloyal, but because "they" knew the difference between right and wrong, legal and illegal, honor and dishonor. "They" had a pesky allegiance to the institution of the presidency rather than to any particular incumbent. It was only a matter of time before my world and the Clintons' would collide.

I am not sure why strenuously objecting and then exposing the methods of the Clintons is considered partisan. As apolitical as I have always been, the politics were of little interest. For me, while I worked in government, politics would never would be an issue of left or right. It was always about right and wrong. And it should have been important, not spun away like so much murky glass. I was successfully branded a right-wing lunatic nevertheless. Shoot the messenger and move on. The "Clintonoids" were almost, in an odd way, impressively good at doing this. I suppose because they had a lot of practice, it seemed to work every single time.

Back in the early days, Hillary was a work in progress. From her appearance to her command of the issues, her efforts were a series of experiments with a significant learning curve. She was the single most intimidating personage in the White House. People seemed to genuinely like Bill; they also seemed to shake in their boots around Hillary.

As her "look" evolved and then evolved yet again, she mastered things that were somewhat obscure to many of the American people. She could reel off the names of every country in the world and the names of their difficult-to-pronounce leaders. Names of exotic and faraway places like Kyrgyzstan would roll off her tongue, and tricky names such as Raja Pervaiz Ashraf rolled easily from her lips. We have all heard the names over the years, and we loosely know to whom they refer. But most Americans care only vaguely where Kyrgyzstan is on the map and have never bothered to learn the pronunciation of the names of obscure foreign heads of state—if they even know who they are.

There is not a country, regardless of size, that Hillary cannot discuss intelligently. She knows how each country affects the United States. She knows the geographic locations of the most obscure lands and the political situations of each country. She knows the major and even the minor players and can effortlessly pronounce their names. She knows the issues facing each country, what our policy should be in that regard, and how she can make a difference. She can pronounce all of it now. She is a quick study. People are rightfully in awe of Hillary. There are few like her. But when God was handing out brains, grit, determination, and zeal to Hillary, he simply omitted a few other key elements. Perhaps He thought one person shouldn't have it all.

I am certain her abilities are important. Hillary can, in many ways, be quite impressive. I value other characteristics, such as integrity, character, values, truth, ethics, morality, legality, and statesmanlike behavior. These are not mere words; they represent issues of significance to all of us. Or they should. These are words that should have mattered just as much as the impressively tricky and seamless rhetoric for which both Bill and Hillary are so lauded. That these words became a series of disposable letters strung together in an abstract sort of way served only as an irritant to both the Clintons. These words smacked of boundaries, of rules, of accountability, and of consequence. None of the elements in that list of characteristics were present in the Clinton White House. They were empty words with no meaning, summarily disposable and discarded.

I have never seen before or since the level of loyalty these people garnered—such that under oath, one would lie, and the others would swear to it. Happily. Convincingly. As Bill famously said, "They can't prove anything if you lie and I lie." The result was an overflowing cesspool, emanating from the example set at the top of the heap.

The Clintons' friends and staff had a unique bond: they were all willing to cover for the Clintons. Many had known them for years and were complicit in different events over those years. It was as though they had checked their consciences at the door and morphed into robotic Clinton zombies. Many struck me as good and decent people, which made this reality even more stupefying to me. It was as though they had been brainwashed in a sense, with no remaining memory of right and wrong. It simply did not apply. This was Clinton World, after all.

This characteristic was not limited to old friends and old staff. It was clear that new staff were carefully chosen to ensure their blind devotion as well. The most wildly successful of these new appointees went on to have stellar long-term careers with the Clintons. The requirements were minimal. For starters, the appointee had to be a member of the über-elite intelligentsia with impeccable credentials. Most important, he or she had to be willing to sign a blood oath, albeit figuratively. At least I think it was figuratively. The process reminded me of my childhood, when neighborhood boys would nick their hands and become blood brothers—creating a bond literally woven through the exchange of blood.

A willingness to doggedly defend the Clintons no matter the circumstances was a written-in-stone requirement. Check your conscience at the door. A perfect example of this would be Cheryl Mills. A young lawyer in the Office of Counsel to the President, she was an attractive, smart, mild-mannered Stanford Law School grad with an eye to the future. She was one of many young associates. It was rumored that she was the girl-friend of the married counselor to the president, Bruce Lindsey. I don't know what she was like before, but I know when I met her, she had become the most desirable of Clinton staffers. She had a zealous blind loyalty, and she had hitched her star firmly to both Clintons.

Cheryl was bright, quick, and willing to lay down the gauntlet for the Clintons, right or wrong. If you follow her career, you will see she went on to numerous top-level positions with both Hillary and Bill. Her assignments included the plum position of deputy White House counsel and chief Bill Clinton defender during his impeachment. Later, in 2008, she was senior advisor and counsel for Hillary's presidential campaign, and counselor and chief of staff to Secretary of State Hillary Rodham Clinton. She also served on the board of the William Jefferson Clinton Presidential Library Foundation. Few know the dark secrets more than Cheryl. But her wild success by any standard could not be attributed even in part to her rumored personal relationship with Lindsey, one of the Clintons' closest advisors. It is attributable wholly to her choices. Loyalty of this sort is not only demanded by the Clintons; it is always handsomely rewarded. The personal cost must be staggering.

For me, this was astonishing to see. Had the devotees all made a deal with the devil? I understand zealous advocacy, the premise that everyone deserves a defense. I acknowledge that even serial killers and child molesters are entitled to an ardent defense. I simply could not understand how so many good people could look the other way in the face of so much. Because, in their signing of the blood oath, complicity inevitably followed. I guess for some that was a small price to pay.

I have come to understand the questionable world of politics. I quickly learned that spin is king and that often in the political arena, things are not as they seem. While this may be no revelation to Beltway insiders or political junkies, it was startling to me. It is merely the way of the world in present-day American politics. Simply everything is spun for ultimate advantage, and no political party is exempt. But as unpleasant as this truth may be, spin is one thing; a pattern of blatant lying to the American people is quite another.

My experience in the Clinton White House was of a daily exposure to lies and corruption from the very beginning. Spin was a distant cousin. In a perverse way, it was almost fascinating to watch the monumental lies unfold and the corruption ensue. The Clintons, chiefly Hillary, and the Clintonoids who slavishly followed them were amazingly good at it. Most impressive were the masterful methods unleashed to ensure that truth tellers were wholly decimated. I watched again and again as the Clintons managed to turn themselves into the true victims of their political enemies. Somehow it worked. Every single time.

Chapter 4

THE MAIN CLINTON SCANDALS

In Hillary's never-ending quest to avoid any responsibility for anything, in 2016 she tried to explain away the lack of the public's trust of her. Of course, she blamed it on years of wild accusations and conspiracy theories. The all-encompassing, very handy "vast right-wing conspiracy" was apparently still at it. With a straight face, she said she would have "work to do" to turn things around. Heavy lifting to be sure—but if anyone could do it, Hillary could. Sorry, Hillary, it is the stench that has always surrounded you and Bill that you cannot do much about.

The truth is that there has always been an enormous ethical cloud hovering over Hillary since the late 1970s, and for a very good reason. Her pattern of behavior is as familiar and predictable as it is disturbing. Secrecy bordering on paranoia is a hallmark of the Clinton couple, as noted previously, and literally all the Clinton-related scandals had at their core one focus. Now and as always, that focus has been the accumulation of power and wealth. There is never enough of either for the Clintons. None of the scandals was made out of whole cloth; rather they were scandals brought about by the Clintons themselves. That "vast right-wing conspiracy" was actually the efforts by the people who were appalled by the Clintons' lack of morals and ethics, and their attitude that the laws apply only to the "little people"—those unwashed masses they so thoroughly despise.

When I reflect upon my time in the West Wing of the Clinton White House, I realize I can't speak to the Arkansas-based scandals. Lumped together, these came to be known as Whitewater. What I learned about much of that came secondhand from longtime Clintonoids. To them the various scandals that occurred in Arkansas were just good ol' boys' business as usual. Normal people (that is, noncriminals) would have seen this behavior for what it was: corruption—which swirled around then governor Clinton and his lawyer wife, who was a legal representative for much of it. Fifteen people went to jail for various crimes and, magically, none of the criminality touched the couple in the middle of it.

When Whitewater began to surface like a toxic gas from a swamp in their early days in the White House, I began to get a look at the real Clintons. Far from this being business as usual, it could only be termed public corruption. The Clintonoids, a.k.a. the Little Rock Mafia, were prepared to take on any attack, believing that there were literally no laws that applied to their bosses, and no controlling legal authority who would or could ever stop them. It was a "you lie, I lie, we all lie" cover-up. This was symptomatic of their true loyalty to the Clintons, not to the institution of the presidency or to the rule of law. Naïve me, I would come to realize this *was* business as usual. The most disturbing thing was that there was no accountability or responsibility, and there were never any consequences.

I do not believe there ever was a couple like them in the White House. The Hillary-initiated scandals in the early nineties went from Filegate to Travelgate to Whitewater to Vince Foster and more. Her paranoia brought about spectacular cover-ups and showcased her willingness to routinely break the law. At the end, when Hillary was looting silverware, tableware, furniture, and a good supply of other things from the White House, her husband and her brother were also selling pardons. By then, the country was numb to it. The country was much too scandal weary to hear any of it. It smelled to high heaven, but the Clintons always seemed to get away with it thanks to their special friends. Despite the stench, they became the most powerful couple in all of politics. Later Hillary would claim they were leaving the White House dead broke. Most of us would love to be "dead broke" with only two book deals valued at $20 million to fall back on. She was apparently worried about making the mortgage payments on their houses. Plural.

Chapter 5
WHITEWATER

At most, I can present only a very brief encapsulation of White-water, the highlights of the multitude of shady business dealings in Arkansas while Bill Clinton was governor. There are any number of books available by people with far greater knowledge of these events than I have.

The scandal that became known as Whitewater is multifaceted and quite complicated. In fact, I never entirely understood all of it, as is true of most people.

It involved what can be described only as a lot of shady, behind-the-scenes, illegal business dealings. It came with the usual assortment of suspects that always seemed to orbit around the Clintons. It involved fraud, illegal loans, and speculative land deals that failed and yet somehow, some people profited from them. The worst of it was a failed savings and loan association through which there may have been money laundering. For those of you who remember the savings-and-loan meltdown during the eighties, you won't be surprised to hear about it.

The original Whitewater was a land development project—in and of itself, perfectly legal. A married couple, James (Jim) and Susan McDougal, proposed the project to the Clintons around 1978, while Bill was Arkansas' attorney general. The idea was to buy approximately two hundred acres of land along the White River near Flippin, Arkansas. It's a beautiful vacation area in the Ozark Mountains. They were going to subdivide the property into lots and sell them for vacation homes. Unfortunately, a recession hit, and interest rates skyrocketed to 20 percent. This made the bottom fall out of the vacation-home market, and the deal went bust.

In fact, the Clintons claim they lost money out of their own pockets on this—although Hillary did manage to make it up in a cattle futures deal. She invested $1,000 which returned $100,000 in about eight months. Nothing to see here though.

About the same time as Clinton's gubernatorial loss in 1980, Jim McDougal decided to go into the banking business. He purchased the Bank of Kingston in 1980 and Woodruff Savings and Loan in '82. He renamed them the Madison Bank and Trust and Madison Guaranty Savings and Loan Association, respectively.

In 1985, McDougal held a fundraiser at Madison Guaranty's Little Rock, Arkansas, office to pay off Bill Clinton's campaign debt from the year before, which was supposedly $50,000. McDougal raised $35,000, of which $12,000 was in Madison Guaranty cashier's checks. Nothing to see here.

Later that same year, McDougal invested in a construction project called Castle Grande. It was for the development of one thousand acres of land near Little Rock. He needed $1.75 million for the purchase. Legally he could borrow only $600,000 from Madison Guaranty. McDougal used others, including an employee of Madison Guaranty, to funnel the rest of the money, $1.15 million, from Madison Guaranty. The money was moved around to various entities to make tracing it very difficult. This, of course, smells strangely like money laundering to cover up what were illegal loans. The lawyer handling all of this just happened to be Hillary Clinton, then an associate at the Rose Law Firm.

You may recall an investigation involving a subpoena to Hillary by attorney Kenneth Starr for her billing records from the Rose Law Firm. He was looking for her involvement in what was clearly a fraudulent loan scheme. Those records were mysteriously missing and never produced. Magically, they turned up in the White House residence several years later. Nothing to see here.

In 1986, federal investigators called the Castle Grande scheme a sham. Somehow, Castle Grande earned $2 million in commissions and fees for McDougal's business associates as well as an unknown amount in fees for the Rose Law Firm. Castle Grande collapsed for good in 1989, costing the taxpayers $4 million. This, in turn, triggered the collapse of Madison Guaranty, which cost the taxpayers another $73 million.

Although all the people involved were friends of Bill Clinton and/or contributors to his campaign, none of this touched him or his wife, the lawyer for Castle Grande.

A federal investigator, L. Jean Lewis, was investigating the Madison Guaranty failure. In September 1992, she submitted a criminal referral to the FBI naming both Clintons as witnesses. The Little Rock U.S. attorney (Charles Banks) and the FBI declined to pursue it. From 1992 to 1994, during the time Clinton was president, Lewis issued several more referrals. All were declined.

There were numerous investigations into the business dealings swirling around then governor Bill Clinton, all of which involved very close friends and business associates. There were only two people who would point a finger at Bill Clinton.

David Hale, a former municipal court judge and Arkansas banker, became Ken Starr's chief witness. He testified that Governor Clinton pressured him into giving Jim McDougal an illegal three-hundred-thousand-dollar loan. He testified to this at the trial of Jim and Susan McDougal in 1989 regarding the failure of Madison Guaranty. However, he had failed to tell this to FBI agents when they first interviewed him, damaging his credibility.

Eventually, Jim McDougal, angered by Bill Clinton's refusal to help his old friend, allegedly told Susan he would make Bill pay for this. She went to the media with this story, which made Jim look like a bitter, angry ex-friend.

Susan McDougal, a favorite Clinton martyr, refused to answer any questions about the Clintons, thereby providing them with plausible deniability. She did eighteen months in jail for contempt of court. Not surprisingly, Susan was on the list of last-minute pardons Bill gave out. Nothing to see here.

When all was said and done, fifteen people were convicted of forty crimes from what collectively came to be known as Whitewater. Most of these crimes were felonies concerning fraudulent business dealings. All of this swirled directly around the Clintons and yet they would claim they knew nothing about any of it and none of it touched them. Of course, potentially incriminating evidence that might have tied Hillary to at least some of it conveniently disappeared, only to turn up years later.

Chapter 6

THE TRAVEL OFFICE MASSACRE

The travel office scandal has been given short shrift over the years in countless books, all compiled from an outsider's perspective. This story has fallen by the wayside, a side story with little resonance. Travelgate. A term heaped together with all the other Clinton "gates." It has a vague lingering odor but no real significance. It's a concoction of the "vast right-wing conspiracy," a "nothing there, there" story. "Let's move on; nothing to see here," the Clintonoid apologists dutifully informed the nation. And move on, the country did.

There has been no firsthand observation and no accounting from the trenches, so to speak, of this sad tale. Nothing from an insider who witnessed what happened to the professionals in the White House travel office. In the grand scheme of the Clinton corruption, it was a small event. But this story, along with the firing of the entire correspondence unit, is important and accurately represents the person who is Hillary Rodham Clinton. It deserves to be told in detail from a firsthand point of view. It is said that if we ignore our past, we are destined to repeat it. That is precisely how Hillary, relying on people's forgetting the past, has blithely operated during her entire career, and it is important to address—in detail.

"We need these people out; we need our people in!"

I personally saw this statement in a memo in Hillary's handwriting. It was on top of a travel office document in Vince Foster's possession well before the mass firing of the travel office staff. The "out" and the "in" were underlined several times, with emphatic pen slashes across the upper-left-hand portion of the letter, the bold "HRC" there for all to see. Except it was not meant for me to see. I don't recall the specific date of the memo. I do know it was in April 1993, and the faux investigation and firings did not take place until May.

Hillary would put out a statement at the time of the firings when all hell was, once again, breaking loose about the Clintons' treatment of dedicated staff. Those staffers were dedicated to the wrong thing as far as Hillary was concerned: the office of the president and not the Clintons personally.

"I had no role in the decision to terminate the [travel office] employees," Hillary claimed—a chilling statement to those of us who knew better. Ultimately, it became even more so when she lied to the General Accounting Office, asserting in her written answers to twenty-six questions that she did not recall anything about any mass firings in the travel office or the correspondence office and that she had no firsthand knowledge of any of it. She claimed she had nothing to do with any of it. Those answers were signed under penalty of perjury on March 24, 2006, by Hillary Rodham Clinton. The behavior was Hillary 101, as true today as it was then.

After the mass firing of the entire correspondence department, when Hillary's paranoia decided the travel office had to be cleaned out as well, the Clintons needed to avoid the hue and cry those firings created. They were losing the news cycle with each new misstep. This time they would cover their tracks. Their solution was to ensure that the travel office firing was for cause. Since cause did not exist, they simply created it out of whole cloth. A Clinton operative, Catherine Cornelius, was sent into the travel office to find malfeasance or make it up.

Billy Dale was fired after a thirty-two-year stint at the White House, and he and his longtime staff of professionals were given an hour to clear out their desks. They were humiliatingly escorted off the White House grounds in a government van with no windows and with the uniformed Secret Service watching their departure. With a heavy heart, I felt I had let them down. I hadn't warned them. I should have. They deserved so much better. And the tug of war with my conscience that had begun essentially my first week in the Clinton West Wing was now in full swing. I owed my oath of office to the institution of the presidency, not to the incumbent. But I worked for the incumbent. I knew how wrong all of it was. I did not know how I could change it, or how I could share it. Or how long I could stomach it.

And just like that began the character assassination of Billy Dale, longtime director of the White House travel office, and his entire trusted team. But this massacre of dedicated public servants was different than the one involving the correspondence office. Dale was arrested, charged with embezzlement, and publicly humiliated, and would go on to fight the good fight in a court of law much later, valiantly defending his good name and his record. In the end, the outcome—he was acquitted after a thirteen-day trial—did not matter much; Hillary's damage had been long since done. Billy Dale's only crime was being in the way and holding a job that Hillary wanted for someone else, someone with puppy dog loyalty to the Clintons. His life was never the same after that.

Hillary gave decent people's lives and the damage she did to them about as much thought as she gave the dirt under her feet. I remember David Watkins, White House director of administration, prophetically declaring, "There will be hell to pay" if Hillary's wishes vis-à-vis the travel office were not carried out posthaste. Well, that did not quite cover it. Later, as I mentioned, she would swear she had nothing to do with it and/ or did not recall any specifics. This, from a woman who could recall the names of all of the countries on the planet and the leader of each of them.

It was horrifying enough that the Clintons wanted to erase Billy Dale—a man who had loyally served several presidents and their staffs over so many years—and his staff. To reiterate, all White House staff, whether political or that core group of "permanent" career civil servants who traditionally serve presidents over the span of many years, ultimately serve at the pleasure of the president. It is understood. However, no other president had sacked the permanent staff. Clinton's predecessors all understood the inherent value in retaining those who made the trains run on time. They were valued members of the White House staff, and they deserved to be. Until the Clintons. It was that blood oath again. Those who had served previous presidents were thought to be the dreaded "them" whom "we" could not control. I recall Hillary's ousting of those thought to be "them" beginning early on. It was obvious that she had come in with the attitude that "they" had to go and be replaced by "us."

That the Clintons could easily have just fired any of them made what they did even more egregious. Mere removal was no longer palatable for the Little Rock crowd. It would have caused them to appear as cold and callous in the public's eye. The public might well have begun to disbelieve the carefully crafted "I feel your pain" theater. No matter how fraudulent, going forward there had to be reasons given for the mass firing.

By turning the seven dedicated United States federal civil servants into shady and inept characters headed by an alleged crook, the Clintons effectively vacated the travel office, solved that pesky problem, and filled the empty desks with Clinton appointees. Sadly, they were "ridding the government of the bad guys." In one fell swoop, they orchestrated the abomination, implemented it, ruined lives, and later claimed they did no such thing. It was a headliner for a while but quickly lost steam, given the twenty-four hours of news to fill. The country moved on, but lives were destroyed. The Clinton mantra worked. I'm certain it still does.

Catherine Cornelius was a twenty-three-year-old brash blonde variously described as Bill's cousin or friend of the family. That it was said with a knowing wink and a nod did not go unnoticed by anyone. One irreverent staffer tried to set me straight by quietly throwing "You know, they marry their damn sisters in Arkansas, so a cousin's not a stretch" over his shoulder as he left the room. It is my understanding that Catherine is, in fact, Bill's third cousin.

Early in the first administration, Catherine proudly informed me that she would be heading the travel office in the very near future. How could she possibly have known that? Because of the respect and affection I had developed for the professionals in the travel office, this statement was quite disquieting. Surely, they would not put this silly young girl at the helm of that office.

I originally met her in her basement West Wing office. She was working in the office of David Watkins, who was at the time the assistant to the president for administration. He was a key figure in implementing Hillary's demands that the entire travel office staff be fired. Watkins, along with the ubiquitous Harry Thomason—Hollywood producer, Clinton crony, and fellow Arkansan—spearheaded this travesty for Hillary.

Thomason seemed to be a constant presence in those early days. He was a guest in the residence and seemed to have carte blanche to be anywhere he wished inside the West Wing. He was always roaming the halls. Some said he had an office in the residence.

He was known around the White House as a big FOB (friend of Bill's) who happened to be good at theatrical productions. Since everything the Clintons tended to present publicly was pretty much an elaborate act, his services were invaluable. It's no wonder he stuck around. And like most of the Clinton staff, he was allowed free rein without the benefit of a security clearance. It's little wonder Hillary did what she did with her email server years later when she was in the State Department. Convenience for a Clinton is far more important than such trivial matters as the nation's security.

Thomason's hand was always behind the scenes, orchestrating the message, the image, the lie, like a magician conjuring a new reality from thin air. I believe that it was he who years later, in 1998, orchestrated Bill's feigned outrage during the debacle that was the wagging-finger episode—I did not have sexual relations with that woman—in the Monica Lewinsky saga. That was when Bill Clinton lied unconvincingly on national TV. I'm certain Thomason directed Hillary's pained expression—along with everything else, including her defiant Easter-egg yellow pantsuit—when, as the "betrayed" wife, she was forced to stand stoically by Bill's side for all the world to see. It was political theater at its worst, and it had Thomason's name all over it. That was one production I'm thinking he wished he hadn't produced.

It was during the travel office debacle when David Watkins, Harry Thomason, and Catherine Cornelius came together. Their agendas were one and the same: first and foremost to serve Hillary, of course, but also to score a home run or two for their own individual personal gain. Watkins wanted a win for his office. Cornelius wanted to leave the rank of administrative assistant behind and head up a real White House office. And Thomason, well, he had his eye on money.

Thomason had an interest in an air charter broker called TRM. It was known that he desperately wanted the White House charter business, apparently not simply because of the financial windfall it would bring but also because of the bragging rights and prestige such a contract would bring. Plainly put, it would be good for business. So, Thomason's goal was a lucrative White House contract. Hillary was likely orgasmic at the opportunity. She could score a "twofer" by ridding the White House of some potential disloyalists while shoveling taxpayer money to a Clinton lackey—getting rid of the "them" and placing loyalists in those slots.

Soon, with the blessing of both Watkins and Thomason, Cornelius was sent on a covert mission to document malfeasance in the travel office. And, as with all other Clinton business, when there was none to be found, it simply had to appear as if there was. A later accounting review by KPMG found careless record keeping but revealed no graft at all. But that didn't matter to the Clintons.

When Cornelius brought Thomason the fruits of her cloak-and-dagger reconnaissance in the travel office, manufactured evidence as it was, they both knew it would be enough to oust the entire office for cause. Thomason brought this ostensible evidence of malfeasance directly to the Clintons. By this time, Hillary already had been pressuring White House chief of staff Mack McLarty to act, but the process wasn't moving fast enough to suit her. And Vince Foster, deputy White House counsel, was caught in the crosshairs, seemingly walking a tightrope between his conscience and Hillary's demands.

It was Bill Kennedy—William Kennedy III—former Rose Law Firm managing partner, who called the FBI and sicced it on the travel office, telling the FBI that this directive "came from the highest levels." Eventually, Kennedy and Watkins were officially reprimanded by the White House. They were soldiers who fell on their swords for Hillary.

After the trial for embezzlement, it took a jury less than two hours to acquit Billy Dale. But the age-old question lingered: "Where do I go to get my good name back?" He never did. The soiled hands of those who played a nefarious role in this shameful debacle were never exposed. By the time the truth came out, no one cared. It was old news. They were never punished. As we would see in the decades following, the Clintons would continue this tried-and-true MO with virtually everything they touched. If it ain't broke, don't fix it. Yet it is all so broken.

But Dale wasn't alone. Hillary removed the barber who had been cutting presidential hair for years, along with White House chef Pierre Chambrin and two other chefs. We wondered how the Clintons could appear so empathetic and compassionate publicly, and so vindictive privately. I came to know that their sense of paranoia about "them" was born of their own dirty tricks, which required a fealty unheard of by most.

Eventually, Hillary came under scrutiny for allegedly having played a central role in the firings and making false statements about her involvement in them. In 2000, independent counsel Robert Ray, having taken over for Kenneth Starr, issued his final report on Travelgate. Ray declined to prosecute her. He concluded by saying that while some of Hillary's statements were factually false, there was insufficient evidence that these statements either were knowingly false or that she understood that her statements had led to the firings.

In plain English, she lied about her involvement in the firings, and those of us inside the White House knew she lied about it, but proving it in court would be unlikely. She would simply continue to lie, and others would lie on her behalf, creating reasonable doubt.

Chapter 7
FILEGATE

Most people probably do not remember much about the Clinton scandal that came to be known as Filegate. In fact, most of the country did not pay much attention to it at the time it happened. That was, and still is, unfortunate. It was another item on a long list of instances when the Clintons and their pals showed their disdain for the rule of law—or even for right versus wrong. This case demonstrated an abuse of power that makes anything President Trump may have done seem trivial in comparison. Most fair-minded people do not believe that the alleged abuse of power for which Trump was impeached even occurred, let alone that it rose to the level of treason or a high crime or misdemeanor.

Filegate began shortly before I left the White House to go back to the Pentagon in the spring of 1993. It did not come to light until 1996, when Whitewater special prosecutor Kenneth Starr found hundreds of FBI files stacked in the office of Craig Livingstone, director of personnel security at the White House. Livingstone was a former bar bouncer who got his job at the White House from Hillary when he wore a chicken costume to harass George Bush during the election campaign. How those files came to be at the White House, let alone in the office of Hillary's White House featherweight security chief, has never been discovered or explained. The best the White House ever came up with was to claim it was a "bureaucratic mix-up."

Bill Kennedy—as mentioned, one of Hillary's cronies from the Rose Law Firm—was an associate counsel to the president. His office was across West Executive Avenue in the OEOB. When FBI agents were brought in to investigate the travel office and go after Billy Dale, it was Kennedy who had warned them that if they didn't do it, he would get the IRS to do it. He was another one of Hillary's toadies.

Kennedy's White House job was to vet applicants for appointments as staffers. At least that was his day job. His real job was to be on call for Hillary's bidding 24/7. Kennedy's office was a spacious one, with tall windows and traditional White House mahogany furniture—at least what you could see of it. His desk, and every available surface, was covered floor to ceiling in files—real paper files obtained illegally from the FBI. More than nine hundred of them. Most of the files were on Republicans, Hillary's favorite "them" enemies. The files contained personal information that should never have been released at all, let alone to partisan politicians.

Since Kennedy's job was to vet applicants for appointments, why did he need FBI files on Republicans such as former secretary of state James Baker; Kenneth Duberstein, chief of staff for President Ronald Reagan; and Marlin Fitzwater, press secretary for President George H. W. Bush, to name just a few? Had these people applied for jobs in the Clinton White House for which they needed to be vetted? Pretty unlikely. And that is just the tip of the iceberg. It turned out that there were also hundreds of FBI files, legitimately obtained by the FBI, on Republicans stacked in the office of two Hillary-appointed political operatives.

What was the White House's explanation for this? A bureaucratic mix-up. Imagine even having the nerve to claim that hundreds of FBI files on political opponents—Hillary always referred to them as enemies— turned up in the offices of two political hacks such as Kennedy and Livingstone due to a simple mix-up, and to get away with it. They also managed to convince the independent counsel that none of these files were perused for any political purpose. Of course, since it was just a simple mix-up, they never had to explain just what they did with the files and why they kept them for three years.

The administration did come up with a story to explain the bureaucratic mix-up: an Army official detailed for temporary duty to the White House, Anthony Marceca, had made a simple mistake in requesting the files from the Department of Justice. He supposedly used an outdated Secret Service list of personnel who had formerly held White House passes. Why wouldn't everybody believe that? Later, the Justice Department conceded that it had erred in releasing the files. Oops. You lie, I lie, we all lie, and everybody swears to it. Then keep your mouth shut. The Mafia calls this code of silence *omertà*, and it works.

Marceca's immediate superior, Craig Livingstone, claimed he did not know that Marceca had obtained the files at all. Apparently, he never asked Marceca, or anyone else, what the nine hundred files lying around the office were and where they came from. Again, why wouldn't you believe that? In my opinion, since Craig Livingstone was not blessed with a superior intellect, that is not as hard to believe as it would be coming from someone else. Fortunately, this was the final straw of his incompetence, and he resigned shortly thereafter.

The revelations finally came out three years later in 1996 and provoked a strong initial political and press reaction. The Republicans were not quite that willing to simply buy the nonsense about a bureaucratic mix-up having caused the transfer of nine hundred files from the FBI—likely because many of the files covered White House employees from previous Republican administrations, including top presidential advisors. Further, allegations were made that senior White House figures, including Hillary, may have requested and read the files for political purposes, and that the first lady had authorized the hiring of the underqualified Livingstone.

Despite investigations by the House Committee on Oversight and Government Reform, the Senate Judiciary Committee, and the Whitewater independent counsel, the matter more or less petered out. Eventually, in 1998, independent counsel Kenneth Starr exonerated President Bill Clinton as well as the first lady of any involvement in the matter. In 2000, independent counsel Robert Ray, having taken over from Starr, issued his final report on Filegate. His report found no credible evidence of any criminal activity by any individual in the matter. He also concluded that there was no credible evidence that senior White House figures or the first lady had requested the files or had acted improperly or testified improperly regarding Livingstone's hiring.

The ending finally came on March 9, 2010, when a separate lawsuit on the matter brought by Judicial Watch, a conservative watchdog group, was dismissed by federal district court judge Royce Lamberth. Lamberth found there was no intentional misconduct and that the acquisition of hundreds of FBI background files on political opponents of the Clintons was simply a mix-up. When people testify under oath, they are given the benefit of the doubt. It is presumed they are telling the truth. If everyone testifies to the same story or cannot recall anything (Hillary's personal favorite answer), the investigation will end up going nowhere.

During my time at the Clinton White House, I learned that if everyone commits perjury but there is no forensic or documentary evidence to prove it, it is virtually impossible to prove that anyone committed perjury. It is a foolproof system that works remarkably well. I don't know that a White House administration before or since was or has been this committed to its own version of events—all for one and one for all. I do know that the Clinton White House's efforts in this regard were impressive to watch. They were sad, of course, in the greater scheme of things, but impressive nonetheless.

Chapter 8
HILLARY CLINTON AND VINCE FOSTER

I was a young bride of a junior Army officer when Hillary was working on the Richard Nixon impeachment inquiry. All these years later, I can't help but compare the startling similarities between the Clintons and Nixon—they're rich with irony. The exact same things a young and formidable Hillary apparently found illegal in the early seventies appear to have become veritable hallmarks for the way the more seasoned Hillary operates. Political enemies. Dirty tricks. Obfuscation. The denials. The lack of conscience. "The rules do not apply to us." "The ends justify the means." Or it could be that Hillary simply picked these traits up from the man who was once known as Tricky Dick.

All the things she found abhorrent about President Nixon appear to be the selfsame characteristics ingrained in her psyche. Hillary, the operator, carefully selected her own plumbers. These were the individuals who could best be relied on to do her dirty work, leaving her hands squeaky clean—except, to those of us around her who didn't drink the Kool-Aid, she could never quite get rid of the stench. Further, her plumbers could be relied on to lie for her. Falling on swords was an unspoken but crucial element of each job description, and often outside help was necessary.

No one said no to Hillary. No one, including or maybe even specifically, the president, would dare. As volatile as he was—as I mentioned, his temper when the cameras were off was legendary—he was a kitty when it came to the volcano that was Mount Hillary. If he wanted to keep doing his sexcapades, Hillary had to be placated.

The foot soldiers knew their marching orders and knew, too, that she would not tolerate a paper trail leading back to her. It did not need to be said. Everyone understood—well, except perhaps David Watkins, whose long-standing familiarity with Hillary's method of operation meant he would stubbornly put pen to paper. His memo to Hillary making it quite clear she was in the loop of the travel office fiasco was conveniently found in the residence years later by another erstwhile foot soldier, Carolyn Huber. But by then, it was too late to make a difference.

Hillary escaped Travelgate consequences the way she has always escaped all the scandals. She lies, her toadies swear to her lies, and by use of threats and intimidation. Also, back then, by relying on her position as first lady to provide cover, she knew how to play the victim with the best of them. After all, it is somewhat unseemly to go after a first lady for criminal behavior, isn't it? But what if the first lady is a crook?

Of course, many years later, she was no longer first lady. But in 2016, as a former first lady, former senator, and former secretary of state, as the Democratic presidential nominee, she was "too big to jail." That was when she blatantly used a personal server for everything, including top secret classified information, which would have sent anyone else to jail. How does anyone know how many times her server was hacked and how much classified information went to, well, let's just call them people who were not on the dissemination lists? We can believe such stalwarts of truth as James Comey, John Brennan, and James Clapper, can't we?

As I've mentioned several times, the public Hillary bore no resemblance to the private. For all her wide-eyed gazes and enormous smiles on the campaign trail, Hillary's presence behind the scenes was quite intimidating. Even those who had known her for many years felt the formidable and threatening pressure. Theirs was a lockstep response to her bidding, with no thought to ramifications or to simple right and wrong. It is what has allowed her over the decades to orchestrate anything she wants, in the end blaming the hue and cry on her perceived political enemies—on that good old, extremely convenient "vast right-wing conspiracy" she so cleverly invented and then, over time, convinced herself really existed.

When David Watkins wrote there would be "hell to pay" if her wishes were not carried out in the firing and subsequent maligning of the travel office, this sentiment captured fully the atmosphere in the White House. No one could dole out horrific fear better than Hillary. Everyone wanted to avoid the icy stare. We all stayed out of the shotgun blast. Most of us ducked. When she was around, the entire staff literally kept their heads down so as not to be noticed by her. It is no joke. If you looked at her in a way she did not like, you could be gone the next day. Nice atmosphere to work in. It was even more vile for me after I had worked with the professionals in the first Bush administration.

A perfect example of how childishly petty, vindictive, and just plain mean she could be occurred in March 1994. Chris Emery, one of the White House ushers, who had served in that capacity for eight years, was summarily fired at the behest of Hillary. A side note: she never fired anyone personally. She always had someone else do her dirty work. Emery's professionalism was above reproach. What was his egregious crime that brought about his firing? He had recently spoken on the phone with his highly regarded previous boss, former first lady Barbara Bush, about a computer he had helped her set up.

Of course, the Clinton spin machine came up with a bunch of lies, claiming he was passing on personal information about the Clintons—an allegation Chris Emery vehemently denied. Being a professional and doing an excellent job did not matter. Puppy dog loyalty was and still is the only thing that matters.

I had gotten to know Vince Foster, who was dignified, reserved, and distinguished, while working in the immediate office of the president during the first three months of the new administration. He was a serious, earnest man. He was also Hillary's "go-to" guy, known to be her willing lackey. I believe he was so much more. While he had dirtied his hands in the service of Hillary, he did so reluctantly, but at the same time he was eager to please her highness.

Vince's go-to guy, in turn, was his former managing partner of the Rose Law Firm, Bill Kennedy. Arriving a bit later than the rest, Kennedy became an associate counsel to the president and quite a bit more. It was easily believable that this down-home, "aw, shucks" good ol' boy didn't mind routinely getting his hands dirty. That's why they make soap, right? Essentially, the heavy hitters from Little Rock's Rose Law Firm were ready, willing, and able to make a difference—at any price.

Rumors abounded in the West Wing, but one that seemed to have legs was the rumor about Vince and Hillary back in the day. Well, not so long ago, but before they got to the White House. The rumor claimed that they had had a long-standing affair while both were partners at the Rose Law Firm. I don't know if this was true or not. I do know that if it had been true at one time, it was clearly no longer so when they arrived at the White House, although holding that over his head would help explain his behavior toward her. She treated him as her personal whipping boy. And boy, could she whip.

There was a level of intimacy in her abuse toward him; the situation was reminiscent of a couple fighting with one holding all the cards. There were many times when Vince became almost concave looking and pale faced while he quietly endured countless strident and obscene dressings-down in Hillary's office area. He seemed to melt in shame during these occasions, his usually ramrod-straight posture simply crumbling. I felt sorry for this good, kind, decent man and vowed to avoid Hillary at all costs. If she could not see you, you might just avoid being hit by the shotgun blast.

Bill Kennedy's go-to guy for dirty tricks was the incredibly unqualified, newly branded head of White House personnel security, the aforementioned Craig Livingstone. As mentioned, he was a former bar bouncer; he was a rough-around-the-edges toady who knew he had won the lottery when he was given the White House job. As I said, his background experience for this position was that he had worn a chicken suit during much of the '92 campaign to heckle George Bush at various events. Seriously.

This is how this ludicrous nonentity solidified his position with the most important person in the administration, bar none. No, not Bill. Hillary. And this ridiculously unqualified person was so grateful to be given this quite lucrative opportunity that he would have done anything that Kennedy—or Hillary, by extension—wanted. And he did. That was always the point.

I used to chuckle, despite being a little bit horrified, when in the beginning, Livingstone routinely walked from the OEOB to the West Wing appearing to talk into a device on his wrist. Only there was no wire or earpiece. He was simply speaking down his sleeve. Head of security. Secret Service. I think he thought it made him look important. I know he thought it made him more marketable as date bait. He often asked us to fix him up with one intern or another. He sure liked those type of props. They did not help. Go figure.

It would be Livingstone's and Kennedy's fingers that were caught in the Filegate cookie jar, when those nine hundred raw-data FBI files of former Republican appointees found their way to them. The two made good use of them. As was always the case with the Clintons, Filegate, which should have been an alarmingly gargantuan news story, became a temporary dustup before eventually petering out to nothingness. I mention this again in this chapter about Vince Foster for a reason.

I would personally become one of the Clintons' victims in 1998, when they attempted to smear me with information from my FBI file. In the end, I sued the Pentagon and the White House and won. Still, the damage was done—of course, that was always the point.

Livingstone was a brilliant choice when you consider that Hillary chose him knowing he couldn't hope for a job as head cashier at a gas station, let alone as head of personnel security at the White House. His filial-style devotion was guaranteed. Oh, and how do I know this? He told me himself. Hillary later claimed she didn't even know who he was. I'll bet he loved that. Later, during one of the countless investigations of Clinton wrongdoing, an intern testified that she saw Hillary greet Livingstone warmly and by name. Oops, someone forgot the "I lie, you lie" Hillary cover-up creed. I wonder where *that* intern ended up.

During the various depositions, congressional investigations, and lawsuits over the FBI files, the White House stonewalled to the bitter end. People steadfastly refused to answer who had hired this featherweight to head one of the most sensitive offices of the White House. Eventually, they came up with an answer, despicably blaming it on the dead guy: Vince Foster, who was found dead in 1993. Yup. The White House spin machine later tried to claim that it was Vince Foster who hired Craig Livingstone. Said with the straightest of faces, of course. Aside from being ridiculous on its face, it was a pathetic Hail Mary pass to finish the subject off once and for all. You cannot question the dead guy.

Hillary Clinton, a woman who was supposed to be at least a close friend of Vince's, had her lackeys cover for her by blaming him for her screw-up.

Attorney Bernard (Bernie) Nussbaum, Vince's boss in name only, could never remember Livingstone's name. Vince looked askance at Livingstone with raised brows whenever he encountered him. Having nothing to do with the campaign, Vince would have had no opportunity to know scum like Livingstone. Had Vince known Livingstone, the bouncer would have been the last person he would have hired. Correction: he would not have been the last; he simply would never have been hired.

Craig Livingstone, ex-bouncer and chicken-suited heckler, was hired by Hillary. Of course, she lied about this—in fact, she said she had never heard of him. This was the type of loyalty she demanded and never recip-rocated. Professionalism, ability, experience, competence? Little wonder the White House under the Clintons ran like a frat house filled with liberal partiers.

The Clinton Little Rock gang was a close bunch. And I do mean gang. Little Rock is a relatively small place, and this bunch seemed almost incestuous from the start of the administration. Right away there was a noticeably real sense of "us" versus "them." In the beginning, "they" began as anyone who did not come from Little Rock. Later it came to include all those who refused to take the blood oath and, above all, those who would dare cross the Clintons. "They" became anyone who was not one of "us."

As in every White House, the hours are grotesquely long. I spent many a night on a White House office sofa, when in the wee hours of morning it simply made no sense to try to get home only to turn around moments later and head back. Thank God for my parents, for my former husband, and for good friends who generously helped fill in for me at home during these times.

This White House was no different. Tuesday nights were the Little Rock gang nights. Armed with the latest Zagat guide, they tried out various culinary locations en masse recommended in the guide, with the hope that they would ultimately hit all of them. Sometimes the president and Hillary joined them. As I recall, the group of regulars included Vince Foster; Webb Hubbell, an assistant attorney general; Bruce Lindsey; Marsha Scott; Bill Kennedy; Deborah (Deb) Coyle (the president's current secretary and a former Rose Law Firm secretary) and her husband, Bill, who had been given a job at one of the agencies; and sometimes Nancy Hernreich, the president's personal assistant and a class act. Getting together and trying out D.C.'s finest restaurants was a regular weekly event, but it seemed to slowly peter out after Vince Foster's funeral.

I thought it was sweet that this tight-knit social group crossed the professional divide and included the hottest of the hot shots and the worker bees as well. They all had one thing in common: they came from Little Rock. They all knew the score. They were each fiercely loyal to Bill and Hillary Clinton. Each possessed a sort of blind loyalty—a loyalty so intense that it went without saying that one would lie and the other would swear to it. I found it somewhat incongruous that they were, for the most part, individually decent people. Collectively they represented the Little Rock Mafia. They were not gun toting—not that I noticed, anyway—but they would have done just about anything on behalf of their misguided bosses. In the beginning, it was endearing but with intimidating undertones, and then it became frightening.

They all had something else in common. Months after arriving at the West Wing, all still had temporary security badges. None of them had bothered to fill out the extensive security forms to begin the intensive background evaluation required for anyone—and legally, everyone—working in the West Wing. And this in the president's house. Hillary concerning herself with protecting the nation's secrets? As I've said, not when it interfered with convenience for her.

Nancy Hernreich was an enigma to me. She was the first Protector—one of three categories of people surrounding Clinton; Protectors, Facilitators, and Graduates—I came to know. Elegant and quietly efficient, Nancy was unfailingly pleasant and warm. The director of Oval Office Operations, she was a single mom, startlingly beautiful, completely professional, soft-spoken, and efficient. She often spoke of her daughter who was attending the National Cathedral School.

In the beginning, she had the office immediately adjacent to the Oval Office Dining Room. From there, she could not monitor the comings and goings in the Oval Office—a necessity in protecting Bill from Bill, probably Nancy's most important job. Nancy eventually switched offices because she needed to be front and center near Betty Currie, the president's secretary, to better monitor and keep track of Bill. I'm sure she saved Bill from Bill many times, but Bill scheduled Monica Lewinsky only when Nancy was not there. Bill and Monica even used her tiny office once for an assignation, or so Monica said. The man was like a child who needed a nanny to always keep an eye on him and monitor his behavior—notoriously when it came to women.

At first, I had no idea what prompted the move out front to be by Betty Currie. Some say it was because George Stephanopoulos or maybe Rahm Emanuel, a senior advisor to the president, wanted her space. I believe it was because Nancy could control nothing from the "back door" and needed to be closer to the gate in the front. I could not figure out if she was a long-ago graduate who had dedicated herself to this politician, a Protector, or simply an efficient professional who had landed a great job over the years. I will say that of all the Little Rock Gang, I admired her the most. She seemed to want to keep everything aboveboard. Later I determined that Nancy was a significant Protector. Protecting Bill from Bill was a full-time job. Nancy, and a host of others, tried valiantly but failed each time. He was lucky to have her. I remember thinking that Nancy Hernreich and Vince Foster shared something more than their time in Little

Rock in common: they were the two individuals close to the Clintons who, without a doubt, would have been more at home as Bush appointees than Clinton ones.

Bruce Lindsey, senior counselor to the president, was hard not to like. He was the chief Protector. With his Arkansas drawl and his "aw, shucks" kind of personality, he was instantly your friend. Or so he could make you believe. He arrived in D.C. with the rest of the Little Rock gang, but did not arrive with his wife, Beth, and the rest of his family.

Lindsey, a nice guy with an easy smile, was fiercely loyal. He was at once a Protector, Facilitator, and friend of the Clintons. It was to Lindsey's law practice that Bill Clinton went to lick his wounds when he lost his first election for governor of Arkansas. In fact, Lindsey was probably the chief Facilitator as well as the chief Protector. He was, I believe, the only individual who wore all three hats, Protector, Facilitator, and Graduate, and he wore each exceptionally well. With his wide grin and open and disarming charm, you just could not imagine him doing dirty deeds for his boss. As I found out myself much, much later, looks can be deceiving.

I very much liked and respected Vince Foster. As I said, I always thought he acted more like a Bush appointee than a Clinton appointee. Buttoned up and reserved, this man had an elegance seldom seen in the Clinton West Wing. He was always courteous, unfailingly polite, and considerate— virtues that were anathema to Hillary unless it suited her or the cameras were on. I have a feeling that he became involved in some of the more cloak-and-dagger things at Hillary's direction under duress, not by choice.

Still, choice or not, I believe he self-flagellated to literally the point of death. For some inner reason (love?), he simply could not endure failing Hillary. And thanks to her, he felt he had failed her, across the board. Vince was a man with character. He should never have allowed his loyalty to supersede his value system, but he did. For whatever reason, he tossed aside his integrity and tied his star to Hillary's.

For a man who had never even tasted failure, his short time in the White House spoke of little else but failure—at least according to Hillary, and she never missed an opportunity to berate him viciously and publicly, using the most vile and vulgar language. Vince must have been racked with enormous inner turmoil. The things she demanded of him had to have clashed severely with his belief system. Most don't know that Vince graduated first in his law school class and had the highest score of anyone in his class on the bar exam. Taken separately, each was no mean feat. Together they show a snapshot of his determination. He was a serious achiever. And, whether he had an affair with Hillary or not, he seemed to have an exceptional moral compass, quite unusual for the Clinton White House.

The West Wing is some of the most coveted real estate on the planet. But it is small. In fact, it is hard to comprehend just how small it is. The feeling of the space is of genteel wear; it's a gracious but minuscule series of comfortable rooms surprisingly housing the most influential staff for the president of the United States.

The counsel to the president's office was on the second floor of the West Wing. It felt like the upstairs of a spacious house. For a house, it would have been spacious. As office space, it was ludicrously tiny. In the outer office was Bernie Nussbaum's assistant, Betsy Pond; Vince's assistant, Deborah (Deb) Gorham; me; and usually an intern, a volunteer, or a staff assistant in the back. There were two offices off this space to the right as you entered the suite. One was Bernie's spacious office, with a handsome desk, a comfortable sitting area with sofa and chairs, and an oversized conference table. The other was Vince Foster's very small office. It had a small window, a desk, a chair, some shelving, and a small loveseat. That office could hold two comfortably; more would be a stretch.

Chapter 9
VINCE FOSTER'S DEATH

July 20, 1993, started out as a normal day. As it happened, it was the six-month anniversary of Bill Clinton's inauguration. And, as always when Hillary was safely elsewhere, the overall mood was less tense, less edgy. From the Oval Office Corridor to the counsel's office upstairs, there would be a subtle but noticeable lightness in the air when Hillary wasn't around. That was true on this day.

Hillary had been out of the White House for some time, having traveled extensively to Japan and Korea with Bill. He had returned to the White House more than a week earlier, but Hillary traveled on, still accompanied by her mother. Their Pacific travels culminated with a week-long stop in Hawaii, where Chelsea joined them. On this day, they had flown from Hawaii to Arkansas to drop off Hillary's mother.

The White House was moving at its normal, hectic, and chaotic pace. The extended absence of Hillary was like a breath of fresh air on a sunny spring day. No one had to avoid eye contact with her for fear of annoying her and getting fired. And, more important, the president's immediate staff did not have to constantly monitor her position or frantically weave and dodge depending on her movements. The atmosphere was far more relaxed. As I write this, I realize how peculiar it all sounds. Yet, that was life in the Clinton White House.

I arrived at my desk at my normal 8 a.m. time. It was already a warm, humid D.C. day. Little did I know that this was going to be anything but a "normal" White House Day. In fact, it is a day imprinted in my memory, oddly resembling a repetitive celluloid loop, at once stark and surreal—every detail forever frozen in time.

"Good morning, Bernie," I said to my boss. "Ready for the big day?"

"Why? What big day? Is there something going on today?" he asked me while sporting a big grin.

"Nice try," I replied.

Bernie knew exactly what was happening that day. Louis Freeh was being presented in a Rose Garden ceremony that morning as the newly minted director of the FBI. Bernie could not have been happier. It was, as he later said, a home run for the besieged counsel's office.

While Freeh was being vetted, I noticed he and I had been born in the same hospital within weeks of each other. Quite a coincidence that two people born of Italian American parents in a Jersey City, New Jersey, hospital around the same time would end up at the White House, albeit in wildly disparate positions, working for the president of the United States. Before the ceremony, soon-to-be-director Freeh and I got a chuckle out of it. The mood was light.

The appointment of Freeh as FBI director was a bigger deal then than it now seems. The Clintons had been in office only six months to the day. But when it came to significant appointments in that short time, they looked like the Arkansas Hillbillies. They already had blown appointments for the attorney general and a Supreme Court justice, among others—more on that below.

The appointment blunders were also a huge problem for Vince Foster. Hillary had laid the job of vetting significant appointments on him. As noted above, the first few months regarding those appointments had those in the administration looking like they couldn't get out of their own way. They were not able to get much of anything right. Much of this was squarely on Hillary, and she constantly brought her wrath down on the head of Vince. She would dress him down, screaming and bludgeoning him, in public spaces, using the most vile, obscene, and offensive language imaginable. Vince, probably the most professional of the Little Rock gang, quickly became Hillary's favorite scapegoat. When she needed someone to blame for her mistakes—which she could never admit to, let alone be responsible or held accountable for—Vince would get a foul-mouthed verbal flogging.

A perfect example of this scenario was finding a nominee to be the new attorney general. Hillary insisted that it be a woman. Her first choice was Zoë Baird. The administration blew this one when it came to light that she had used illegal immigrants as nannies and failed to pay Social Security taxes for them; the scandal became known as Nannygate.

Next up was an old college friend of the Clintons', Kimba Wood, a federal district court judge for the Southern District of New York. It came to light that she also had an illegal immigrant as a nanny but before it became illegal to do so. She had also had training as a Playboy Bunny and this, it was feared, would be the subject of too many jokes.

Finally, the administration settled on Janet Reno, who was being pushed by one of Hillary's brothers; I cannot recall which one. It is generally conceded that Reno was, at best, a mediocre attorney general. Also, it was her doing that the Branch Davidian massacre took place.

Louis Freeh was a big win. That morning, Freeh and his party met with Bernie, Vince, and several of the senior associates in our office. We were all milling around before going downstairs to join the president in the Rose Garden. As our guests overtook our small office suite, work as we knew it ground to a screeching halt. As the time approached for the announcement to begin, we all went down to the Rose Garden.

Some of us stood in the vicinity behind the cameras, well back in the small garden, while others stood off to the side. It was packed. Vince stood back on his own under the colonnade joining the West Wing with the residence, observing from a bit of a distance. He was present but obviously chose to not be part of the hoopla. This was in stark contrast to Bernie, who beamed from ear to ear. Vince also had a preoccupied look on his face, but he was quiet and dignified as always. His demeanor gave no cause for concern and did not portend what was shortly to come.

The previous evening, working a bit late, I had poked my head in Vince's office and asked him if he would like me to get his children cleared to attend the next day's event. He looked at me and thought for a moment, then told me not to bother. I assured him it was not a bother, but he simply and pleasantly told me it was okay and not to do it.

This surprised me because he liked having his children attend events at the White House. He always seemed to be a dedicated dad doing his best with crazy hours in a new city. Lisa, his wife, and their kids had recently moved from Little Rock to Washington, D.C., and we heard that she wasn't thrilled about it. Vince was seldom home. He was totally consumed with "the client," and Lisa was on her own. Who could blame her?

When the ceremony for Freeh was over, back in the office there was a sense of ebullient joviality and celebration. There had been so little to rejoice about previously, with all the nomination missteps, the tension, the behind-closed-doors drama with Hillary, and the bizarre events unique to this White House. The Rose Garden event had gone off without a hitch. Bernie was in high spirits. Since it was close to lunchtime, he and some of the staff made plans to go have lunch outdoors at the White House, a novel concept in the West Wing. Vince did not join in.

When we returned to the office, Deb Gorham, Vince's private secretary, approached me and said, "I have to leave to take care of some business to become a notary. I'll be gone for a while, but I'll be back later. Will you keep an eye on Vince? Get him some lunch in a little while and help him with anything he asks?"

Since "the client" of Vince's was Hillary almost exclusively, most of Deb's work was for her. It also required signatures to be notarized. Getting a notary stamp would make Deb's work much more efficient, since Hillary could not be bothered with the current process; Deb would have to get a notary from the White House staff to go with her to obtain Hillary's signature on whatever needed signing. Now Deb could just do it herself.

"No problem," I replied. "What's on his calendar?"

"Nothing at all. Her highness is gone, so he has an unusually easy day."

"Okay, no problem. I'll see you when you get back."

Most of us simply ordered our meals from the White House Mess by phone. The staff there would call back when the food was ready, and we would go pick it up. It was a good system. The food was terrific and reasonably priced, and we each had a White House Mess account with an invoicing system and would pay once a month. All in all, it worked great—except, of course, that it generally meant that most people ate at their desk while working, so there was not much of a break. It's just the nature of the beast.

On this day, I must have had a bit of a concern. There was nothing, of course, that could in a million years have predicted the later events of the day; I just observed that Vince had a less-than-happy demeanor. He seemed a bit down when I went into his office.

"Hey, Vince. I'm going to order some lunch. Would you like something?" I asked.

"Yes," he quickly answered. "Get me a cheeseburger, please."

"No catfish today?" I asked, teasing him a little and hoping for a smile.

I asked about the catfish because he could wax poetic about this popular Arkansan delicacy, one that had been added to the White House Mess menu once a week when Clinton took office. Vince never missed it. He was always trying to get me to try it, but I could never bring myself to do so. Normally he would kid me about it a bit and humor himself.

"No, thanks," he flatly said. "Not today."

I did not wait for the call from the Mess to pick up our lunches. Instead I ran down to get them when I thought it was about time. When I got there, Vince's was not quite ready. While waiting, I took a phone call.

"Hey," said Tom Castleton, a young man working in our office. "Vince wants his lunch. I'm going to come down and get it."

"Don't do that. It's almost ready, and I don't want you to leave the office alone. I'll be along in a couple minutes," I said. "Stay there."

Tom Castleton—or Castillo, the name he'd used to further his Harvard aspirations (it had worked)—was exasperating on a good day. He was our plodding intern/paper pusher and seemed to lack common sense. He was, however, a Harvard product, so affirmative action notwithstanding, he had to have something.

During both the Bush and Clinton administrations, there was a preponderance of M&Ms all over the place, including in silver bowls at the entryway to the White House Mess. I picked up the two lunches, quickly dumped an excessive number of M&Ms on Vince's tray, thinking it might make him smile, and ran upstairs.

Vince seemed to be engrossed in a newspaper when I walked in with his lunch. I believe it was the editorial page of *The Boston Globe*. He was seated on the loveseat in his tiny office. His back was to me, and I remember noticing he had removed his suit jacket. I placed the tray on the small table and, unfailingly polite, he thanked me.

"My pleasure. Enjoy those M&Ms!" I said with a laugh as I returned to my desk.

I was surprised not to have found him busy at his desk, but then, that day was the one relaxed day we had ever experienced, and I was glad to see him unwind.

Before too long and somewhat to my surprise, Vince walked out of his office carrying his tray. As he put it down, I noticed he had left a lot of the French fries and had removed the onion from the cheeseburger. I remember making a quick mental note to make sure to have the Mess hold the onion next time.

I note these little details because every one of them seems engraved in my mind, likely due to the traumatic events that followed—the same way everyone remembers where they were when JFK was assassinated.

"Thanks, again," he said. He smiled slightly, then joked, "There sure are a lot of M&Ms left here. Help yourselves."

He tossed his suit jacket over his shoulder and, carrying nothing, walked through the doorway, saying, "I'll be back." I never saw him again.

That was the last thing Vince Foster is known to have said to anyone.

I had never known anyone who had killed himself or herself. I had never known anyone who had died in such a violent way, by gunshot. Hindsight being what it is, I later wished I had pressed him, or paid more attention, or done something to determine where he was going. After all, I had assured

Deb that I would do so. She had said he had no engagements, nothing on his calendar.

I thought maybe he was going across the street to the OEOB. Or that he was off to run a last-minute errand, but all of that seemed somewhat strange in retrospect. Later, when we couldn't reach him over a period of hours, I remember thinking that while it was unusual for him to leave, that day itself had been significantly more laid-back. Perhaps he was taking advantage of the slower pace for once and running errands, taking a walk, getting air, any of the above. It seemed possible. I made a note for Deb of the time he left, which as I recall was right around a few minutes after 1 p.m., and promptly went back to my work.

After he left and with Deb's absence, I took a few incoming calls for Vince. The ever-efficient Deb had a computerized message log, so I logged the incoming calls on her computer. There weren't many. I recall thinking there were no obvious kook calls at all. We routinely received weekly calls and faxes from those who received ominous messages in their dental fillings, ostensibly from aliens. They all wanted their news to be relayed to the president. These nuisance calls were instantly identifiable and quickly but graciously dismissed.

Under the heading of "just plain weird," and since it occurred on this of all days, oddities seemed magnified. One such oddity was an incoming phone call I took on Vince's line. I didn't think much about it until I tried to log it in.

There had been no problem with any of the messages until I tried to log in a somewhat unusual call from a man who identified himself, as I recall, as George Stein. The voice on the other end of the line was modulated and professional; I didn't immediately classify this caller as a potential kook. Additionally, the kook brigade generally called on Bernie's line, the number that was more publicly available.

Vince's number was less known. The caller, Stein, was somewhat disturbed to hear that Vince was not there. He went on to say that he was supposed to meet with Vince, needed to speak to him, and when pressed, said all he could tell me was that Vince knew him.

Pressed for the subject, he said, "Look, Vince knows, he knows me. It's about Mena airport. Tainted blood." It meant nothing to me. While he seemingly didn't fall into the kook category, I supposed he could be in it. Whether or not this call would have significance on any level was hard to know.

But when I tried to log in this caller's full name, as I had done with other calls on Deb's computer, something surprising occurred. Each attempt was stubbornly met with the message "password protected." I then tried "Mena airport" and got the same result. I tried at least three times and then gave up.

It was peculiar. It immediately confirmed to me that this was a legitimate caller. Deb's computer had recognized not only the name but also the subject. It also confirmed that Deb's computer containing all things Hillary had a level of protection staff computers did not. Unable to log this message into her computer, I left a written note on her desk. She later shrugged her shoulders, providing no explanation for the stubborn "password protected" message, and we dropped the subject.

One by one, my coworkers returned: Deb, Betsy Pond, Bernie. I explained that Vince had left earlier. He had not taken his briefcase, so we knew he would return for it. As time went on, eventually we all began to wonder aloud where Vince was. We called him but got no answer. As the day went on, our concern mounted. It was not long before everyone else seemed to be concerned as well, and that was not good. Eventually, Vince's wife, Lisa, called. No one knew where he was. She called again a bit later. We still didn't know where he was.

When I was getting ready to leave for the day, Vince had been incommunicado for close to four hours, something that had never happened before. All the way home I wondered where he had gone. My mind wandered, recalling all the contention and upheaval that seemed to constantly fall squarely on Vince's shoulders. It wasn't just Travelgate, or health care reform, or the Clintons' finances, or the first inkling of Whitewater; Hillary dumped myriad issues in Vince's lap.

As my mind wandered, I recalled the many explosive Hillary meltdowns directed at Vince. One concerned Kaki Hockersmith, a Little

Rock interior designer Hillary had brought in to redesign the family quarters. Vince appeared to be concerned that under Hillary's tutelage, Hockersmith was spending indiscriminately and that the allocated budget was ignored. Vince tried raising this with Hillary which resulted in a shockingly obscene blowback directed at Vince. He was her whipping boy yet, somewhat ironically, it was clear that it was Vince whom she trusted the most.

I recalled the mounting tension as it pertained to the redesign of the residence, but Kaki Hockersmith also redesigned the Oval Office, the Treaty Room, the solarium, the family dining room, and the music room. Since Vince worried about the excessive spending, it had to be raised with Hillary. Repeatedly. And to no avail.

Unfailingly, she dressed him down in her signature style, once saying: "Fuck the fucking cost; this is what I fucking want. Make it fucking work, no fucking excuses." It was an alarming scene I witnessed in the hallway between their two offices, but just one of so many. It was always quite painful to see.

Kaki Hockersmith went on to redesign "Aspen," the president's cabin at Camp David, as well as "Laurel"—the lodge and presidential dining hall there. The staggering costs for all of it far exceeded budgeted allocations, and once again, assiduous Vince was left holding the bag.

These thoughts and others filled my mind on that day Vince left early, July 20, on my two-hour homeward commute.

I kept coming back to one fact. It was out of character for Vince to leave early, let alone leave without a word; to then be unreachable for hours was unheard of. I worried about accidents but realized he had his White House badge with him. With that to identify him, it was likely we would have heard something if there had been an accident.

I suddenly recalled that Vince had said he had done something over the previous weekend that he had not done since coming to Washington. He and Lisa, along with his former law partner Webster Hubbell and his wife, Suzy, had gone to visit friends at a house on the Eastern Shore of Maryland. I remembered thinking at the time, *Okay, this is good; he's settling in, finding time for himself.* Maybe the disappearing act was just a sign of a new way forward, a good thing, but an ominous niggling undercurrent stubbornly lingered, leaving me unsure. Vince was simply too much of a gentleman to disappear without giving anyone an explanation.

Much later, after a routine evening at home, I went to bed, hoping to read before falling asleep. I had just begun to doze off, book in hand, when sometime around midnight the silence was suddenly shattered. The blaring of the telephone on my bedside table awoke me with a start. No one ever called that late. It was the president's secretary, Deborah Coyle.

"I have some terrible news. Vince is dead," Deb told me.

I was barely awake, and what she said was almost incomprehensible.

"What? What are you talking about?" I cried, loud enough to briefly awaken my daughter in her room across the hall.

"He committed suicide. He was found this evening in Fort Marcy Park," Deb replied very firmly, as if it were a settled fact.

"What? How?" was all I could think to ask.

"He shot himself in the head," Deb answered.

Of course, I was absolutely stunned. I remember thinking, *Quiet, dignified, gentlemanly Vince Foster shot himself in the head with a gun?* Stunning. Incomprehensible. Tragic. Suicide? Pills, maybe. Carbon monoxide in a car, maybe. But a gun? Amid a fog-like utter sadness, I wondered about all that blood. His kids would have to know about this.

"There was no suicide note, no nothing," Deb said. "But definitely suicide. I just wanted you to know before you heard it on the news in the morning on the way in."

During a restless night, I could not sleep. How did the authorities know it was suicide? This was a high-profile death, possibly the highest-profile White House-associated death since the Kennedy assassination. Surely there would be an investigation. My thoughts swirled around my head, crashing into one another and making sleep impossible.

I remember thinking how bizarre it was that the president had called Vince just the night before, on a weeknight, to invite him to come to the residence to screen a movie with him. I had taken the call and vaguely remember telling the president I thought Vince would have liked that. I know I told him to try Vince at home because, again in an anomaly of sorts, he had left at a relatively civilized hour and so was not in the office, as he usually was. The president later said the invitation was to cheer Vince up.

Later, after Vince's death, I thought how odd the timing of that invitation was. The president had never done that before. Vince had been included in movie groups, but Bill had never personally singled Vince out for a screening. Would it have made a difference if he had done it every now and then during that time? I don't know. But he didn't. For whatever reason the president extended the invitation then, it seemed to be a strange coincidence that he did it on the evening preceding Vince's suicide.

Arriving at the White House the day after Vince's death was a surreal experience. Everything looked the same. The West Wing was ablaze with lights. The residence stood as quietly regal and stately as it had since 1800. I guess I expected something, somehow, to appear different. A senior member of the staff was dead. Everything had changed. But everything looked the same.

As soon as I arrived, I raced upstairs. While everything might have appeared the same on the outside, everything on the inside had forever changed. I saw the darkened office of Hillary Clinton immediately adjacent to ours. Remembering that Hillary was still out of town, I went through the double doors of the counsel's office, where I was shocked to find Betsy Pond busily rummaging through Vince's desk.

Picking my mouth off the floor, I cried: "Betsy, what are you doing? You have to get out of here. The Secret Service needs to come up immediately and cordon off Vince's office."

I added in frustration, "This could be a potential crime scene. You can bet all sorts of investigators are going to be in here, and the last thing we should do is disturb anything."

She stood there, looking as sad as I felt, her puffy face and red eyes streaked with black eyeliner and mascara, tears still falling copiously, and looked at me as though I had lost my mind.

"I'm, ah, just, um, you know, straightening up his office," she barely managed to say.

"Well, stop it," I told her, more calmly now. "We need to get the Secret Service up here."

"Oh, um, yes, you're right," she finally gathered herself enough to say.

Sometime later, I do not remember exactly when, she would claim she was looking for a suicide note.

Before long, the lookie-loos began to show up with their condolences. It was all too much, a horrifying and unreal situation that felt exactly like an episode of *The Twilight Zone.* We had no information, and we were all devastated. We were in no position to answer the inevitable questions. After a while, we finally closed the double doors. Only those with a need to come in could enter. If we didn't have to talk about it, maybe it hadn't happened.

We had so many questions. They would remain, for the most part, unanswered. Bernie had not yet arrived; his office was still dark. We anxiously awaited his arrival, hoping he could provide some sort of clarity. When he did arrive, clarity was not forthcoming. Confusion reigned. He went into his large office adjacent to Vince's small one and firmly closed the door.

The situation spiraled out of control, and it would get even worse. Reeling from the reality of Vince's death, regardless of how it had come to happen, kept us all off-kilter and in a state of raw emotion. There were questions and more questions. But no one was there to answer them, and no one ever would.

Soon after Bernie's arrival, several lawyers from the OEOB office began pouring in, and everything began to get weird. As the associates arrived, one by one they all converged in Bernie's office, and the door remained firmly closed. No one said anything, and no one had yet come to cordon off Vince's office. The door to it was still wide open.

At first, I was completely unaware of the nocturnal exploits of Maggie Williams, Hillary's chief of staff and someone with whom Vince had daily contact, and Patsy Thomasson, the White House director of administration, hours before in that same office. But later it all made sense. Williams and Thomasson had been going through files in Vince's office; long before I found Betsy "straightening" his office, it had been ransacked.

A little context is helpful and illuminating. A longtime "right-hand man" to Dan Lasater, Patsy Thomasson was part of the Little Rock gang and accustomed to how things worked in the underbelly of Clinton politics. Her loyalty to both Clintons was rock solid.

Lasater was a successful Little Rock business owner; his business was named Lasater & Co. Patsy had been executive vice president of this company and had also been the head of the Democrat Party in Arkansas. Lasater was a longtime and major Clinton donor as well as a personal friend of Bill Clinton's. In fact, Lasater was a major financial supporter not only during Bill's campaigns for governor but also during his 1992 presidential campaign.

In 1986, Lasater was indicted and convicted of drug dealing, and he received a thirty-month jail sentence, most of which he never served. He was also suspected of being heavily involved with laundering drug money. Bill Clinton's brother Roger was also involved in the Lasater drug scheme and was convicted as well. In 1990, Lasater was pardoned by none other than his buddy, Governor Bill Clinton.

At the time of Vince's death, the Clintons had had a long and storied history with both Patsy and her boss. Clearly, neither the criminal behavior nor the total lack of ethical conduct disturbed either Clinton. In fact, it made Lasater and Patsy more desirable. Patsy took over the reins of Lasater & Co. during Lasater's forced absence. She was closely associated with Lasater before, during, and after his conviction for cocaine trafficking.

Unabashed and without shame, the same man who was neck deep in the periphery of Little Rock drug dealing became the one the Clintons put in charge of White House drug testing. Given that, it was only natural that Patsy was one of the "soldiers" directed to ransack Vince's office before law enforcement of any kind had a chance to enter. The act was in blind service to Hillary.

I knew nothing then about the removal of files. But apparently the ubiquitous Tom Castillo did. He mentioned later that "they" had asked him to carry boxes of Vince's files over to the residence. Loyal Clintonoid that he was, he did as he was told.

You don't have to be Carnak the Magnificent to figure out who told Patsy and Tom Castillo to get in there to look for specific things. And much later it would be learned that many of Vince's files, all having to do with

Hillary, had indeed been removed the night before. Remember, Vince was almost exclusively working for Hillary. No one other than Hillary could have directed her closest aides to remove the files, and no one else would have been able to authorize the moving of the files to the residence.

It was all business that early morning following Vince's death, but clearly the work had started the night before. In fact, as soon as Hillary got off the phone with Chief of Staff Mack McLarty, who had informed her of Vince's death, she got down to business. In her book *Living History*, Hillary claims she was so frantic, she called everyone she could think of. Anyone who knows Hillary knows how absurd this claim is. The truth is, she went into full-on attack mode and called her most trusted aides to do her bidding. It was not about the tragedy. It was about protecting Hillary and her political viability, and nothing—not even death—could be more important.

When I first learned of this, I wondered about it. It was yet another oddity. In the face of this horrific tragedy, could it be that these files, of all things, were even on her radar? It seemed ludicrous. But she was brutally efficient, and it was a stark reminder of the focus, the emphasis, the priority that became all-important as soon as Hillary knew that Vince was dead. The insensitivity was incomprehensible, but by then I should not have been surprised.

At the time, I believed that except for Betsy's "straightening up" early that morning, Vince's office was in the same condition as when he had left it the afternoon before—another wrong assumption. Much later, with people from other offices coming in and peeking into Vince's office, and with Bernie and the associates still behind closed doors, I finally called the uniformed division of the Secret Service, and eventually an agent was sent up to guard Vince's office door.

Bernie and his colleagues, when they emerged from behind the closed doors, seemed stunned and taken aback when they realized what I had done, but then thanked me for "taking the initiative." Of course, making the call should not have fallen to me. The assistants to the president, the special assistants to the president, or the deputies to the president are the ones who should have done this immediately. If you are wondering why they did not, wonder no more: the queen bee had issued her orders, first through others and then personally via telephone from afar. Having the ever-present, annoying, intrusive, and downright vile Secret Service goons stick their noses into her business simply was not going to happen. And the park police? That was laughable.

Hillary would later say she was not going to allow "fucking squirrel chasers" "unfettered fucking access" to the "fucking office" of the late Vince Foster.

She owned Vince Foster. No one crossed Hillary. She ruled the school. I knew only some of this at the time.

All day the phones were ringing off the hook. That morning I took several calls, including from Susan Thomases, a frequent visitor to the White House and a New York-based lawyer who served as a close personal counselor to Hillary. I also took a call from Hillary herself.

Both Hillary and Thomases were all business—hard as nails and in a hurry. Both were on a mission. They urgently wanted to speak to Bernie immediately. I remember feeling that these two should have been devastated. After all, each had had a long history with Vince. On the phone, however, the gloves were off, if behind closed doors they had ever been on. No emotion. No tears. This was in stark contrast to those of us in the office. Neither offered condolences or any personal touch whatsoever. It seemed appropriate to briefly relay my condolences to each of them.

"I'm so sorry for your loss," I said to each.

Then things became even weirder. Hillary said nothing, did not acknowledge my condolences at all. After a moment of silence while I waited for an acknowledgment, I finally gave up and said I'd put her right through to Bernie.

When I said the same thing to Susan Thomases, her response was, "Yeah, put Bernie on." Again, she was all business. My brief offer of condolence, while not exactly rebuffed, was seemingly more a superfluous nuisance. The siege mentality was ratcheted up even higher that day, and it never changed.

The president showed up at our office later that morning. His appearance and behavior at the time seemed a little bizarre. I had known Vince Foster on a strictly professional basis for a total of six months. Bill had been friends with Vince since Miss Mary's nursery school in Hope, Arkansas. In fact, Chief of Staff Mack McLarty had also been a classmate.

As the story goes, Bill's grandparents' house, where he lived for a spell, was across from Vince's family's larger home. After Bill moved to the racy city of Hot Springs in 1952, he occasionally visited Hope and would sometimes see Vince—who, unlike Bill, did in fact grow up in Hope. In any case, in later years, Vince became a close friend of Hillary's at the Rose Law Firm. So, Bill renewed contact with Vince in Little Rock when he was governor.

You would never have guessed about that full history by how Bill was acting now. Maybe it is because people grieve in different ways.

He made the rounds of the outer office, charming all of us one by one. Betsy, Deborah Gorham, each individually. Eventually the president landed at my desk and stood there for a while. He did that thing he does so well. It is his unique talent. He effortlessly makes each and every person in his periphery think they are the only people on the planet. He never forgets a name, and if he only had time, he'd love to get to know each person much, much better. This talent was spread liberally throughout the office that morning.

He made a comment about the ancient walled city of Colombia, having seen a piece of art on the wall above my desk that piqued his interest and evidently his memory. In fact, he queried us on some forgettable and at-the-time innocuous historical fact that he seemingly pulled out of his hat. All I could think was, *You've got to be kidding. His lifelong friend is dead. Dead is permanent. There are no do-overs. And he could not resist the opportunity to pontificate on this ancient walled city? WTF!*

I skipped the history quiz and paid my condolences by saying, "Mr. President, my deepest sympathies. I can't imagine why this awful thing happened."

His only reply was oddly dry-eyed: "It's just one of life's mysteries."

From the "I feel your pain" president, not a quivering lip or teary eye in sight. He went on to say more, but I was so floored by his acceptance of the suicide ruling without the slightest hesitation that my mind flew back to the late-night call from Deb Coyle. "He committed suicide." End of inquiry.

The reaction of both Bill and Hillary astounded me. As I've said, Vince and Bill had been in preschool together. Vince was supposedly a dear friend of both Clintons' and may have been Hillary's onetime lover. Yet, Hillary and Bill seemed about as upset at the news of Vince's death as they would have been upon hearing that the neighbors' annoying parakeet had died. Looking back, I know that the reaction of Hillary was emphatically in character: get her toadies into his office to pull her files before the authorities could find them. Again, perhaps we all grieve in our own way.

The Office of Counsel to the President was never the same after that. Little things were disturbing. The actions on the part of Bernie, a boss I respected and held in high esteem, were a prime example. Secrecy and a sense of paranoia reigned supreme. I genuinely liked Bernie. A lot. He was a brilliant litigator and a mensch. When he was cast aside later, he was simply the next in a series of sacrificial lambs who fell by the wayside in the clutter that was the Clinton graveyard. I hear he is still a Hillary supporter, so he's a mensch and a masochist.

Sent to identify Vince's body were Bill Kennedy and Craig Livingstone, both indisputably Hillary henchmen. Sending Kennedy made sense, since he was the former managing partner of the Rose Law Firm. He knew Vince well. But Livingstone was another story altogether. The former bar bouncer was considered a clown and was the butt of jokes.

Bill Kennedy struck me as a bulbous Clark Kent on steroids and a Dunkin' Donuts aficionado. He played the part of a good ol' country boy, the country mouse in the big, bad city. In reality, he was a happy enforcer for all things Hillary. You simply could not make this stuff up.

The oddities just kept coming. There was an official form listing all the personal effects found on the body and in the car. I remember holding it in my hand as I read and noticed a glaring omission. I wondered, *Where were his keys? If the car was found and he was found, where were his car keys? Where was his key to our office? To his house?* It was a loose end that didn't make sense. I mentioned it to Bill Kennedy, but I need not have worried. The keys turned up the next day after all, apparently in the hands of the former bar bouncer, Craig Livingstone, and the Hillary fixer, Bill Kennedy. The body had been identified by this duo, and the keys were also found by them—the same keys that were not included on the initial personal property inventory of things found with the body or in the car. By the next day, this same type of form showed up on my desk again. This time the keys were on it. How was this possible?

I fully understand that the investigations all concluded that Vince died by his own hand. I don't dispute that. After all, it would be impossible for a layperson to know anything definitively. But what has always struck me most was Vince's behavior on the day he died. I knew so little about suicide back then, but certain questions still nag at me. That a loving father did not leave any sort of explanation or even a farewell for his three children utterly stymied me. It was so out of character for the considerate human being he was. And who casually asks for lunch and eats it while reading a newspaper, knowing the utter finality of death awaited him that same afternoon? Did he simply not care for raw onion, or did he remove it so as not to reek from onion that afternoon, which might indicate that he was planning to be with others? What was he doing at Fort Marcy Park? And how did this recent Arkansas transplant who was at work seven days a week from dawn to dusk even discover the existence of this little-known park? None of us had ever heard of it before. It's not really a park at all. It is more a scenic overlook along a highway overlooking the Potomac River; a highway that was nowhere near Vince's house in Georgetown and is not even close to a route he would have taken to go home. In fact, it was on the opposite side of the Potomac River. There remain a lot of unanswered questions about the tragic death of Vince Foster.

The days began to blur. We went through the motions in a sort of fog. At some point, the president called an "all hands on deck" staff meeting. It was held in a large room in the OEOB, and he and others informed and ministered to the entire White House staff about the loss of Vince Foster. That meeting remains a blur to this day. The president's words seemed inadequate, and random images are all I recall.

The sense of loss and the heavily surreal nature of our new reality continued to hover over us. I generally left the office at 5 p.m., but at one point during this time, Bernie asked me to stay later in the outer office in case I was needed. So I did. Bernie was never alone anymore, and his door was almost always firmly closed. The old back-and-forth we had was a thing of the past.

One day I learned that twenty-seven pieces of a note Vince had written had been found in the bottom of his briefcase. But before I learned this, Steve Neuwirth, a young lawyer on Bernie's staff (with twenty degrees of separation, Monica Lewinsky briefly dated this guy a few years later), came out of Bernie's office late in the day and, obviously flustered, said: "Linda, call around and find me a typewriter. I need it right away!" No explanation.

I responded, "I can try, but I doubt I'll find one. I can do whatever you need on the computer, Steve."

In frustration he brusquely said, "No, I said I need a typewriter, and I need it now!"

Well, okay then, I thought. I called around the compound, but since it was late, few support staff were still at their desks. No typewriter was to be found. By the time I buzzed that information to Bernie, he and Steve had come up with a better plan. I had no idea about the fragmented note yet; I would learn about it the next day. I did know that the entire brief-case had been searched on July 21 by the extremely efficient Deb Gorham, who somehow failed to see those twenty-seven pieces of paper at the bottom. She was as genuinely surprised as anyone when they seemed to magically appear.

Bernie and Steve had planned, I would later learn, to type up the contents of the note once it had been painstakingly pieced together. For whatever reason, a computer would not do. I knew nothing of this that night. That Bernie was now holed up in his office behind closed doors and keeping the support staff out, when the doors had always been open before, told me that things had now changed in a significant way.

Chapter 10
THE MAIN BILL CLINTON SEX SCANDALS

This and the following few chapters are about some of the women Bill Clinton abused, at least those I know of from my time inside the White House. There were literally hundreds, if not thousands, of other women over the many years whom he and his chief enabler, Hillary, used, abused, and tossed aside. It shocked my sense of decency how many women, even just those I personally knew of in the White House, consensually went along with this. At least once each day, Bill needed "servicing" by someone. And let's be clear, this servicing had nothing to do with how pretty, attractive, or sexy a candidate was. Pretty much anyone with the female chromosomes was allowed in to do the job. Why these women allowed themselves to be debased like this, I will never know.

The following chapters are accounts regarding the women whom I know were not consensually involved with Bill Clinton. These women were abused by a sexual predator who just happened to be the president of the United States. Yes, even Monica Lewinsky. Despite the number of birthdays she'd had, she was not on an equal playing field with the president. Their involvement with each other was not just a marital affair between two consenting adults. Monica was, at best, an immature child, and he grossly abused her.

The Clintonoid gang, their media supporters, and the entire Democratic Party provided cover for him. Even the #MeToo movement, had it been around at the time, might have wanted to let Clinton slide and get away with it. Many of the women who are now on the #MeToo bandwagon did just that at the time all this abuse happened.

Juanita Broaddrick

Juanita Broaddrick is a former nursing home administrator who alleges that Bill Clinton raped her in 1978. At the time, Clinton was the Arkansas attorney general and Broaddrick was a Democratic Party activist.

During Bill's 1978 gubernatorial campaign, Broaddrick met him when he stopped to visit her nursing home. Broaddrick claims she asked him about volunteering to work for the campaign, and that he told her to stop by his Little Rock campaign office. A few weeks later, she was near his office and contacted it. Clinton told her he would not be in his office that day. He then suggested they meet at her hotel's coffee shop.

She alleges that when he arrived, he suggested they talk in her room to avoid the press. They went to her room and talked for a short time. Clinton suddenly kissed her; she pushed him away, telling him she was married and not interested. The following is a portion of a statement from Broaddrick in an NBC interview on February 24, 1999.

> Then he tries to kiss me again. And the second time he tries to kiss me he starts biting my lip. He starts to, um, bite my top lip and I tried to pull away from him. And then he forces me down on the bed. And I just was very frightened, and I tried to get away from him and I told him no, that I didn't want this to happen, but he wouldn't listen to me.... It was a real panicky situation. I was even to the point where I was getting very noisy, you know, yelling to "please stop." And that's when he pressed down on my right shoulder, and he would bite my lip. When everything was over with, he got up and straightened himself, and I was crying at the moment, and he walks to the door and calmly puts on his sunglasses. And before he goes out the door he says, "You better get some ice on that." And he turned and went out the door.

When asked if there was any way Clinton could have thought it was consensual, Broaddrick said, "No, not with what I told him, and with how I tried to push him away. It was not consensual."

Broaddrick was sharing the hotel room with a friend while they attended a nursing home conference. The friend, Norma Rogers, came back to the room and found Broaddrick still on the bed in a state of shock.

Rogers said Broaddrick's pantyhose were torn at the crotch, and her lip was swollen. Roberts further says Broaddrick told her about the rape. She said that Clinton had forced himself on her.

They left Little Rock shortly after this, and Rogers says Broaddrick was quite upset and, like a lot of rape victims, blamed herself for the attack by letting Clinton into her room.

Broaddrick did not tell her then husband, Gary Hickey, about the rape. Again, not unusual. Three other friends—Susan Lewis, Louise Ma, and Jean Darden (Rogers' sister)—all claim that Broaddrick told them about being attacked and raped by Bill Clinton.

Three weeks later, Broaddrick was attending a fundraiser for Clinton at a private home. Broaddrick claims she was still in denial and blaming herself. Both Clintons attended the fundraiser, and Bill totally ignored her. According to Broaddrick, Hillary took her aside, took her hand, and said, "I just want you to know how much Bill and I appreciate what you do for him."

Broaddrick says at that point she tried to take her hand back and move away. Instead, Hillary firmly held her hand and, while looking at her very seriously, said, "Do you understand? Everything that you do."

Broaddrick says she felt literally sick to her stomach. She interpreted what Hillary had said as a veiled threat to keep her mouth shut.

From my observations of Hillary Clinton in her capacity as Bill's number-one enabler, it is easy to believe that what she said to Broaddrick was meant to be intimidation. Over the years, Hillary had a lot of practice at it.

Being thoroughly bullied, intimidated, and terrified by the Clintons, chiefly by the great self-anointed champion of women, Hillary, had done its job. For almost twenty years, Juanita Broaddrick went further than simply keeping her mouth shut. She actively, almost vehemently, denied that the event ever happened.

Over the years, especially during the time when Bill was president, this story made its way around the media grapevine. Most of the media, then as now, liberal and a little burned out by the stories of Bill's behavior, ignored it. In 1999, NBC interviewed Broaddrick, and she finally admitted it on camera. It was the day after Clinton was impeached.

Having what should have been a significant story, NBC sat on it. Given NBC's attitude about covering up for well-connected sexual predators—see Harvey Weinstein—initially spiking a story about Bill Clinton should surprise no one. NBC did not put it on the air until February 24, after Clinton had been acquitted by the Senate on February 12. Even then, the broadcaster did not air it until the *Wall Street Journal* interviewed Broaddrick. Disgusted by the way NBC was sitting on it, had Broaddrick agreed to another interview. That interview was published on the *Journal's* editorial page on February 19, 1999. Five days later, NBC finally aired the Broaddrick interview.

Typically, the media downplayed the story as an old, unsubstantiated claim. Broaddrick was portrayed as victimizing poor Bill. It was another great example of the Clinton propaganda machine's working its magic. Once again, Bill and Hillary came off as a loving couple, fighting to save their marriage in the face of that relentless "vast right-wing conspiracy."

Interestingly, Bill did not deny the allegations of rape himself. He hid behind one of his numerous Clintonoid lawyers, who denied it for him. In 1999, attorney David Kendall said, "Any allegation that the president assaulted Mrs. Broaddrick more than 20 years ago is absolutely false. Beyond that, we're not going to comment."

Later at a press conference, Clinton would continue to dodge and hide behind his lawyer by saying, "Well, my counsel has made a statement about the issue, and I have nothing to add to it."

Juanita Broaddrick was a Clinton supporter, a loyal Democrat, and a professional woman in the state of Arkansas. It would appear to be difficult to apply the "nuts and sluts" label to her. In the end, no one had to. This credible accuser, who experienced firsthand the horror of rape at the hands of Bill Clinton, was simply summarily dismissed as ho-hum news. The liberal media decided that any more coverage would be piling on poor, victimized Bill and not worthy of belief. Let's move on.

Paula Jones

Along with the rest of the world, I first heard the name Paula Corbin Jones in February 1994. She was a former entry-level Arkansas state employee, and she was suing the president of the United States for sexual harassment. That eventual lawsuit would lead to a landmark legal precedent set by the United States Supreme Court, which ruled that a sitting U.S. president is not exempt from civil litigation for acts committed outside of public office.

Ultimately, Bill agreed to an out-of-court settlement, paying Jones $850,000 to drop the suit. His lawyers asserted that he did so to get on with his life. Even as he settled, he continued to deny her allegations. Jones and her lawyers asserted that the substantial payment was evidence of Bill's guilt. Jones continued to maintain that Bill sexually harassed her. Her testimony of what she claimed he actually did reads more as predatory assault than harassment. But it didn't matter in the end; the Clinton spin machine had effectively nullified anything she had to say. But that's getting ahead of ourselves.

When Paula Jones first burst onto the scene, I had no idea how important she would become. I was still working for the counsel to the president in the West Wing, but I was hanging on by a thread. My antipathy toward all of the Clintonoids was becoming difficult to hide. The Paula Jones case was just one more sordid scandal. I knew it would trigger the same tired counterattack measures ripped from the pages of the dogeared Clinton playbook.

It all began when Jones held a news conference claiming that then governor Clinton had made unwanted advances almost three years earlier, on May 8, 1991, to be precise. She went on to nervously say that she had been invited to meet Bill in a hotel room in Little Rock during a state-sponsored conference. It went downhill from there.

A deer in the headlights might well describe the unsophisticated Paula Jones on the day she became a household name. I felt sorry for her, knowing what she would face, but at no time did I doubt her veracity. It was helpful to the White House, of course, when the usually vocal feminists abandoned her. Still, chaos ensued in the West Wing. The usual bunker mentality followed. More cloak-and-dagger secrecy enveloped the White House, but I knew by then what was coming. Nothing less than total eradication would do.

It was going to be full-on destruction for Jones. Hillary went into overdrive. No one, least of all Hillary, cared if her allegations were true. In fact, Hillary was likely delighted. As I mentioned, she always used these "bimbo eruptions" to verbally, emotionally, and publicly slap Bill around to keep him in her doghouse. This made him very pliable and allowed Hillary to run the presidency. Of course, it did not hurt that the accusation was always true. His lifelong pattern made it impossible for him to deny it to her. But the truth of any accusation didn't matter. To preserve the "eight years for Hill," it simply had to go away. As Hillary had said so many times before, "We'll just have to destroy 'em." This case was no different—just another entry on a long list of Bill's difficulty with keeping his pants zipped up. Attack swiftly and decisively.

Paula Jones was an adversary for sure, and she definitely got the attention of the White House. In the grand scheme of things though, Hillary considered her small potatoes, ranking right up there with Gennifer Flowers, whom Bill admitted under oath to having a sexual encounter with. This simply meant that this latest revelation would be easily dismissed with minimal repercussions to the Clintons. Hillary seemed confident that they could handily dispose of this latest bimbo with little effort. They had done it before; they would do it again. In fact, they were becoming quite proficient at it.

Hillary had handily brushed aside the Gennifer Flowers eruption during the '92 campaign, and Flowers had tape recordings. The enablers made Flowers' claim of a twelve-year affair with Bill Clinton evaporate into thin air, saying she was lying and the tape recordings were doctored, and then Hillary took to *60 Minutes* to stand by her man. What few realized at the time was that Hillary's defense of the indefensible was not designed merely to get Bill elected. Instead, there was a further-reaching and much more important goal: getting Hillary elected eight years down the road.

In the early nineties, she still needed his coattails. Her political viability always depended on his, and she would do anything to preserve it.

Predictably, the White House immediately denied the accusation with the standard media-accepted lie that President Clinton "did not recall meeting Ms. Jones." If I only had a dollar for every lapse of memory the Clintons and their pals have had, I would have Clinton-level wealth.

The playbook also called for the usual behind-the-scenes character assassination of Bill's latest problem. With that, the office of the presidency would shield him—and of course, Hillary—from something so frivolous, so easily disposable. There was a heady sense of confidence that the less-than-worldly Paula Jones would be swiftly dealt with. Little did anyone know that this lawsuit would ultimately bring out much more damaging evidence and put the president through an impeachment.

On May 6, 1994, Jones' lawyers filed suit in federal district court in Little Rock claiming, among other things, that Bill's advances negligently and intentionally inflicted emotional distress and that he had defamed her. This got the Clintons' attention. I didn't hold out much hope for Jones. The Clintons were unfailingly unscrupulous. They owned countless talking heads whose coordinated attacks would resonate, and they had the most expensive lawyers on the planet. I believed Jones didn't stand a chance.

By this time, I was on my way out the door at the White House. Within days, the West Wing would be off-limits for me. My testimony during various depositions had shown the Clintons that I was not a blind loyalist, that I was not willing to fall on my sword for them, and that I was not willing to lie and commit perjury for them, as so many others were. My days were numbered already, but I believe that with the filing of this lawsuit, my departure was swiftly accelerated. The last thing they wanted was for me to have another ringside seat to what they were going to do to Paula Jones. Since Bill Clinton had taken office, I had been sitting at ground zero during every single Hillary-created scandal. That was not going to be allowed this time.

I believed Paula Jones. Everything I knew to be true about President Clinton informed that belief. His inconceivable recklessness knew no bounds. His callous self-serving abuse of women as sexual objects was legendary. That which would be impossible to imagine with other people became easily believable when it came to Bill Clinton. He simply believed his entourage would provide cover for him.

I also knew what was coming. The champion of women, the "Every woman must be heard and believed" advocate for truth and justice for all women, Hillary Clinton, would mastermind the full attack targeting Paula Jones. As always, this talented maestro would orchestrate whatever she deemed necessary to ensure her and Bill's political survival. It is what she did best, and let's face it, she had decades of experience in this arena.

Predictably, the annihilation quickly took shape, and it was brutal. I am sure Jones never knew what hit her. It was a never-ending cacophony of verbal attacks. She was resoundingly ridiculed for everything from her looks to the way she dressed to her accent. You had James Carville bemoaning on national TV that this was what happened when you "dragged a hundred-dollar bill through a trailer park." I personally found this to be priceless. James Carville, a man who looks like an escapee from an Area 51 display case, has no business criticizing anyone for their appearance or background.

The contrived character assassination that painted Jones not as a victim but as a gruesome villain, grew exponentially within hours. In one fell swoop and with the full power of the White House behind them, Bill and Hillary Clinton handily reduced her to nothing more than a money-grubbing loser—a woman who, if they were to be believed, was not all that far removed from serious promiscuity anyway. And this was just the first shot across the bow. Imagine fighting that.

As familiar as I had become with Hillary's tactics, I was still horrified at these extreme steps and felt sorry for Jones. I knew that no matter how her lawsuit turned out, she would not emerge whole. She had committed the mortal sin of being sexually harassed by Bill Clinton, not quietly accepting it, and not going away. For that, she would pay on a grand scale.

Bill was using Robert (Bob) Bennett, a supposedly highly regarded D.C. lawyer. Bennett gleefully dove into the gutter with what should have been, for any adult, an embarrassing, almost adolescent lie on behalf of Bill. He disparagingly assured reporters that there were nude pictures out there of Jones. In fact, he personally orchestrated the subpoena of men who would allegedly attest to his claim concerning her promiscuity, and made sure that information became public. The "nuts and sluts" strategy. It had never let the Clintons down before.

Of course, in addition to the character assassination, Bennett tried valiantly through all legal channels to stop the suit from going forward. His main claim was that a president's duties were too important to spend time on a civil suit. It was his job to try every possible legal channel. Unfortunately for Bill, he failed miserably.

Paula Jones had filed her groundbreaking lawsuit in 1994. But the arrogance of Bill Clinton meant that he believed Bob Bennett would dispose of this nuisance lawsuit. No need to be concerned. He went on his merry way, his pattern intact. That all changed in May 1997 when he learned that Paula Jones could, in fact, sue a sitting president. As it finally turned out, the Supreme Court did not buy Bennett's argument and ruled nine to zero that the suit could go forward. All bets were off.

Before this Supreme Court ruling, I knew about Monica Lewinsky and was feeling more and more helpless about what Bill was doing to her. The ruling was a game changer. I dared to hope that Bill could finally be held accountable for his atrocious actions. At this moment, I fully understood that the world needed to know about Monica Lewinsky. More precisely, Paula Jones' attorneys needed to know. While the ramifications were enormous, what was going on was so much worse.

Monica's quick and one-sided liaisons with Bill began in November 1995 and continued on and off through—surprise!—May 1997. Certainly not a coincidence. With the ruling against him, he finally realized his behavior could be a problem, and Monica's services came to a screeching halt. I imagine that end date is significant, in that even "the Big He," as

Monica sometimes referred to Bill as, had come to realize that the irksome Paula Jones was now really coming after him.

Right in the middle of a groundbreaking lawsuit concerning his abuse of Paula Jones, who had been a young woman when he did what he did to her, the sitting president was doing what? He was still recklessly flaunting his arrogance, carelessness, and stupidity by using and abusing yet another young woman, Monica Lewinsky.

This series of events makes for startling reading. If nothing else, it highlights Bill's supreme arrogance, his belief that he could get away with virtually anything. With Monica, beginning in late 1995 and going through May 1997, he did this with the full knowledge that a sexual harassment lawsuit had been filed more than a year earlier and was looming over his presidency. His unconcerned response was to continue doing more of the same. Apparently, he was so used to having cover provided for him that he did not believe anyone would not do so again. Restated, it was hubris on a massive scale.

Paula Jones' accounting of precisely what happened in a hotel room with Bill and the grotesque circumstances of what he did would defy credulity for anyone. It was so outrageous, so specific that it defied logic. It was something one might expect of a sexual predator, not the governor of one of our fifty states. She was not alleging a long-standing affair, or even a brief affair. In fact, before that moment, they had never met. What kind of a sick, twisted person exposes himself to a woman he has never met and asks her to perform a sex act on him? And what kind of wife knows about this behavior, enables him, and provides cover for him?

I never had any doubt that Jones was telling the truth. As soon as I heard about her, I silently wished her fortitude and luck. And that was long before I met Monica. Now, in May of '97 after the Supreme Court ruling, I wanted to somehow make public what I knew about Bill's abuse of an extremely emotionally immature young woman. Before this court ruling, I had no idea how. I knew now I would have to do something to get Monica Lewinsky in front of Jones' lawyers. The pattern was there. I simply had no idea how to do it.

Kathleen Willey

One victim of Bill Clinton's turned out to be arguably the most tragic figure in this entire sordid mess. Her name is Kathleen Willey, and I must admit to being at least partially culpable, inadvertently, for the destruction of her name and reputation. For this I am now, and have been for many years, terribly sorry. If she reads this, I hope she can find it in her heart to forgive me. Kathleen did not deserve what happened to her.

Kathleen's story reminds me of a truism that seems to have always blessed the Clintons. They are fortunate in their enemies, for we are all flawed. This story concerning Kathleen Willey is a tale of entirely conflicting versions, allowing the Clintons to dismiss the case as a fabrication and an agenda-driven attack victimizing Bill once again. The conflicting versions allowed the truth to be diluted and, in the end, ensured that he walked away scot-free on this case, too. That's why it is worth going into detail here. Bill and Hillary Clinton are no one's victims.

Many will not even remember the name Kathleen Willey. Some may only vaguely remember her name, but she was an important part of the documented predatory behavior of a U.S. president, and her story deserves an in-depth look. Bill Clinton's behavior toward Kathleen was so egregious that today, it could easily have landed him in jail. Unfortunately, because he was the leader of the free world—a term for him that to this day makes me shudder—his conduct was casually dismissed, and instead Kathleen was excoriated.

Kathleen Willey was the subject of the infamous "talking points" that Monica presented to me in the days leading up to when the news of Monica and Bill broke, in January 1998. As the Paula Jones lawsuit against Bill Clinton loomed, it was Kathleen who we were all being pressed to lie about. In December 1997, the focus was on repressing and or destroying Kathleen's story because that was the name that had stirred the pot as it pertained to Jones' lawsuit.

Kathleen's name appeared in a *Newsweek* article in August 1997. At that time, the name Monica Lewinsky wasn't on anyone's radar—except mine and, of course, Bill Clinton's. Worse, Monica was on Hillary's radar, since Hillary's White House spies kept her well informed about Bill being Bill. The *Newsweek* article made all of this dangerous.

Of the books written about the Clinton circus, some were authored by journalists, others by significant participants, and a few by extremely peripheral players. None of these were at all accurate. It is difficult to be accurate if you were not there, if you have an agenda, or both, which was true for most of them. Everyone jumped on the Bill-as-a-victim bandwagon. It was no surprise in 2007 when Kathleen's ghostwritten book, *Target*, came out in 2007. What was surprising, however, was that in her recounting of her version of events, Kathleen was the victim of both Bill Clinton and myself. In fact, she reserved most of her substantial venom for me. After all, the saga had long since established me as the true villain.

It was sometime in March 1993 when Kathleen and I first bumped into each other. This was still the early days of the Clinton presidency. I was working in what was referred to as the immediate office of the President, and Kathleen was volunteering in the mailroom in the OEOB.

By then I was becoming acclimated to the brave new world of the Clintons. Their casual, no-rules-apply approach had all but overtaken the staid complex. It started at the top, and everyone had taken their cue from both new bosses. It meant change at every level, from the smallest of changes to the most significant.

I genuinely liked Kathleen. In fact, she was hard not to like. Her great sense of humor and dry wit made her enjoyable to be around, but she was way too hooked-in for me to be forthcoming. As time went on, we became friendlier. This should not be confused with becoming friends. We were friendly acquaintances but not real friends. If either Kathleen or Monica could have risen to the level of our being in an actual friendship, it would have been Kathleen. It would *never* have been the narcissistic and childlike Monica Lewinsky.

As I mentioned previously, one of the more noticeable changes in the Clinton White House was the dress code. Or, more precisely, the lack of a dress code and the behavior that engendered. After the professionalism of the Bush administration, this was a sea change from what most people with any sense of decorum would want to see in the White House.

The new dress code favored jeans, sneakers, and shirttails. A permeating sense of "Out with the old, in with the new" overtook the place. It included everything from obscene language to even littering. Some of the obscene language in the open spaces was remarkably coming from Hillary. She didn't seem to care where she was or who she was talking to or dressing down. The woman could make a Marine drill instructor blush.

Respect for the institution of the presidency disappeared overnight, replaced by a collective disdain that seemed to spearhead a mission to tear down what had come before. Rings left by soda cans appeared on beautiful mahogany furniture; takeout boxes and trash piled up on others. The frat boys had moved in and started to party.

This total lack of respect for the institution had taken over. Rules were for the duds who had come before. The new normal ushered in by the cool kids who thought they were in charge was a runaway train, and we were all along for the ride. While those of us on the permanent staff had no real choice but to acclimate to the dramatic changes, the new reality in the entire White House compound was disturbing and shocking. So right away Kathleen stood out.

Polished and impeccably turned out, she looked like she had stepped right out of a bandbox. She might have been the only person among the new arrivals at the time who looked like she had arrived to work at the White House. She was a startling anomaly in what looked like a veritable sea of latter-day Woodstock leftovers. It was not just that she dressed in designer clothing. It was also her perfectly coiffed hair, understated makeup, and demeanor—and it was not vanity. She cared about her professional appearance. Kathleen was a breath of fresh air in a White House filled with staff who seemed contemptuous of any semblance of professional proprieties. It was Hillary herself who set the tone.

Kathleen was quite pretty and projected effortless elegance. She had a soft, sort of breathless voice and manner of speaking. She was charming, gracious, and above all poised, and very likeable. In contrast, the hordes of new volunteers overall looked like they had collectively come in from weeding their gardens, and obscenities prevailed. Despite the lengthy train ride from her home in Richmond, Virginia, and the subsequent cab ride, she always arrived perfectly turned out and beautifully dressed. She was also clearly smitten with Bill Clinton—but not in the way he would have wanted.

I don't recall when, but at some later point, I mentioned that her talents might be better utilized as a volunteer in the Social Office. She seemed underutilized and ill-suited for going through thousands of pieces of mail. I knew she would excel in any social setting, and I knew the Social Office could use her in several capacities. Bill Clinton had also suggested the same thing and, of course, his input worked.

The Office of the First Lady includes the Social Office. I had occasionally floated to this office in the Bush administration, and I remember being impressed with the professionalism of the well-oiled machine it was at that time. There was a serenity to the place that belied the monumental and quite labor-intensive events they so meticulously planned. It seemed it would suit Kathleen.

The Social Office coordinated with various departments within the White House. Everyone from the in-house florist to the White House chief usher, White House chef, and chief of protocol of the United States, an official within the State Department, was there to help plan state visits and state dinners. For the people who represent the United States, this should be—and always was before the Clintons—a very important function of the presidency.

Ordinarily, the first lady was an active participant in the planning and preparation of these important events. Until Hillary Clinton. It was beneath her to do what she so callously disdained as woman's work. Hillary washed her hands of the whole thing and abdicated this role to a hand-picked social secretary. Because Hillary was nowhere in sight, it quickly became an office with no direction, no discipline, no sense of propriety.

Upon landing in the Social Office, Kathleen quickly became friends with several of the women already there, but she was taken aback by the lack of discipline and the melodrama that seemed to overtake the office. According to Kathleen, it had been in freefall since the inauguration. By all accounts, the office was flailing and in unchartered territory because the first lady was simply MIA.

It was not long before the undisciplined atmosphere and sloppy attire began to offend Kathleen's sensibilities. Worse was the obscenity-laced venom routinely spewed by Ann Stock, the director of that office and a Hillary person to the core, markedly in her behavior and foul mouth. Despite the unseemly behavior of her boss, Kathleen persevered in the East Wing. Fortunately for her, Hillary had taken up residence in the West Wing. No first lady had ever done that before.

Over time we learned that Kathleen and her husband, Ed, were substantial Clinton donors and early supporters. They had gotten to know Bill on the campaign trail and became friends. They had created Virginians for Clinton, had attended many fundraisers, and Kathleen had even orchestrated a local fundraiser herself. Between the fundraisers and the social events with Bill, Kathleen and he had enjoyed a good bit of personal contact. She mentioned what a flirt he was, and that he seemed unusually interested in her. There was no doubt it was immensely flattering to her. She knew of no other women in the Social Office who received this level of intense attention from the president. Obviously, she wasn't looking too hard.

On election night in '92, with Bill victorious, Kathleen and Ed took a charter flight with other party activists to Little Rock for the festivities. That night, the Excelsior Hotel was the site of a private, by-invitation-only event with exorbitantly expensive tickets. Still, the place was packed with supporters, donors, and, of course, celebrities. The Excelsior Hotel was also the local playground for the former governor Clinton in the furtherance of his not-so secret life. It was where Paula Jones had endured predator Bill a couple of years before. More later on Bill's big night and his inability or unwillingness to control himself and behave like an adult, married man.

Kathleen's obvious adoration of Bill meant that I had to be careful around her. I kept quiet about my observations and how repulsive his behavior was to me. Later, she would claim I encouraged her, and that the thought of pursuing Bill on anything other than a platonic level had never entered her mind. Nothing could be further from the truth. I never discouraged her in her plans to see him more, or to get together with him. I did not share my belief that her involvement with Bill would have been an unwise career move. I listened, all the while marveling that so many seemingly adult women had fallen under his spell. The allure escaped me.

In her eyes, Bill could do no wrong. Kathleen had total contempt for Hillary on every level and did not hesitate to say so. She was offended by Hillary. The proper Kathleen could not abide Hillary's crass and constant obscenities, her callous behavior, and her slovenly appearance when the cameras were not around. But her disdain of Hillary did not offset her admiration of Bill.

Kathleen spoke of an intense flirtation between herself and Bill that had gone on since the day she first met him. I remember she even asked me and others if this intensity was typical of him. As time went on, the stories became more layered, and indicated to me a level of friendship of which Hillary would not approve. More than once, I laughed and said: "Well, it's not exactly a surprise; you fit the bill." I meant because she was female. I was always careful to appear neutral around her and others, and even to appear accepting of the president's sexual addiction run amok.

I did not let her know that his serial philandering in the Oval Office was pure anathema and highly offensive to me. And that feeling grew exponentially as time went on because the philandering just got worse and worse—in fact, it seemed to be a clinical addiction. It also showed a profound disrespect for the office that I could not get past. How Bill Clinton ever fulfilled his countless duties given the sheer amount of time he spent on his "problem" was an ongoing puzzle.

Bill's need for being sexually gratified was a constant, daily thing. It was hardly just Monica or even a flirtation with Kathleen. There were daily occurrences of women slipping into his office to service him. There were literally dozens of them just during the time I was there. He seemed to have an insatiable need. He put an extraordinary amount of time and energy into it, as did his staff to provide cover for him. Women other than Hillary were involved with Bill. Nothing new there. Hillary *involved* with Bill would have been the news flash.

At forty-seven years of age, Kathleen Willey was first and foremost an adult. She was not a working professional, and by that I mean she wasn't a careerist of any kind. She had been a flight attendant much earlier in life, when flight attendants were glamorous and charming, so that fit. She was more a glamorous version of Martha Stewart than a hard-charging career woman.

She was a "lady who lunched" and who did good works. She volunteered her time while participating, through her political activism, in Richmond's affluent social scene. She did this while actively supporting her husband and children and while keeping a fastidiously clean and well-appointed house. That was the world of Kathleen. A gracious person, she was a bona fide lady at a time when that term had long since fallen out of favor. In a world of women, Kathleen seemed to be a lady to her core. Hillary, the reluctant first lady, could have taken a lesson or two from Kathleen.

I saw a woman who was smitten with Bill and clearly enjoyed the attention. As time went on, I began to grasp the depth of the flirtation that had existed between the two of them since the campaign. That was also all it was, flirtation. Why Bill did not act on it seemed strange, since he was not shy with others about doing so. It did not seem to be Kathleen who held him back either. In fact, I had the impression she would have been all for it.

Looking back, I now think I was likely mistaken about my impression. Assumptions are interpretive, and other people's intentions are ultimately known only to them, regardless of what they say.

Something I did not fully appreciate until years later was Kathleen's innate innocence. It was there; I saw it but somehow missed its significance. Kathleen was a dyed-in-the-wool romantic, a true Southern belle debutante who believed in hearts and flowers. Having lived a bit of a sheltered life in upscale Virginia society, she had very little exposure to the workplace. Powerful, predatory men were unknown to her because she had not dealt with them. Not that Kathleen was not intelligent; she was. Her lifestyle and exposure just left her a little naïve when it came to people like Bill Clinton.

Upon reflection and with the advantage of hindsight, I found years later a level of clarity that had been missing. Her believable appearance on *60 Minutes* in 1998, during which she accused the president of assault, had me reconsidering everything I had always believed about her—although, despite all evidence to the contrary, there were times when I wondered if Kathleen ever intended for her fantasy to ever really happen. In the ambiguity that was Kathleen, eventually her television appearance helped me reinterpret the mixed signals she sent.

She always spoke well of her husband, Ed; her children, whom she absolutely adored; her marriage; and her life. But, after twenty-plus years of marriage, the embers had probably cooled. Kathleen was looking for romance. But not just romance. She wanted all that went with it: true friendship, companionship, hand-holding, roses and, most important, fireworks.

She had an obvious schoolgirl crush on Bill. She was taken with him, and she spoke often of him. Her crush seemed clear, but she was not stalker-like in any way. She shared her feelings about Bill with several people. I just happened to be one of them. I don't think she had even figured out how her feelings for Bill squared with her happy marriage. I believe now that they likely had nothing to do with her marriage or Bill's, for that matter, nor could it in her eyes. She could flirt innocently, all the while imagining Bill as her special savior, a powerful knight in shining armor.

I had lost sight of this back then, if I ever understood it at all. By then I had become jaded about Bill's behavior. His many trysts were poorly kept secrets in the West Wing, probably because the participants could not help sharing their excitement with anyone who would listen. I made assumptions regarding Kathleen based on his pattern, helped along by her fascination with him. If it looked like a duck, walked like a duck, and quacked like a duck, it was likely a duck—except, as it turned out, Kathleen was not a duck.

Kathleen was likely going through a female midlife crisis. She wanted Bill Clinton, president of the United States, to be her boyfriend—at least emotionally if not physically. In fact, despite the signals she put out, I now do not believe she wanted a physical relationship at all. That would have meant cheating on her husband. And she absolutely did not want what predatory Bill had to offer. Saying "thank you," zipping up his pants, looking at the door, and saying "next" were all Bill was interested in.

On November 29, 1993, after repeated attempts, Kathleen finally managed to get an appointment to meet alone with the president—but not for what he wanted. Nancy Hernreich, director of Oval Office Operations, had said she could fit her in his schedule that afternoon between appointments.

This came none too soon because just that previous weekend, her comfortable life had fallen apart right before her eyes. There had been rumblings in the weeks leading up to this, but now it all erupted. She had just learned precisely how dire her and Ed's situation had become. As she explained it, not only were they in dire financial straits, but they might have also been in physical danger—caused by Ed.

The resultant blowup had been so severe that her husband had packed a bag and left without a word as to where he was going. Worse, the future looked exceedingly grim. It looked like there was no way out, so catastrophic were the circumstances. Ever since she started, Kathleen had been looking for a paying job in the White House, but now she was desperate.

She fully believed her good friend Bill would make that happen with a snap of his long, bony fingers. Kathleen headed for the Oval Office, hopeful she would leave with the promise of a good job. I am sure she believed this would be easy for the most powerful person on the planet, and surely something he would do for a friend who had campaigned so vigorously for him.

Unfortunately for Kathleen, a job was not on the president's mind. Instead of the warm reception and helpful posture she expected upon entering, she met the dark and even fearsome predatory Bill Clinton known only to a few.

Over the many years, Kathleen's account of what happened would remain consistent. The question of whether it was welcome or unwelcome would hound her for years. What we all need to understand is that the reason her story remained consistent is because she was telling the truth. It is easy to keep your story straight if you are not lying. Unless you are as good at lying as Hillary Clinton is, it's better to just not lie.

According to Kathleen, Bill offered her a cup of coffee, which she accepted. He then led her into his personal office space attached to the Oval Office. She described the surroundings perfectly, so I knew she was telling the truth about where he took her. It is an area few people ever see, even White House staff. He then pushed her against the corner in the private hallway off the Oval Office.

The female head of his Praetorian Guard and Bill's number-two enabler, the all-knowing Betty Currie, was at her post right outside the Oval Office. With her was Secretary of the Treasury Lloyd Bentsen, cooling his heels and awaiting his own appointment of a somewhat different nature. Inside, things were either going from bad to worse mere feet away, or they were going roughly according to plan, depending on whom you ask.

I fully believed that Kathleen saw what happened next as a first step toward a relationship of some kind. I now think it is entirely possible that if she had merely harbored an innocent crush before, a romantic illusion, it likely died a quick death that afternoon. If so, tragically it would not be the only death in her life on that day.

According to Kathleen, in the inner sanctum Bill turned purple as he grabbed and molested her. Breathing heavily, he forcibly kissed her, grabbed her breast, and shoved his tongue down her throat. At the same time, he forced her hand onto his erect penis and then, grasping, reached up her skirt. As he did, he gasped, "I've wanted to do this since the first time I laid eyes on you."

Kathleen later said he was utterly out of control, overwhelming her physically, going from zero to sixty in an instant. She said his coloring changed so dramatically, he looked like he might burst a gasket. He became something wholly unrecognizable incredibly fast.

Bill might not look it today, but in 1993 he was a big and imposing man. Kathleen was a petite woman who fully expected to meet her white knight. Instead, I now know, she met a violent predator who sexually assaulted her. I have absolutely no doubt that Kathleen was telling the truth. Luckily, she dove for the door and made her escape.

Upon fleeing the Oval Office, Kathleen had to run past Betty Currie and Lloyd Bentsen. Betty would not have been the least bit shocked at

Kathleen's appearance. Bentsen was an old-school gentleman but never said a word.

I was the next person she encountered upstairs in the counsel's office. Kathleen was totally disheveled and breathless, and there was redness all over her face and neck. I remember seeing her without her touching up her lipstick, and she was carrying a coffee cup. The cup had more lipstick on it than she did. Looking back, I think it's odd that I would remember those small details. I had never seen her without lipstick, and I had never seen her so disheveled. I can still see the image clearly because Kathleen's appearance was so out of character for her. I should have realized that something bad had happened to her.

She quickly explained in detail what had happened. Considering her and Bill's ongoing flirtation, and the level of importance she placed on that, I interpreted—or rather, misinterpreted—her reaction as a positive one. Mistakenly, to me Kathleen seemed oddly both overjoyed and stunned. She was intermittently smiling even as she described the brutality of his attack. It was her seeming excitement that instantly resonated with me more than anything else. Everything I had seen and heard leading up to this day supported that belief.

When, years later, she finally went public with her accusations, she became the victim of real intimidation tactics. These escalated when it became known that she was a cooperating witness in the independent counsel investigation headed by Ken Starr. The tactics struck me as the work of Hillary's trusty dirty tricksters. From the tires on her car being shot out with a nail gun, to the fate that befell her cat, to the jogger who threatened her and more, they sounded like something Hillary would sanction. Can I prove it? No.

Now, when I look back on it, I have no doubt that my first reaction was totally tainted by Kathleen and Bill's flirtation. Kathleen may have encouraged that, but she did not send out a signal that she wanted to be sexually assaulted. This was obviously not a case of "she asked for it." When these events were publicized, Kathleen was resoundingly mocked. The self-appointed champion of women and self-proclaimed prominent feminist Gloria Steinem dismissively declared that if Kathleen's claims were true, it was only proof that Clinton "took no for an answer"—Steinem's reasoning being that Kathleen had been able to fight him off and escape. And she is one of those loudly proclaiming that women should always be believed. Hypocrites.

Unfortunately, I testified to my belief that Kathleen's reaction had been positive, and even testified to all the planning she had done to get closer to him. I fully believed all of it to be true, and I would have scoffed at the suggestion of another possibility. It would be years later when I began to see the real possibility of another explanation.

On the day the incident happened, however, events were unfolding in Richmond that changed the subject, and Kathleen's life, permanently. That day, she was in for something far worse.

All day she had been trying unsuccessfully to reach her husband, Ed. The longer it went on, the more worried she became. It was very unusual that she couldn't reach Ed. Their recent blowout fight in front of their kids had deeply upset her. It was then that he had fully admitted the calamitous reality of their financial situation.

Ed, a lawyer, was facing certain disbarment for what he had done with money belonging to a client. Ed had embezzled money—or as he had put it, "illegally borrowed"—hundreds of thousands of dollars from a client's escrow account. Kathleen's shock was great because she had known nothing about any of it. Ed had built a house of cards, and when he could no longer pay for their extravagant lifestyle, he was looking for a way out and the client was demanding the money.

Worse, Ed had previously pretty much forced Kathleen to cosign a note in the amount of $274,000. He pressed her to sign, nervously saying, "These aren't nice people." She was terrified and at a loss as to how they could come up with that kind of money by November 29. Ed told her not to worry because he was handling it. It was now November 29, and she was unable to contact her husband.

Back in Richmond, Kathleen searched everywhere she could think of for Ed. She never found him. She later learned the devastating news that at some point after he left their house that day, Ed had driven to a neighboring county, walked into a marsh, and on a hunter's path shot himself.

In utter shock, she called me at some point. She simply could not take in what had happened. She knew of no gun, had never seen a gun, had never seen ammunition. Even the location puzzled her. It was more than sixty miles away and, according to her, in a remote part of the state. She was stunned, in disbelief, and heartbroken.

We spoke several more times as she prepared for Ed's funeral and during the days after it. I tried to be available to listen for as often and long as she needed, but I wondered if that was a good idea. Even in her overwhelming grief, she was still speculating on how all of what had happened would impact her relationship with Bill Clinton.

Our conversations about Ed and this enormous tragedy all found their way back to Bill. In fact, Kathleen always brought up Bill in our many telephone calls during that time. She was totally devastated about Ed, and her grief was genuine. But her obsession with Bill was alive and well. I'm sure this seemed normal to her, one having nothing to do with the other. I wasn't so sure.

Ed had left individual notes in his own hand for Kathleen and the children, but she kept saying, "He just would never do this, Linda, no matter how bad it got." She was sure of this. In fact, years later, she would speculate about whether his death had in fact been a suicide. I'll leave that to the experts, but I will say that his name was included on the list of Clinton-related deaths that was left on my office chair mere weeks before I went to the independent counsel. The sticky note attached read, "Thought you might find this of interest."

Years later, Kathleen tried to inform Paula Jones' lawyers of her experience—anonymously, for fear of Clinton retaliation. I knew all too well that going up against any president would be overwhelmingly intimidating. But going up against the unscrupulous and ruthless Clintons was downright terrifying.

Enter journalist and author Michael Isikoff in March 1997. Hot on the trail of a Clinton sex scandal story, he had spoken to Kathleen, who gave him my name as someone who could verify her story about the sexual attack. Kathleen also gave him the name of a friend of hers, Julie Hiatt

Steele. Steele was supposedly Kathleen's best friend, in whom Kathleen confided. Steele would eventually turn on her and claim Kathleen told her to lie. Steele did lie, but on behalf of the Clintons.

At first, I told Isikoff, "You're barking up the wrong tree." Eventually, in the August 11, 1997, issue of *Newsweek*, he used my one and only on-the-record quote. And it created quite a stir. I had said that Kathleen, emerging from the Oval Office, had come upstairs to my office and appeared "disheveled, happy, joyful," not necessarily in that order—which at the time I believed to be true. In fact, I had believed it all along. But I had not taken the time to give it much thought or to put her reaction into any kind of context. My quote tended to cement the consensual nature of the incident and got Clinton off the hook as it pertained to workplace harassment or assault.

Bob Bennett, Clinton's lawyer, was quoted as saying, "Linda Tripp is not to be believed." It seemed an odd thing to say, since what I had said seemed to exonerate his client of sexual assault. This is the way of the Clintonoids, though. Attack and never concede anything—not a possible consensual incident; nothing. It was a scorched-earth approach, and blanket, vehement denial was the MO.

That statement was my official wake-up call. Proof. It always came down to proof. No one ever had proof. Gennifer Flowers had Bill's voice on countless tapes, and it had not been enough proof—the Clintonoids claimed that the sleazy tapes had been altered. That distinctive Clinton voice? Not his. Proof was never available to Clinton's accusers, until Monica's infamous semen-stained blue dress. Even the Clinton slash-and-burn propaganda machine had trouble denying DNA.

Let's review some of the cases.

Juanita Broaddrick, who alleged she was brutally victimized by Bill Clinton—the man whom Clinton attorney Bob Bennett would one day proclaim "has done more for women than any president in history." After Bill raped Juanita Broaddrick, she was then threatened by Hillary, the champion of women, to keep quiet about it and to sacrifice herself to the political ambitions of the Clintons.

For twenty years, Broaddrick denied what had happened out of fear from Hillary's threats and, like most rape victims, embarrassment and shame. Of course, the Clintons' fans, political allies, and media lackeys went after her anyway to make poor little Billy the victim.

Paula Jones was hustled into a hotel room, a regular occurrence, by a Clintonoid toady and subjected to a nauseating experience by Bill Clinton. At least she finally received some measure of justice for an offense that would have led to a jail term for any other man.

Kathleen Willey was clearly, viciously, and sexually assaulted by Bill Clinton. I have no doubt about this at all. She was not a victim of the same first-degree sexual assault inflicted on Juanita Broaddrick, but she was unquestionably a victim of a felony sexual assault.

This reminds me of a question I have pondered from time to time all these years. How many other women are out there who were likewise victimized by the Clintons? I honestly do not know. I admit there may not be any. But let's be adults about this. What are the odds that there are no others? No other women threatened by Hillary to protect her political ambitions. No other women too embarrassed, frightened, and ashamed to come forward. No other women unwilling to have their lives shredded by a media all too willing to cover up all the sexual transgressions of Bill Clinton and other powerful Democrats. I will leave that to you, the reader, to ponder and decide for yourself.

"Drag a hundred-dollar bill through a trailer park, you never know what you'll find." So said James Carville, showing what the Clintons and their allies truly think of women. Carville is a Clintonoid to his core, with so much shoe polish on his tongue he will never get it all off. Protect and serve.

How would you like to have that trailer park statement aimed at you and spread through the media coast to coast to protect a man who should be a registered sex offender?

Chapter 11

KATHY SHELTON, GENNIFER FLOWERS, AND MARILYN JO JENKINS

There are three other women in the background of the Clintons who went public: Kathy Shelton, Gennifer Flowers, and Marilyn Jo Jenkins. I do not know any of them personally, nor have I ever met any of them. My information is based solely on what is in the public domain.

I believe there are dozens, if not hundreds, of other women from more than thirty years of Bill Clinton's behavior. As I mentioned earlier, why these women allowed themselves to be abused by Bill is something I will never understand.

Kathy Shelton is now a fifty-eight-year-old woman living quietly in Arkansas. You have probably heard things about her as they relate to Hillary Clinton, then Hillary Rodham.

In 1975, Shelton was a twelve-year-old girl who had been sexually assaulted by two men. One of the accused was Thomas Alfred Taylor, an indigent who had a court-appointed lawyer represent him. The lawyer was Hillary Rodham.

It has been reported over the years that Hillary sought out this representation. Hillary has denied this, claiming that he was assigned to her while she was working in a legal aid clinic at the University of Arkansas. Hillary further claims that she asked the judge who assigned Taylor to her to dismiss her as counsel, and that the judge denied her request. Subsequently the prosecutor confirmed this.

Over the years, the story also came out that Hillary badgered the young girl, forcing her to submit to multiple polygraph tests and a psychiatric evaluation. Because of this, Hillary was able to get greatly reduced prison time for a clearly guilty man.

Media reports, primarily done by *The Washington Post*, could find no evidence that Hillary played a role in Shelton's taking a polygraph. Hillary did request the court to order a psychiatric examination. It was denied by the judge.

Taylor, the defendant, and Hillary's client took a plea bargain. He pleaded guilty to fondling a minor under the age of fourteen. The judge sentenced him to five years in prison, suspended four years, and gave him credit for two months' time served. Taylor did eight months in the county jail.

Hillary has also been accused of laughing about the outcome. Again, no one has corroborated this. In a taped interview for the magazine *Esquire*, at one point Hillary did laugh about the vagaries of the criminal justice system while discussing the Shelton rape case.

Kathy Shelton was quoted in a 2007 interview as saying that she bore Hillary no ill will and that Hillary had only been doing her job as the court-appointed attorney. In an interview in 2014, Shelton refuted this, saying she had been misquoted in 2007—that in fact, "Hillary put me through hell. I had been stomped into the ground." Shelton further said she decided to speak out after hearing Hillary claiming differently in unpublished tapes.

This entire affair about Shelton and Hillary came to the surface again during the 2016 election. Most of you probably heard about it then. Each offered a different version of the same event. I have no idea which one is true. I personally knew a lot of people willing to lie on behalf of the Clintons. You can decide for yourself.

The entire country was introduced to Gennifer Flowers during the campaign of 1992. She was an extremely attractive forty-two-year-old woman at the time. She came forward during the '92 election campaign stating she had been in a twelve-year sexual relationship with Bill Clinton. This would have covered the entire time he was the governor of Arkansas.

Per standard procedure, Bill denied it. During a highly publicized interview on *60 Minutes*, he denied having a relationship with Flowers. With Hillary playing the part of the ever-faithful, all-suffering little woman, they oozed indignation. This was also the first time the public got a good look at the public Bill and Hillary—the chameleons that I would come to know.

There was a little problem.

Gennifer Flowers then held a press conference, during which she played audiotapes she had secretly made of phone calls with Bill. This was when Hillary turned the hounds loose. Bill's political life was in jeopardy—and worse, so was Hillary's.

Behind the scenes, phone calls and "leaks" were made to pliable, gullible, and willing reporters. When this happened, news reports routinely appeared saying that the tapes were doctored. Of course, there was no evidence of this. None of the reporters or media outlets reporting this had seen the tapes, let alone had them checked. This was a long-established pattern that continues to this day. Democrats lie to their media lackeys and the lackeys in turn will do their duty and report it as gospel.

No one, not even Bill Clinton, could deny it was his voice on the tapes. The claim was that they had been altered to make the conversations sound lascivious when they were in fact perfectly innocent. None of the media enablers ever asked the rather obvious question: why was a married man, the governor of Arkansas, making these calls to a beautiful, single woman? Perfectly innocent, they all parroted.

Years later, I had a weird and disturbing front seat to overhear why. One evening during the Monica Lewinsky fiasco, Monica almost begged me to spend the night in her Watergate apartment. I agreed, and shortly after I went to bed, Bill Clinton called Monica. I knew it was him because of the way Monica was talking to him.

While lying in bed, I could not help overhearing a mostly one-way sex phone call. Monica was doing almost all the talking. Without going into the grimy details, she was talking pretty dirty to him.

The next day I asked her about it. Monica laughed and told me they did it all the time. It helped him get turned on to, ahem, relieve himself. It took me weeks to get out of my head the image of the president of the United States with his pants down to his ankles, having phone sex.

The denials, the media claims of doctored tapes, and the image of the loving couple on *60 Minutes* worked. It was not long before the image of Gennifer Flowers' allegations began to fade. After all, it was a marital problem that many presidents were guilty of having, notably the sainted Jack Kennedy, the man the East Coast media were comparing Bill Clinton with.

Years later, Bob Bennett, Clinton's lawyer during his impeachment, would express the same lie, that the tapes obviously had been doctored. Even George Stephanopoulos, being interviewed by Tim Russert, made the same claim: that it was Clinton's voice but the tapes had been edited.

Russert, overall, was generally regarded as an excellent interviewer. Even he decided to provide cover for Clinton. How could he not ask the rather obvious follow-up questions? "How do you know that? Have you seen the tapes? Had them examined?" Nope. He let it slide.

Finally, there is Marilyn Jo Jenkins—the one woman who frightened Hillary. She was supposedly the love of Bill's life, the one he supposedly wanted to take Hillary's place.

Jenkins was a marketing executive for the Arkansas Power and Light Company. She was also an attractive woman and likely—this has been rumored, but the story has never been corroborated—had an ongoing affair with Bill for almost ten years, during which he was governor of Arkansas. It was also during the time he was having an ongoing affair with Gennifer Flowers for twelve years.

On November 3, 1992, election night, the night that saw him reach the pinnacle of political power, Bill Clinton was being true to himself. He was busily planning for Hillary's one real nemesis, Marilyn Jo Jenkins, to again be secretly ensconced in the governor's residence before dawn the following morning. They were to have their exclusively private victory celebration while Hillary slept. It would happen again three more times leading up to the Clintons' departure from Little Rock for the White House and the inauguration, although I must admit I never saw Jenkins in the White House.

It is believed that Hillary finally put her foot down on one of Bill's paramours.

It has also been reported that Jenkins' name came up during Bill's deposition in the Paula Jones lawsuit. Bob Woodward, a reporter for *The Washington Post* reported that when Jenkins' name came up, Bob Bennett believed he had found Bill's Achilles' heel. When her name was mentioned, Bill's facial expression gave away his true feelings. A gambler's tell.

Bill, being true to himself, denied having had a sexual relationship with Jenkins. Lying to your own lawyer is quite common and quite stupid. Bennett smoked him out immediately and warned him about lying during his deposition. If he lied under oath during his deposition, that would be an impeachable offense. But Bill, being a Clinton, lied under oath and got others to do so as well. Fortunately, the Clinton cover-up held. Many of the same Democrats who impeached Donald Trump for fake crimes let Bill Clinton off the hook for real crimes.

Chapter 12
INTRODUCTION TO MONICA LEWINSKY

Where to begin explaining the phenomenon that was Monica Lewinsky? Allow me to put forth my best efforts.

To start with, don't be fooled by the images you have seen of her, or you may remember her as the beautiful young woman gracing the pages of *Vanity Fair*, the well-coiffed woman in photos snapped by the paparazzi, or even the poised adult on TV. These are the images of the Monica Lewinsky the world met in 1998. This Monica was created by the Clinton-friendly media to portray her as a consenting adult, to provide cover for Bill Clinton as a sexual predator. This was a Monica I had never met.

Monica Lewinsky was a Jekyll-and-Hyde-style study in contrasts. For one thing, she was a psychiatrist's dream patient. By herself, she could make a psychiatrist's career, leading to peer-reviewed journal articles, a book deal, a TV tour (including appearances on late-night comedy shows), and a seat on the lecture circuit. For a shrink with a desire for fame and TV time, and there is no shortage of them, Monica could have been a ticket to fame and fortune. She was one of those people whose mother never convinced her the world did not revolve around her. But then, get to know her mother and you'll realize that it is likely mom not only never tried, but may have fostered Monica's belief that the world did, in fact, revolve around her.

Nothing was ever simple with Monica. She was a likable young woman, pleasant, affable, even sweet and kind. In fact, over time, I grew quite fond of her. She was also the center of her own universe, believing she controlled events even as they swirled around her, totally out of control. Like the incredibly egocentric Clintons, chiefly Hillary, she had no boundaries, no brakes, no little voice sounding alarms. There was no such thing as wants versus needs. Her wants were all that mattered. Of course, she also had no sense that there are other people in the world, oblivious to the fact that they also matter.

Monica was larger than life. Being the center of the universe around whom all things revolve, she had to be. A Broadway stage was far better suited to Monica's persona than the remarkably ill-fitting, staid, and regulatory atmosphere of the Pentagon. In any case, the Pentagon was simply the building where she was forced to sit, a limbo of sorts, while she waited for her return engagement at the White House. The Pentagon is two short miles from the White House as the crow flies, but a world away.

It is difficult all these years later to adequately capture the essence of who Monica was during this time. Perhaps it is easier to describe what she was not. She was not the polished and poised person the world might encounter today as she swiftly approaches her fiftieth year.

She wasn't even the person the world met in January 1998. By then she, too, was playing a part. She played it well. It was a Monica I barely recognized. There was no sign of histrionics or outward appearance of certifiable breakdowns, and there were no threats of suicide. She had metamorphosed into just a lovely, if somewhat confused, rather innocent young woman whose ill-advised affair with a married man had captured the interest of the world—and the victim of a busybody in the form of a villain named Linda Tripp.

It was not long before I began to understand that the Monica I had known, the naïve, immature child, had been effectively erased. In her place was an unfamiliar public persona appearing on center stage—a stable, centered young lady who had simply had a boyfriend with a big job, who was now claiming she had been inexplicably abused by a friend.

Her obsession with Bill Clinton would not, at that time, allow her to see that this "abusive" friend—me—had saved her from a sexual predator. These twenty-two years later, it is still the public Monica the world knows.

This story is about the other Monica, the one I knew for close to two years before she became a household name. And as you will see, the difference could not be more dramatic.

The Monica Lewinsky I knew, and I knew her during this time better than her absentee mother and father, was far from a sophisticated adult. Instead, what I had to deal with was a young person of stark contrasts. She was a mass of complexity with a bevy of glaring contradictions. A true study in extremes. I had never met anyone like her, nor would I ever meet anyone quite like her again.

While I have often referred to her as a naïve and misguided kid, that is the simple explanation. The reality is far more complex—while she was those things, she was ever so much more. Most important, she was not my peer. She was, most assuredly, still a child.

Back to Bill Clinton, the narcissistic sexual predator. Because he treated women like Kleenex—using them and then tossing them in the trash—at first, he was unable to see Monica for the potential psycho stalker that she became. It would be perfectly in character for him not to pay any real attention to her at all. It wasn't until after he tried to dispose of her like all the others that he saw the real Monica.

There were times when she absolutely brimmed with enthusiasm. Those were the days she believed things were looking up with "the Big He." On other days, when he was being "the Big Creep," she was a study in melancholy with intermittent threats of suicide that became increasingly credible. There was no such thing as too much attention to be paid to Monica Lewinsky. Her unpredictability, coupled with her no-holds-barred approach, meant nothing was off the table. She was simply unlike anyone else, and she totally lacked any filter.

On her best days, Monica was her own high-wire act flying without a net. The rest of the time, she was pure mayhem. As the president became increasingly aware of her instability and tried futilely to disengage, the never-ending roller coaster seemed to jump the rails. The airborne ride left me breathless and alarmed, but for Monica—whose loose grip on reality was, during this time, already questionable—the jump signified the beginning of her decline, leaving the ever-tenacious Monica an unhinged powder keg ready to blow.

One sure thing about her: she never failed to rise gloriously from defeat. Defeat was merely a temporary setback to her. As she experienced Bill's repeated rejection, she dealt with it in her own unique way. For the longest time and well before he tried to officially disengage from her, she plotted and planned all manner of scenarios every day. Plotting was her real job at the Pentagon, where she had been transferred to in 1996 from the White House, with the goal of landing back in her rightful place: the Oval Office Study. She knew if she could just be seen, be in his presence, she would achieve this goal. The problem was getting into a walled fortress with armed guards actively engaged in keeping her out. And I don't mean the uniformed Secret Service. I mean the Praetorian Guard who surrounded the president in a futile attempt to save Bill from Bill—and, far more important, to keep Hillary informed.

Optimistic through much of it, Monica cheerily worked on what she considered to be foolproof plans. She always had a daily Bill plan. The meltdowns occurred when these intricate, "foolproof" plans failed. Then she could go from zero to sixty in the blink of an eye, from euphoria to despondency. It was the highest of the highs when she thought she could get in to see him, followed by the lowest of the lows when the plan invariably failed.

I asked her to discuss these severe mood swings with her psychiatrist, and more than once I encouraged her to discuss the increasing suicidal threats with her as well. This was her Los Angeles-based psychiatrist with whom she claimed to have a long-standing doctor-patient relationship. In those days, the bicoastal sessions were held by phone, and they had been since she had moved to Washington. Or so she claimed.

Monica assured me she told this psychiatrist virtually everything. There came a time when I wondered why this professional was not doing something, anything, about her patient's highly volatile situation. I recall being underwhelmed with whomever this psychiatrist was. What I as a layperson was observing seemed to be the farthest thing from normal or healthy. If Monica had been in treatment for so long, it did not seem to be effective. Why was she spending so much time leaning on me?

I recall researching the clinical definition of "manic depressive" because Monica's mood swings were so severe, so powerful, and so swift. They were occurring on such a routine basis that I wanted some insight as to why. And the meltdowns just got worse and worse. There came a time when the hopelessness of her situation with Bill finally sank in. That was when the hysterical sobbing and the frightening threats of suicide began. Beginning in late September 1996, this pervasive hopelessness, and the alarming instability it caused, would be constant right up until the day the story broke.

To understand all of this, one must consider the dichotomy at play here. Obviously, it concerned this mixed-up young girl, but also and not incidentally, it concerned the most powerful person on the planet. "Lopsided" does not begin to cover it. And for that most powerful person on the planet, Monica was just another in a decades-long string of malleable and eagerly enthusiastic sexual service providers.

For Monica, what she had with Bill was something altogether different. In her naïveté, it was romance. Her ten minute "visits" were the equivalent of romantic dates. He would talk to her just before and just after "business" was taken care of. She cherished that, as though those fleeting moments gave real depth of meaning to these meaningless sexual encounters. He gave her crumbs, but they were crumbs she cherished.

Monica convinced herself that the president of the United States was her boyfriend, and that he loved her and wanted to spend his life with her. This boyfriend came with an annoying job, and the annoying job came with tiresome people who, against his will, were keeping them apart. Above all, he had an irksome domineering wife whom he was forced to keep, at least until he was out of office. "Delusion" does not begin to cover Monica's concept of the situation. And Bill Clinton, sexual predator, took blatant advantage of this naïve child.

As acutely reckless as he always was, as self-centered as he always was, he saw nothing wrong in frolicking with a girl so clearly much younger than her years. In fact, she didn't have much more maturity than Chelsea Clinton, who was in her mid-teens at the time. This is important. It was one of the most startling aspects of Monica, this extremely childlike affect, the girlish exuberance and even naïveté vying for space in the body of a young woman. At that point in her life, you could not spend five minutes in her presence and not notice this. Bill noticed. He was simply reckless enough, self-consumed enough, arrogant enough not to care.

Bill saw her as simply disposable, like so many others. But dismissing Monica was playing with fire. For the longest time and amidst the Russian roulette he was playing, he did not recognize the powder keg this young girl was. Monica was not like the others, and Bill Clinton did not see it—probably because of his enormous narcissism. Monica was not one who was willing to play a temporary and ultimately disposable part, then go away gracefully as he expected.

What seems a little strange is that he hadn't run into this before. He had been playing with women, this particular brand of fire, for decades. Why did his behavior take so long to catch up with him? A significant reason for that can be laid right at the feet of the champion of women, Hillary Clinton. We will likely never know how many women she threatened to destroy, but she was not shy about doing so. There is even more to come on Hillary's role in Bill's sexcapades as we go along.

In his callousness, Bill never once considered the emotional damage he inflicted on Monica or any other woman. As entitled as he was, it simply was not on his radar. Monica's insignificance was total—at least until much later, when he knew definitively that what he had done with her stood a chance of being made public. Suddenly, he cared. She could finally get back in to see him. He showered her with regifted gifts. It was a full-court press. The turnaround wasn't based on any concern for this young girl; it was all about his own preservation. Monica had to be seduced into protecting him. He needn't have bothered; she was eager to protect him. She would go to her grave protecting him. How else could they have a future once he was rid of "the Ba Ba" (Hillary)? Monica was in it for the long game, as ridiculous as that may sound today.

("The Ba Ba" is a name Monica picked up from her aunt, her mother's sister. It is also used by her mother. It is a generic name they used for the wives of the married men with whom the three of them had affairs.)

Monica protected Bill brilliantly in the end. She lied by omission when she simply left out so much. That is what brought me to the conclusion to which I eventually came. Any reasoning person would have come to that same conclusion.

No one, no father or mother, Democrat or Republican, could have stomached what he did to this vulnerable child and remained unmoved. On a human scale alone, I know of no one who could have borne her excruciating cries of uncontrollable anguish without feeling an element of anger at the adult causing them, or perhaps even without feeling compelled to do something about it. I know of no one who could have endured her utter despair, threats of suicide, and crushing pain and remained neutral. Well, the Hillary I saw behind the mask could. I could not.

What I did is part of the historical record of the impeachment of a president. I never wanted to achieve this notoriety. I did not seek it, but I do not regret it either. Bill and Hillary Clinton are responsible for their behavior, even though neither will ever accept any responsibility for anything they have done. I merely outed them. Given the same set of circumstances today, I would do it all again—not to betray a young girl, but to save a young girl and at the same time, to expose a dangerous predator once and for all. We all know how that turned out. Suffice it to say that the dangerous predator became one of the more popular presidents of all time. I went on to be roundly hated. And that's how things work in Clintonland.

Monica's later recounting of all of Bill's abuse became a bit of a walk down Primrose Lane. Suddenly, and seen through new rose-colored glasses, things were far more pleasant than I remembered. All at once, the truth was whatever Monica wanted it to be, and it resembled nothing that had come before. The ugly part had to stay buried, away from prying eyes. She had to be viewed as a romantic partner, a bona fide mistress, in a simple affair between consenting adults. This new version would benefit both Monica herself and, more importantly, the Clintons.

So, yes, bury the ugly part she did—the cruelty, the ugliness. The raw truth, that which had driven me in large part to take dramatic steps, simply disappeared. It was as though it never existed. The Clinton propaganda machine simply couched the entire thing as a consensual relationship, a romantic transgression between a man and a woman. Monica simply hit the delete button on all the rest. It worked for her and for him. It was what finally saved him. No one is punished for a mere affair. The never-ending Sturm und Drang, the hopeless despair, the suicide threats, the emotional wasteland that became her life for a period of three years—all of it just ceased to exist.

The nation bought the story because the media sold Monica as an adult and not the fragile, immature, naïve child she was at the time. Her affair with Bill became a private matter, a moment of weakness by a president turned victim, and Bill was not removed from office. It would be something everyone providing cover for Bill would pray about. Jessie Jackson helped. That this beautifully orchestrated theater had nothing to do with reality seemed beside the point. It was their story and they were sticking to it. Does this not make the senators who voted to acquit Bill guilty of enabling a serial sexual predator?

Today, so many years later and possibly having been awakened by the growing #MeToo movement, Monica has finally conceded that Bill took advantage of her. But unfortunately, she is still wearing the rose-colored glasses and "burying the lede." She simply cannot acknowledge the most crucial point of all. Because these twenty-two years later, she still doesn't see the all-powerful man who almost destroyed her as the villain. That role, she reserves for me.

Chapter 13
MONICA IN 1996

I first met Monica Lewinsky in April 1996, when she was transferred from the White House to the Pentagon's Public Affairs Office. I had been transferred to the same office in May 1993, long before Monica had started at the White House. Her immediate superior was Ken Bacon, assistant secretary of defense for public affairs, a title with real teeth and authority. He was also my boss, and I had come to know him as a partisan political appointee, fiercely loyal to the Clintons. Apparently, because of Bacon's willingness to accept them, the Public Affairs Office at the Pentagon had come to be the depository for White House undesirables.

Political appointees generally owe their allegiance first and foremost to the president who appointed them. That is how they got the appointment in the first place. This is true of all administrations. There is nothing necessarily sinister or corrupt about it; any new president needs trusted people in certain positions. There are, however, degrees of loyalty. Let's just say that some people are more fiercely loyal to the president than others.

Ken Bacon fell into the über-loyal category. His allegiance was not to the institution of the presidency or even the Department of Defense. He was more partisan than anything else; his loyalty was first and last to the Clintons for putting him there.

This level of allegiance is a bonus for an incumbent because it can be used for damage control. It can also be a disservice to the institution and to the various cabinet agencies. If there is a conflict between what is best for the person who is the president and the office of the president or

129

the institution that the appointee is working for, things can become very problematic.

The only thing of which I was absolutely certain was that Monica's White House connection had to be someone of enormous influence. As to whom, I had my suspicions, but I couldn't imagine that even Bill Clinton, with his predatory reputation, could be so blatantly foolish, reckless and, let's face it, stupid as to get involved with this flighty girl. No way. At least that was my initial reaction.

Monica's arrival at the Pentagon meant that political appointees had better tread carefully where Monica was concerned. She had clout and was not shy about letting us know it. She belonged to someone with influence. There was simply no other explanation for how or why this young woman landed at this particular desk in the Pentagon. Ken Bacon was Bill Clinton's boy at the Pentagon, so he accepted her without a peep.

Within a day of meeting Monica, I was stunned that anyone would consider this flake for a security clearance. But then, this was the Clinton White House. I recalled my time in the OEOB and how the Clintonoids acted toward protecting the nation's security. Basically, security was a nuisance to be treated as little more than a mere suggestion, especially when it might interfere with personal convenience.

During this time, Monica knew me only as someone who knew the president. She did not doubt my loyalty to this president, and I was careful not to give her a reason to doubt my loyalty. It wasn't just me; everyone in the office, given Hillary's propensity for spies, walked on eggshells and watched what they said around her, including Ken Bacon. For all we knew when Monica first arrived, she could have been Hillary's girl in the Pentagon.

What Monica didn't know was why I had departed the White House, and I was determined to keep her in the dark. I saw no reason to let her know that I was likely on the White House enemies list. She also knew nothing about the various and sundry scandals that those in the White House had brought upon themselves. I made sure she learned nothing of my hidden contempt or how much that had led to the Clintons' distrust of me and my eventual banishment. It became obvious very quickly that

Monica had no interest in anything not directly related to Monica and her quest to return to the White House.

It wasn't long before I realized that Ken must have known more about why Monica was dumped not only on him but on the rest of us as well. Ken came to be known throughout the Pentagon as the dude who took in not one but two White House rejects and installed them in his office, one right outside his door. I kept my mouth shut, took everything in, and kept my disgust to myself. Monica was a Clinton loyalist, as was her immediate boss and my ultimate boss, Ken. With one phone call, my job would disappear. I was under the Clintons' thumbs and I knew it. So, a tried-and-true Clinton loyalist I would appear to be.

Monica made sure that everyone in the office knew that her current position—which apparently involved filing and polishing her nails, styling her hair, and checking her makeup—would only be temporary. She was going back to the White House right after the November election. Monica had no intention of being stuck in the Pentagon for long; in fact, she was counting the days. In those first few months, she never explained the reason for the hiatus, why she had been moved to begin with. There had to be a reason she had been shipped out if her benefactor was as high up the food chain as I began to suspect. This also explained why she essentially didn't do any work. Any business outside government would have fired her in a heartbeat. It was another reason why I believed that Ken knew exactly who was protecting her. It still didn't occur to me that it could be Bill Clinton himself.

The late spring and early summer of 1996 was a particularly busy time for me between my program, the Joint Civilian Orientation Conference, which was most intense at this time of year, and life at home. My children and I had a lot of family visiting us during this period, and it was a welcome diversion from what had quickly become Monica saturation.

As summer came and her stories escalated, my sense became that, despite the incongruity and my sheer unwillingness to believe something this contemptible, her White House connection was most likely the president himself. As August approached, and even though Monica had not admitted it, I was becoming more and more certain that her benefactor was Bill Clinton.

For the longest time, I couldn't remember precisely when Monica confirmed this. She testified later that she told me sometime after the November election. That is true to the best of my recollection. My confusion arose from what occurred at the time of Bill's fiftieth birthday, August 19, 1996, which made it all obviously clear that her benefactor was, in fact, the president. Monica had not verified it by admitting it to me, but her behavior made it obvious.

One morning in early August, Monica flew into my office, barely able to contain herself.

"Hey, my mom said they're throwing the president a birthday party at Radio City Music Hall! In New York! And guess who's going to be there?" she breathlessly exclaimed with glee. "It costs two hundred fifty dollars per ticket. But it's so worth it, and my mom said she would pay for it!"

The invitation had come courtesy of her well-connected mother, who lived in New York and was intimately involved with Monica's odd relationship with Bill.

With the approach of Bill Clinton's fiftieth birthday, a splendid gala was being planned in New York in honor of this momentous milestone. It was to take place at the famed Radio City Music Hall. In fact, Hillary was planning a star-studded bash reminiscent of President John F. Kennedy's forty-fifth-birthday party in 1962 at Madison Square Garden. Hillary's New York tribute could not help but evoke memories of that presidential birthday bash so many years before, when Marilyn Monroe purred "Happy birthday, Mr. President" for all the world to see. Hillary was planning a somewhat different musical tribute to her husband's life. Of course, with the Clintons, the real purpose of the big bash was money. This was to be a major fundraiser.

Besides Monica Lewinsky, some 5,300 people would attend the show, and many more would participate via satellite. All of them paid through the nose, netting the Democratic National Committee more than $10 million in one evening.

I was surprised to see the night-and-day change in Monica's attitude. Prior to this, she had moped around, bemoaning the Clintons' lengthy family vacation in Wyoming.

Monica's excitement was so over the top that my suspicions about her White House patron became a certainty. I could not help wondering, if it were true, why was Monica, or her mother for that matter, forced to buy tickets? Surely the friends-and-family discount should have kicked in. Monica pondered the game plan, the logistics, the expense, the dilemma as to who, if anyone, could accompany her. The most important items, however—hair and outfits—began to consume her. Every single detail, every contingency, was considered and hashed out. Any concern about the cost was quickly and easily dismissed.

Then a horrible tragedy struck that should have changed some plans.

A military plane ferrying presidential equipment crashed shortly after takeoff in Wyoming at 11 p.m. local time on August 17, less than two days before the big birthday bash. The C-130 military transport had departed Jackson Hole, where the president and his family had been vacationing at the president's Wyoming retreat, and was bound for New York City, where the president would celebrate his birthday on August 19.

The aircraft was carrying eight Air Force crew members as well as a Secret Service agent. They had reached approximately ten thousand feet when it slammed into a Wyoming mountainside. The enormous C-130 was transporting not only the Secret Service agent and Air Force crew but an automobile used in presidential motorcades. The eighteen tons of fuel aboard created such an enormous explosion that little more than fragments remained.

The president and his family had left Wyoming aboard Air Force One just a few hours before the crash and had arrived safely back at the White House.

By the nineteenth, Monica had long since left for New York, planning on using the time to prepare—to get her hair done and choose just the right dress in one of the many boutiques she frequented. The devastating news convinced me that she had gone to New York for nothing, certain as I was that the event would be postponed because of the tragedy.

I recall thinking there was no reasonable way anyone remotely associated with this tragedy could continue to plan to party, least of all the
commander in chief. The notion that the president would go on with
a fundraiser didn't even enter my mind—it would have been grossly
insulting to the military, the Secret Service, those who died serving the
office of the president, and their grieving families. Who would not see
that? The Clintons, as it turned out.

I fleetingly wondered how volcanically the egocentric Monica would
react to the postponement of the party, having made meticulous plans
for nothing. I knew she would not mourn for the crew. By then, if I had
come to know anything about her, it was that she would see it as "sad," of
course—but to her plans, no more than an annoying inconvenience. Her
tendency to have tunnel vision would simply not allow anything else. If
this implies an unfeeling callousness on her part, that would be inaccurate.
Monica was by no means hard-hearted. She was simply singularly oblivious
to virtually anything or anyone outside her own personal bubble. In her
remarkably self-absorbed world—she is probably the most self-absorbed
person I have ever met—she simply would not be able to help herself. As
it turned out, there was no need for me to wonder how she would react.

The Pentagon houses all the branches of our military. When one
person in the military goes down, they all go down, in a manner of speaking.
It is an excruciating part of being closely associated with the military. To
all branches, their casualties, especially those who have given the last full
measure, are particularly painful. These are not merely faceless statistics.
Every casualty is someone's actual husband, father, son, brother, mother,
wife, or daughter. The list is never-ending, and they are all brothers and
sisters in arms. They mattered and are not to be forgotten.

Safely back at the White House, the president made a short statement
about the crash, saying: "This was particularly painful to us because they
worked for me and did an invaluable service, and I am very sad about it."
This included the weeping of political crocodile tears.

The president promptly left for New York and the celebration. Take
a significant moment to honor the dead? Show true empathy? That he
truly felt their pain in a way that mattered? Get serious. There was money

involved. Keep the priorities straight. On to New York and the celebration of Bill! I had started to believe that nothing could shock me anymore
when it came to the Clintons. This did.

So, the show went on. Monica was going to be there with bells on.
This would be my introduction to Monica's infamous "plans." In this
instance at least, the Pentagon could be proud. Her "plans" were laid out
with military precision worthy of that storied institution.

If I had ever been able to before, I could no longer chalk up her
behavior to merely that of an enthusiastic supporter. Even the groupie
label began to pale. As she plotted and planned and ran back to my office
several times the day she announced the party to me, I knew that with a
little encouragement, she would soon break down and admit the shocking
truth. It was inevitable. And when I reflect on this time, one thing stands
out: I remember thinking that if this ludicrous thing was true, that she was
involved with the president, the country should know. Monica was, for all
intents and purposes, a child.

I recall using much the same remark I had used time and time again
when dealing with women around Bill Clinton. His pattern of behavior
had gotten to be predictable and even hilarious on one hand, but was still
startling on the other.

So, I gave Monica the standard opening: "It's a good thing he was
unaware of your infatuation, or he would most assuredly have acted. You
are just his type."

Monica thought I meant because she was young and attractive. I meant
because she was female and within his periphery. She all but conceded
with a wink and a smile, but did not verbally confirm, that she had in fact
been carrying on what she termed a "relationship" with the president. Yet
it was then that I knew. And while the involvement was repulsive, based
on what I had seen myself, it was no real surprise.

Each and every time I had said something to this effect to one of Bill's
women in the past, an immediate recounting of that woman's Bill Clinton
story followed. It was how I got to know the Graduates—who, to a person,
beamed with the chance to tell their own personal story. They were all so
strangely proud of it.

But before the incredibly detailed recounting could begin, Monica first had to get to Bill's birthday party. And she did. Upon her return from her meticulously planned trip, she immediately flew back to my office, grinning from ear to ear and positively beaming.

"I did it!" she boasted with immeasurable pride. "It was amazing. I'm so glad I sucked up the expense and went; it was so worth it!" The words tumbled out fast and furiously; her excitement was uncontainable. I would come to know this Monica as the euphoric one.

And the euphoric Monica had another reason to be thrilled. The election was drawing closer. It was now fewer than eighty days until she would be whisked back to a job in the White House. Although Monica was fully capable of playing a long game, she was never an overly patient person. But, as I would soon learn, she was able to find joy in the countdown to Election Day, sure as she was that it would be well worth the wait.

What exactly had she done? Monica had taken full advantage of her attendance at the president's birthday bash. She had not only gotten into the party; she had "made actual contact" with him in a peculiarly personal way. Right after the November election, she would lay all her cards on the table and brag to me, relaying all the sordid details about what had happened at Radio City Music Hall months earlier—telling me much more than I wanted to know. She would gush that she had maneuvered into a position to grab his genitals with no one being the wiser, delighted to have given "the Big He" a little love massage. So, there you go.

Eventually, reviewing every contact with him—physical, telephonic, whatever—would become part of Monica's daily Bill Clinton analysis.

"You absolutely won't believe this, but I squeezed his balls right in the middle of throngs of people!" she told me in November, adding her trademark loud laugh, a guffaw that could be heard several offices away.

This was quickly followed by a recitation of the celebrities there ("I'll bet none of them got to squeeze his balls!") and catty remarks about Hillary, who from that moment on was referred to disdainfully only as "the Ba Ba."

She went on: "I saw Chelsea, too; it was so great!"

Monica was, of course, talking about the young daughter of the man whose testicles she had squeezed in the middle of an enormous public event. And this daughter's father just happened to be the president of the United States. All of that was lost on Monica.

Had all of these details been relayed by anyone else, they would have been merely horrifying and hard to, well, grasp. It was as staggering to hear about as the thong incident she had pulled off the year before—she had deliberately bent over so the president could see her, then hiked up her dress to reveal her thong underwear to him. But by now I knew Monica to be a young, misguided girl packaged as something entirely different.

My reaction to this latest news was visceral—in the end, because of her hands. On the continuum of Monica's glaring contrasts, her tiny, somewhat pudgy, and incongruously childlike hands starkly belied her preferred impression of voluptuousness and sexual sophistication. To me, the image of her seemingly prepubescent hands grabbing the president's balls presented a stark picture of abuse that had started so many months before in the White House.

In her exuberance, she threw in a few derisive, but in her mind hilarious, cracks about rope lines and the Secret Service, questioning their thoroughness given how easily she was able to pull off what she'd done: "Okay, there were tons of people, but still, they are the Secret Service! And they missed it!"

I was fairly certain the protection detail hadn't missed any of it, but I didn't mention that. I believe to this day not only that the Secret Service agents witnessed the grope, but also that they were well aware of Monica from day one at the White House, and never lost sight of her right up until the end. That's the protection detail and the uniformed division. These people rarely, if ever, miss anything. They are uncommonly professional but also adaptive to reality, and after three long years with Bill Clinton, the business with Monica would have been business as usual for them. And, as always, the charismatic president was able to cultivate some of them to facilitate his personal needs.

"I had hoped for eye contact, maybe a kiss on the cheek," Monica continued. "I just wanted him to see me. I can't believe I really did it!"

The saddest part was that this grope validated, in her mind, a sort of secret romance between them. She may not have been Marilyn Monroe singing to her guy, but she was Monica and he was the president, and this was good enough. For now.

By the time I officially knew that it was the president, the floodgates had burst, and she couldn't wait to discuss every single detail of the whole series of events that had landed her in the dismal Pentagon. Pardon the pun, but it had been a series of blow-by-blows since the affair began in November 1995 in the White House. There was a lot to tell all these months later.

What struck me immediately was the amount of time since her last physical "encounter" with "the Big Creep"—Monica's pet name for the president when she was mad at him. September was rapidly approaching, and her last physical rendezvous had been on Easter Sunday, April 6, 1996, with the exception of the rope-line grope. Still, she was convinced she had found her special man and they were meant to be together. She was thoroughly convinced it was only a matter of time before everything would be back to the way it had been.

What was the way it had been, exactly? She'd had only had a handful of sexual encounters with the president. She even told me once that she had to remind him of her name; she had the impression he had forgotten it in the six weeks since their last encounter. Yet, to her, this was a romance. I shuddered at her naïveté and at his recklessness in choosing this particular girl, but that was about the extent of my personal involvement at that point. How much more obvious did he have to be? He had forgotten her name! This should certainly give you a sense of Monica's immaturity, naïveté, and delusion. And her mother was encouraging this!

One day after the groping of Bill at the big birthday bash, Monica burst into my office and bellowed with glee, "You won't believe any of it!"

And so, she started opening up to me about him. It was as if she could finally, openly brag to me about what she was involved in and with whom. She was like a high school girl losing her virginity to the cute captain of the football team and then bragging about it to her friends.

Once I knew for certain that her White House guardian angel was the president, it became obvious why the countdown to Election Day had taken on such grave significance. Monica was confident that the president would be reelected, as were most reasoning people by this point. But unlike Monica, I knew what banishment from this administration's White House really meant. It was not a temporary condition. I also believed that Hillary knew about her, which meant the door back to "the Big Creep" was permanently slammed on her. Not that Hillary cared about Bill's dalliances. If Monica was banished, she must have passed her sell-by date, meaning Hillary had had enough and this little tootsie of Bill's had to go.

As Monica shared with others what she shared with me about Bill, I knew he was still the same Bill I had known him to be, just a bit worse for wear. I was certain he and his wife were still pontificating about "the rights of women all over the world" while each of them in their own way not only laid waste to the rights of women in their own home, but also plotted to routinely destroy the inevitable women who surfaced into the public eye periodically.

In the beginning, I was distanced enough to not care. I was tired of all of it. I didn't care about him, and I didn't care about Monica. Months and months later, the distance no longer existed. Now I did care. Helplessness was an unfamiliar sense for me, but this was more than I could handle on my own.

Monica's biggest fear was that he would forget her before the reelection and move on to someone else. There were always pictures of Bill with women. The celebrities in particular angered her. The pretty Eleanor Mondale, who seemed to surface in Bill's presence every now and then, bothered her the most. But even Barbra Streisand was perceived as a threat. And everyone in between.

It was why, despite her banishment, she showered the White House with calls, notes, and reminders of her existence. She realized he was a tactile sort of fellow, that he coveted what he saw. Monica was not being seen, and despite her valiant efforts, her presence was not being felt. She knew she was off his radar. She followed the news carefully, not for campaign content but to ferret out situations in which he could conceivably be tempted to "stray."

She knew full well his weakness. After all, who had more firsthand knowledge than Monica Lewinsky of how easily such opportunities presented themselves to him daily? His life was a veritable candy bowl with a remarkable assortment from which to choose. And most of the opportunities were not covered in the news. Oddly, Hillary was the only female whose close proximity to Bill Monica could accept. That was because Monica had it on good authority that "the Ba Ba" was on her way out the door.

Monica anxiously worried about all the women who worked in the OEOB, West Wing, and East Wing, as well as the congressional staff and even the housekeeping staff. She worried about the parade of donors overnighting in the Lincoln Bedroom, which itself continued to rival the turnaround at a Motel Six. She worried about the plethora of eager supporters, the women of the press. Her paranoia encompassed anyone of the female persuasion with any reason at all to be in the White House. Or Camp David. Or Martha's Vineyard. Fill in the blank. These women were being seen, and she was not. It made for a good bit of worry. And the worry took up a great deal of time. So did the plotting.

In between the obsessive worrying, Monica plotted and planned. And talked. She needed to get in to see him, if only to remind him of better days, with her. Inundating Betty Currie with constant phone calls was simply not working. The guardians of the gates were doing their job. What she didn't realize was that they had been told to keep her away.

Instead of realizing that her make-believe boyfriend had broken up with her, Monica took her stalking to new heights. During this time, she even knew and complained that she was referred to as "the stalker" in the White House. Of course, in her tiny Monica world, the moniker was entirely undeserved. After all, Bill had been an active participant. But as I watched Monica in this quest, it was clear there was no better description than stalking.

To effectively stalk, to be able to closely monitor Bill's schedule, she needed Betty Currie. She also began to cultivate Bayani Nelvis, better known as Nel, the Oval Office Navy steward. Nel had extraordinary access through a back door to the Oval Office not used by anyone else. He had information about the president's movements, and above all, about "personal" visitors who were seen by few. Nel was an irresistible gold mine there for the unearthing.

Monica cultivated him as only Monica could: through a seduction of sorts. As she explained it, Nel was easy pickings. She started with flirtatious chitchat, the batting of eyelashes, and artfully exposed cleavage. Eventually, with her small gifts and frequent visits, he succumbed to all of it.

When Monica was booted from the White House in April 1996, he became essential to her—a lifeline, a font of desperately needed information. In a move that astonished me, she maintained regular telephone contact with Nel. He became her on-site eyes and ears, an invaluable tool in her quest.

Her "boyfriend" had not given her the direct phone number to the Oval Office for a reason. But Monica was incapable of admitting to herself why he hadn't: he simply did not want her to have it. Whatever he'd had with her was over. "Go away." Instead of accepting this, she decided to find allies who would help facilitate her quest. And find them, she did.

The president lives behind an impenetrable wall of security. His office is guarded whenever he is in. He is even accompanied by Secret Service when he moves outside the Oval Office within the White House from one room to another. While this serves as protection, it also provides him with an effective way to ward off unwelcome, even tiresome, "friends"—particularly those once-irresistible "friends" who, within five minutes, would begin to bore him. No one can weave and dodge or even hide better than a president. This didn't dissuade Monica at all. She was well aware of this, but it was no more than a minor challenge to overcome. For anyone else, this would be like attempting to climb Mount Everest blindfolded and without the luxury of limbs.

After the birthday bash in August, most of the rest of 1996 leading up to the election was taken up by attempts to make phone contact and other ways to make him remember her, whether by gifts or notes or calls to Betty Currie. The emotional roller coaster continued. Her entire life revolved around holding on to the postelection promise of a return to the White House and, in a strange way, to her sanity. I knew and dreaded the reality that what she wanted was not going to be the case after the election. This girl, in reality an emotional child, was in serious trouble.

During the summer and fall of 1996, the president and first lady were out of the White House on the campaign trail most of the time. Monica begrudgingly understood this but barely accepted it. To her, this was his "other life" away from where he wanted to be—with her. Monica would impatiently wait, literally counting the days until the magic day, her personal D-Day, November 4, would arrive. The date became all-consuming. It represented her lifeline, without which she would drown. It could not get here fast enough.

The '96 election came and, as expected, the Clintons would remain in the White House. It also brought about the now famous photo, beamed around the world, of a beret-clad Monica enthusiastically greeting her guy on the rope line upon his victorious return to the White House. This picture would become an iconic representation of "the intern and the president."

   That same day, politically appointed employees of the administration were encouraged to come to the White House in a show of enthusiastic support for the returning victor. For days before this, Monica had been almost jumping out of her skin in anticipation of the big event. To finally be there in physical proximity to the center of her world. Monica had harassed me to go with her. But I had something more important to do. I had set aside that day to unsnarl my heap of paper clips, so I passed.

   With all her hopes and dreams centered on a day that had finally arrived, I dreaded the inevitable letdown. Monica's world was nothing if not a series of dramatic extremes. Euphorically high highs and devastatingly low lows. I suspected her promised return to the White House was nothing more than an artificial deadline of appeasement to buy Bill time.

I also suspected that reality would rear its ugly head. It was inevitable. It meant Monica would be forced to face his final dismissal once and for all. And I knew that at that point, all bets would be off. "Hell hath no fury like a woman scorned" came to mind. With Monica, the adage was glaringly insufficient.

As the big day, her D-Day, approached, the plans became the center of her life. You would think she was preparing for an audience with the queen. Hair, makeup, outfit, coat—everything was meticulously planned. Likely even her underwear had to be new and match everything else. I didn't ask, because she would have shown it to me. Everything had to be perfect. She hadn't seen the president in person since the August birthday bash. Her world, possibly her existence, was riding on this day.

Whenever Bill Clinton was involved, Monica was remarkably attentive to detail. She planned everything to perfection ahead of time, thought it all through and left nothing to chance. Ironically, the addition of the jaunty beret was a last-minute thing. She had been frantically looking for ways to stand out from the crowd. So much was riding on her being seen; Bill would surely remember his promise when he saw her. Knowing there would be hordes of enthusiastic supporters jockeying for position on the rope line, she chose the beret as a prop. And knowing Monica, woe unto anyone who might try to keep her away from the rope line. The months of banishment would finally be behind her. Bill's election victory would be hers, too.

Except, she got the now-famous hug and nothing else. As far as I know, and she would have told me, she wasn't even able to give his genitals a little love squeeze as a reminder of things to come.

For the next seven weeks, she continued her stalking campaign. If Bill had been a normal citizen, she could have gone to jail for her behavior: constant phone calls, notes, gifts she sent. Poor Bill. Actually, poor Betty Currie and the other Guardians who had to deal with Monica. Of course, they had known Bill for years. They knew who and what he was. These people were not only enablers of his predatory sexual behavior, they were coconspirators. Not only for his sake but also for theirs, Monica had to be handled delicately. She was a scandal waiting to explode, and would if anything was made public about her. And there was always the specter of Hillary hanging over everything like a cloud of poison gas over the trenches in France during World War I.

By January 1997, Monica was beside herself. For the past two months, since the election, she had been an emotional train wreck. I had to deal with it every day at work and at home. There were evenings when I had barely walked through the door when the phone calls from her started. Some bordered on hysterical, with threats of suicide.

Eventually, Monica decided she would attend one of the inaugural balls in another attempt to be seen. She decided on the New York Ball, one of fourteen balls that year, which would be held at the Kennedy Center, a mere stone's throw from her Watergate apartment.

She placed so much emphasis on the event, and attached such great importance to the hope that her "boyfriend" would see her there. She convinced herself that, in Bill's eyes, in comparison to "the Ba Ba," she would shine this one time for sure. She showed me the dress she planned to wear. It was a beautiful scarlet strapless gown, and with her alabaster skin and raven-colored hair, she did look stunning. But to me, her efforts were all too sad. I knew they would be for naught. Monica refused to think this even for a second.

Once again, the machinations to prepare became all-encompassing. The hairdresser was summoned to the Watergate. The professional makeup and lashes were carefully applied. The right shoes and bag were thoughtfully chosen. No detail was too insignificant. All that effort, yet the result was sorely disappointing. Devastating, in fact. Monica waited amidst hundreds of partying people, beautiful and quite alone at the ball.

All fourteen inaugural balls were jam-packed with hundreds upon hundreds of supporters. Cameras were everywhere, documenting the Clintons dancing at each event. Making an appearance at each one of these made the Clintons predictably late to the one Monica attended. To an impatient Monica, the wait was interminable. When Bill arrived, hours later than expected, he was riding a high that clearly had nothing to do with her. He and "the Ba Ba" were both jubilantly basking in the glow of victory. They looked and acted like a couple—a real married couple celebrating a joint victory. He might as well have driven a stake through Monica's heart.

Monica simply could not process any of it. She believed after all this time she had more than earned some real acknowledgement, if not her rightful place on the stage. That is how delusional she had become. At the very least, she expected some personal contact, some intimate connection that would separate her from the sea of inconsequential people. It did not happen, and it was crushing.

Instead, all her preparations and planning were for nothing. They were a colossal waste of already tight funds and added to her increasing frustration with him over not bringing her back to the White House two months earlier. In fact, she was just another face in the crowd of hundreds, as unnoticed as everyone else. It infuriated her. She was ready to pop. If she had been emotionally distraught before, now she was a goner.

Monica was on a mission and refused to admit defeat. The president's callous stonewalling, his refusal to see her, put her over the edge. Her increasingly frantic days were consumed with how to get back to the White House. Her first choice was to go back as an employee with constant access. I suspect that even she knew this was a long shot at best. Next, she would get in to see him as an "appointment" through the ubiquitous Betty Currie. But none of her plans were working.

During this time, Monica would call me at home almost every night to talk to me about her plans. If I did not hear about the latest plans A through G at night by telephone, I would learn of them early the next day. The newest plan of attack would greet me as I entered the Pentagon each morning, where I could count on Monica's finding me whether I came by car or by Metro.

That was in and of itself telling because the Pentagon is enormous. It was the largest office building in the world at the time. It boasted seventeen and a half miles of corridors, so getting from any point A to point B was generally a hike. God help you if your destination was closer to point Z. Add to that the close to thirty thousand military and civilian staff and defense contractors working in this massive building and you can begin to imagine the vast environment of the Pentagon. Often, Monica would meet me with Starbucks in hand, saving me a stop and ensuring I could give her my full attention on the brisk walk to my office.

The Metro spilled out to a different Pentagon entrance than the one I used when I parked in the Pentagon lot. They were at least a twenty-minute walk away from each other. It would not be a stretch to say that Monica's morning visit would keep her away from her desk for close to an hour, considering the walking distance she was forced to cover just to find me each day. Monica was understood to be a special employee of sorts with few actual responsibilities, so these extended absences posed no problems. She would find me and accompany me routinely on the brisk walk to my office before begrudgingly returning to her desk.

As I mentioned, her moods were dramatic and always extreme. The extremes often occurred during the same day. She could be euphoric and then flip to suicidal. She could be hopeful and then suddenly turn morose. At that point in her life, melodrama was her middle name. And she was all-consuming and exhausting for me to deal with almost daily. If I thought I was under siege, I am certain Betty Currie and the president felt so, too, because all of Monica's plans included contact with them. Imagine that. They had created a monster, and she was sitting smack dab in the prestigious E Ring of the Pentagon. Thank you very much.

Chapter 14
MONICA AND ANDY BLEILER

To give you even more of a sense of the real Monica Lewinsky, here is a story of her behavior regarding one of her quests during the same time she was after Bill Clinton: Andy Bleiler.

I had heard about Andy long before Monica finally admitted her unique relationship with Bill Clinton. Bill was not the first man Monica had become obsessed with. It was not the first time she had convinced herself of a fantasy. Betrayal was nothing new either. In fact, the Andy Bleiler affair may have been even more bizarre than the one involving the president.

After Monica had been expelled to the Siberia of the Pentagon and before I knew about her servicing Bill Clinton, she told me about Andy. As Monica was wont to do in her immature, naïve, middle-school-girl way, she often spoke of her longtime affair with Andy. As she told it to me, Monica had been a student and Andy had been variously a stage production or drama teacher at the Beverly Hills High School, when the affair began. According to Monica, he was dating or engaged to an older woman with a child when it started. She also claimed it had been a five-year affair, and intimated that it was not exactly totally over even then.

During the initial weeks at the Pentagon, when Monica began showing her Bill compulsion, she could not stop talking about Andy. I would come to learn that her Bill obsession had long since kicked in, but somehow Andy was never quite off the radar. She went on and on. And on. The complaints were endless. As she told it, her frustration had reached a boiling point. Andy would not commit. She had waited patiently. The commitment was not happening according to her schedule. She needed a plan. Since there was always a plan, it was time for plan B. What I did not know then is that this same sequence of events would occur with Bill Clinton more than a year later. She simply does not admit defeat.

Much later, she would tell a different story, and provided quotes from friends in her book, *Monica's Story* by Andrew Morton, who backed up her new and improved version of events. She would eventually claim she did not know when the affair began or that Andy had been engaged to the much-older Kate, a young mother with a child from a previous marriage. She also claimed later that she chose to enroll at Lewis & Clark College in Portland, Oregon, to get away from Andy. This is not the version she told me.

The way Monica told it to me, she was looking for a four-year school to transfer to after she finished a two-year program at a community college. She chose Lewis & Clark because Andy was planning to move to Oregon. They both knew the move was going to happen; it was the timing that was uncertain.

Having come to know the immature, naïve, dilettante Beverly Hills child that Monica was, I found her moving to Oregon hard to imagine. I would have less trouble seeing her clean toilets with her tongue than seeing her move to Portland. She must have felt she was sentenced to twenty years in prison to spend two years at a small liberal arts school in Portland—much like Hillary's sentence of living in Little Rock for so long. I mean no disrespect to Oregon; it's a beautiful place. But not for this pampered princess.

Off Monica went, which tells you something about her obsessive-compulsive tendencies. Andy eventually arrived, family in tow, some months later. By now he was married to Kate, the older woman he had been dating when the affair began, who now had two children. Later, Monica would claim she dreaded his arrival, but her story to me was that it was all she had worked and waited for since arriving in what she called a dreary backwater. The Monica I knew would have seen her time there as her being sentenced to Devil's Island. Knowing Monica, I can see it was a small price to pay to be in Andy's periphery, or at least that was the plan she had told to me. She was still in contact with him, and his wife, while I knew her at the Pentagon.

In an almost offhand manner, she openly boasted that she had befriended his wife and children and easily assimilated into life as a Bleiler family friend and babysitter, no less. The assimilation helped with easy access to Andy because instead of just meeting him surreptitiously when he could get away, she could innocently and openly come to him with her friend, Andy's wife, none the wiser. Monica saw no betrayal in this. In fact, I doubt it entered her mind. Andy's wife was an inconsequential player with little impact on Monica at all.

She told me of the countless presents she showered on the kids and on Andy's wife, including a sexy full-length sheer lace negligee. I cannot begin to understand the layers of weirdness that gift represented.

She showed me several pictures of Andy, his kids, his wife, his home—and of herself smack dab in the middle of this happy little family. This bothered her not at all. Monica simply did not see why some people might see this as a problem. She never saw her actions as the true betrayal they were. She was on a quest, and nothing would stand in her way. Monica wanted what Monica wanted when Monica wanted it. Betrayal was only betrayal if it negatively affected Monica. There was no depth to the enigma that was Monica Lewinsky.

She told me that before she moved to Washington, she'd had no real life outside the Andy obsession. She'd gone through the motions at college, but her real life had been time spent with Andy. As with Bill Clinton later, she convinced herself they had a future. Contrary to her revisionist history, being with Andy was the sole reason she had landed at Lewis & Clark College. It was to be a long-term investment well worth the sacrifice. She knew if she could be in place before he arrived, she would be well situated to achieve her goal. Even though she knew it would be a while before Andy arrived, she put herself in place and patiently waited.

The timing, choices, and long-range planning are telling regarding the lengths she would go to achieve a goal. Monica, as I've said, was a meticulous planner, and no obstacle could stand in her way. But she admitted she had paid a high price to be near Andy, so it simply had to pay off.

The fact that he was married to a nice gal now with two children was of zero consequence to Monica. Offering insight into Monica's unique way of thinking, her stories about Andy became progressively more extreme and more incomprehensible.

Imagine insinuating yourself into a family unit while actively sleeping with the husband of your friend in the family home. I do not know any other woman who could do that. Monica's lack of a moral compass did not allow her, on any level, to see this as betrayal. The situation was like one of those weird movie scripts that usually ends with an axe being flailed about and several gunshots.

When Monica's relationship with Andy became public, the left-leaning media did not see it as the betrayal it was. I began to believe in the fundamental differences between political parties, the stark contrast between how each sees right and wrong. The left's view of betrayal, as seen through the media, made me realize that, in general, liberals are incapable of betrayal. In their view, betrayal is only betrayal when perpetrated by their enemies. This explains why the Clintons are never shown by their media toadies as anything but victims. Nice work if you can get it, I suppose.

It was more than a little disturbing to try to grasp Monica's point of view. She found it hilarious that she was sleeping with Andy, often in the house with his wife and kids nearby and admitted it added to the excitement. She found the times they were close to being caught even more exhilarating and humorous. She bragged about a social gathering with guests at Andy's house when they used the bathroom to, ahem, entertain themselves. At least they closed the door.

When she bragged to me about this infidelity, she always referred to Andy's wife as her friend while admitting she wished Kate would simply cease to exist. This friend was in the way, and in an eerie presage of what would come, she schemed about how Kate might no longer exist. The way to Andy and Monica's meeting at the altar had to be paved somehow. But Andy did not leave Kate. At least not then. Had the feckless Andy left his wife for Monica, much would have been different.

When I met Monica and my suspicions were raised about just whom her White House benefactor could be, I was thrown off by her Andy obsession. While her Bill fascination was extreme, the Andy obsession was front and center as well at the same time. She told me she still called Andy frequently and had in fact made numerous daily calls to him from the White House, sometimes four or five times a day.

A birthday letter addressed to Andy from the president seemed to tickle her most of all. It would take a shrink to explain how twisted that was. The man with whom she was currently having oral sex behind the back of Hillary had personally signed a presidential birthday card with personal greetings from him and Hillary, and had sent it along to another man with whom she was conducting a sexual relationship. And that relationship was being conducted behind the back of his wife, who still knew absolutely nothing and who was often included on these lengthy and frequent phone calls. It was a dizzying circle of irony, falling under the heading "Too Ridiculous to Believe." But that was Monica.

Monica was, above all else, relentless. As it pertained to Andy, she was a disingenuous infiltrator who tracked the Bleiler family from Los Angeles to Portland. In her self-consumed and laser-focused way, she charted her course to achieve an end. She wanted Andy. Period. Yet, if you had called her a home-wrecker, she would have been appalled. That could not be her; that had to be someone else. The very convincing Monica logic would leave most people scratching their heads. I have said in the past, to underestimate Monica Lewinsky would be an enormous mistake.

Unknown to Kate Bleiler, her new friend Monica had been sleeping with her husband for the last few years. Andy's wife was the unwitting and grateful recipient of Monica's incredible generosity. Monica routinely arrived bearing thoughtful gifts. What a nice girl this Monica Lewinsky was! Showering attention and gifts not only on Andy and herself but on the children, too.

When Monica finally admitted to me the obvious—something I had known for six months—officially confirming the existence of her presidential affair, she then began filling in the blanks about Andy. It was then that she shared the missing details of those many daily phone calls to Andy and Kate, all made from the White House.

She told them about an affair she was having with a highly placed White House official. That he would insist on only oral sex. In the lengthy phone calls, she went into graphic detail. I asked her why she did that. It was, she said, a twofold plan. It was primarily a way to keep Andy wanting more, as the descriptive narrative of a sexual nature would turn him on, make him miss her, and compel him to leave Kate once and for all. It was also supposed to allay any potential concerns if Kate heard anything at all from Monica's former college pals about Monica's relationship with Andy. Make sense?

To me, as I've said, this was pretty much a betrayal of a friend. Monica not only did not recognize this as betrayal or that it might be wrong; it simply was not on her radar screen. It was during these conversations that her complete lack of remorse, turmoil, and guilt was most apparent. She would even giggle at odd moments in the relaying of the bizarre chain of events, but never showed any feeling of any kind for Kate Bleiler.

She did not despise Andy's wife. To Monica, she simply did not matter. She was collateral damage, a nonfactor and inconsequential. It was precisely how Monica felt about Andy's and Kate's children as well.

It was during this time that I began to see striking signs of her delusional methods of rationalization. Her thinking was perfectly clear to her but more perplexing than anything else to others. Within a few short months, Monica would magically become the betrayed, ostensibly at my hand.

When Andy and his wife surfaced on the national stage days after the story hit, the word "betrayal" was missing from the coverage. In fact, this story got short shrift, and after spending five minutes reporting breathlessly of Monica's other older, married boyfriend, the national media just dropped it. It simply fell to the wayside. Yesterday's news.

No one, least of all those in the media, saw any irony at all in labeling me the betrayer of all betrayers of this young girl while they sat on a story of her actual betrayal that should have stunned virtually everyone.

Monica was portrayed solely as a victim. Andy was just an old boyfriend. Big deal. Everyone has old boyfriends. The media just ignored the story, the ironic similarities with the presidential affair, and went on to further breathless coverage of someone else. In doing this, the newly hatched "fake news" chose to downplay, if not totally ignore, a betrayal of the worst sort while amping up the cacophony against me that immediately ensued.

Andy gave a press conference, and within five minutes, the same newscasters jumped right back into a chorus of lambasting me and protecting poor little Monica. "Linda Tripp, who betrayed her friend for a book deal." They did not miss a beat.

Chapter 15
MICHAEL ISIKOFF: PART ONE, MARCH 1997

It was 1997, and spring had arrived in Washington, D.C. Spring is cherry blossom time in D.C.—a sight that is spectacular, and if you have never seen it, you should make a point to do so. March 24, 1997, was a typically busy day with a good bit to accomplish before close of business. But on this pivotal day in 1997, life was going to take a dramatic turn. And not just for me.

This otherwise unremarkable day was the beginning of the end and would culminate ten months later in international headlines. It was also the day I impulsively grabbed what I thought was a lifeboat. But appearances can be deceiving. When grabbing what you believe is a lifeboat, it's a good idea to check first for leaks. This particular lifeboat I thought I had found didn't stay afloat for long. I would not know this for quite some time, however.

To put the significance of this day into context requires quite a bit of explanation. The long and winding road The Beatles so eloquently sang about was, for me, a tumultuous and rather directionless road. Even so, it took a new course on this day. To put it in perspective, it is fair to say that had the events of this day not occurred, the world would never have heard of Linda Tripp or Monica Lewinsky.

It had been almost a year since I had first met Monica Lewinsky, and what a time that had been. The "all Monica, all the time" show had been going on nonstop since the first day she arrived at the Pentagon. At first,

I listened with indifferent curiosity. But let's be honest, gossipy stories, especially those involving illicit sex and powerful people, are too juicy for anyone to ignore. Be honest: you would not ignore them either. Plus, I was personally vindicated, having learned that Bill Clinton was as disgusting as I had thought he was, and his pattern had not changed.

I began to listen avidly when all hell broke loose after the election. Monica's nuclear meltdown in November was a sign of things to come. And now, almost a year into the Monica drama, I could feel myself slowly beginning to flail in the water. If anything, this period exacerbated an already tough time for me, a time that had been extremely difficult beginning in January 1993, when I first met both Clintons.

Up to now, during the time since Monica had first begun unloading her sordid tale, I had not taken any steps to document any of it. Still intimidated by the wrath of Hillary, I also didn't allow anyone to see the outrage I kept buried. For all outward appearances, I was a loyal Clintonoid political appointee who supported this severely flawed president and his not-so-loving partner. To put it bluntly, I had children to feed and bills to pay, and needed the job.

As the weeks became months, the building outrage and feeling of helplessness began to overcome me. For close to a year, I was subjected to Monica's daily frenzied recital of all the gory details of her incredible story. On top of everything else, the story was still ongoing. She could not come to accept that her dream was over. In fact, the situation was becoming worse and worse. Things were changing at lightning speed because Monica became a bit more manic every single day. It was an interminable, ever-present, and escalating saga.

This was all due to Monica's singular nose-to-the-grindstone doggedness, which brought more and more inconceivable twists and turns in her pursuit of Bill Clinton. The way he had abused this emotionally weak, naïve, susceptible girl and the damage he had done to her were hard to watch. It was grinding on me because I knew that both his predatory abuse and his callous dismissal of this volatile, immature young girl were true. She was consumed by it. He became her life. But if he gave her a thought at all, it seemed it was primarily as to how to safely disengage. It had worked with all the others. He would soon learn that with the tenacious Monica, they had simply broken the mold.

None of this occurred in a vacuum. Much as Monica disliked it, my life outside the Pentagon went on. My responsibilities at work had increased. The Joint Civilian Orientation Conference (JCOC) is the Pentagon's oldest civilian-oriented program. It is how the Pentagon attempts to educate the movers, the shakers, and otherwise influential people on the abilities, strengths, equipment, and personnel of all the branches of the military. It is a weeklong hands-on field trip during which these civilians pay for the privilege of driving and reviewing a variety of equipment. The premise was sound, and its most critical aspect was ensuring that the attendees were people who could not only learn from this experience but share their newfound knowledge to the widest possible audience.

Recently I had been promoted to director. With that title came additional responsibilities. As a working single mother of two children, I was always busy at home with those responsibilities. I tried to make time for my friends, too, and I was still committed to a bridge game one evening a week. And there was always my love for books.

During the months of the emotionally draining Monica saga, without my consciously realizing it, my outside life changed significantly. My passion for extra activities was going away, and even the day-to-day things I absolutely had to get done at home began to fall by the wayside. Apart from the physical toll the bombardment of her phone calls was taking on me, the overriding emotional outrage and helplessness to do anything about it left me exhausted. My physical energy and normal ambition waned. My house and home life suffered as I let things go. My son and daughter also felt the change. I was the only one, however, who knew why. Monica, around whom the world revolves, was consuming me.

In the midst of Monica's daily mayhem, my deceptively calm appearance belied a raging inner turmoil. Always a serious person, I became more so. I smiled less and less. I became preoccupied with things I was helpless to change. At work I was increasingly intolerant of those around me. I was aware of this but felt helpless to do anything to change it. A shrink would have likely diagnosed me as dealing with depression.

I began to deal with the stress in a way I have learned is common. Food had already been my coping mechanism, but this time, in a colossal burst of excess, I was pretty much eating my way into oblivion. Copious carbs became my personal poison. I suppose it was good that I was not drowning my sorrows with alcohol, but I sure wasn't doing much better.

In 1995, a year into my time at the Pentagon, I saw startling clips of my testimony on Capitol Hill and wondered who on earth that person was. The expansion of my body was a sight to behold.

Getting back to March 24, 1997—the day *Newsweek's* Michael Isikoff entered my life, a red-letter day to be sure. First of all, there are no drop-in visitors from the outside at the Pentagon. To gain access to the Pentagon, visitors are met at the entrance and escorted into the building by a badge holder. They are not left alone to simply roam around the place. When they leave, they are then escorted back to where they first entered. Since unaccompanied strangers simply do not appear in Pentagon offices, I was more than a little wary when Isikoff appeared unannounced. He simply strolled, unescorted, into my office.

Although I had never met him, his name was somewhat familiar to me. Years earlier, he had been a reporter with *The Washington Post*. Isikoff had shared a byline reporting on Whitewater for many articles, which had made his name poison in Hillary's White House. At that time, I had been working in the White House counsel's office, and I recalled the siege mentality those articles engendered. As if that was not bad enough, Isikoff's name had resurfaced regarding coverage of Paula Jones in early 1994 while I was still in the counsel's office.

Those seemingly relentless articles about Jones had brought the White House to its knees. After a short while, the Clinton propaganda machine was put on full alert, got fired up, and began to fight back. Bruce Lindsey was intimately involved, and Hillary's big guns, the Darth Vader-like Harold Ickes and the ever-loyal Susan Thomases took lead roles.

As if Paula Jones was not enough to deal with for them, at that time the White House Whitewater task force was born. Fighting that would become all-consuming. I remembered that the face of the enemy was not

Isikoff during Whitewater; it was Leonard (Len) Downie, at the time also of *The Washington Post*. His persistent articles enraged Hillary, and to a White House that had to control the news cycle, it was all-out war. All this flashed through my mind as Isikoff approached me. I didn't greet him warmly.

Monica's story from beginning to end would have sounded wholly unbelievable to anyone else. My normal inclination was to question perceived truths, taking little at face value. But I knew Bill Clinton, and I knew Monica as well by then. I instinctively knew she was telling the truth. There was simply no doubt.

By now, the Monica saga was escalating to the point of no return. I didn't know it, but within five days, Bill Clinton would have his last actual assignation with Monica. This by itself would generate a full-blown Monica nuclear meltdown—in the Pentagon, no less. And then, less than eight weeks later, Bill would futilely attempt to end his abusive relationship with Monica.

If a nuclear blast had occurred before, we would now be entering Chernobyl territory. Monica's frenzied wrath and rage would escalate to ever-new, frightening heights. The fallout would be intense. Monica would make it clear, specifically to me, that she was not like the dozens (hundreds?) of other women. She would not go quietly into the night—in fact, would not go at all.

But even before all this happened, my nerves were strung tightly, as if I were awaiting some sort of implosion. It was in this context that Michael Isikoff entered center stage.

On the day I first met Isikoff, I was knee-deep in preparations for the JCOC. I was working with several deadlines and had planned to hold a JCOC meeting later that day. It was one of those days when I could keep myself busy and block out the Monica drama with real work. As I've said, by this time it had been months of Monica's all-consuming and constantly escalating saga, leaving me drained, anxious, helpless, angry, and above all, terrified. It would still be several months before, grasping at straws, I began my attempts to document all of it for the record.

When Isikoff entered my office, I looked up to find a somewhat rumpled man asking me about Kathleen Willey and Bill Clinton. It was so wildly out of place and took me by such surprise that I quickly blurted out, "You are barking up the wrong tree." Kathleen's name had surfaced in the context of the Paula Jones case as a possible additional example of sexual harassment on the part of the president.

I don't recall meeting Isikoff before this day. I knew of him by reputation as a tenacious reporter who'd had a fascination with Clinton since 1992. I knew this fascination extended to Jones, whose story had surfaced to much dismay in the White House in February 1994. At that time, the Clintonoids had a "batten down the hatches" mentality, as they confidently envisioned this newest bimbo eruption fading away like all the others.

By the time I met Isikoff, Kathleen was a vague memory to me, and I believed she was just another female fling for Bill that was somewhat par for the course with him. I'd had no contact with her since I had left the White House counsel's office. Isikoff's interest in Kathleen seemed surprising. If his story was about Bill's conquests, why single out Kathleen from the cast of thousands? I thought, at the time, it could be safely argued that whatever had happened between Bill and Kathleen could be construed as consensual. But Isikoff seemed to loosely correlate Kathleen with Jones, and that seemed to be his hook.

I didn't know that later Kathleen would become one of the accusers of the president to whom Isikoff might give more credence than the others. She had the requisite "class" that he equated with credibility regarding her accusations, as opposed to the less sophisticated accusers he quietly disdained. Isikoff had the same class-based attitude toward Clinton accusers that the White House did: the less sophisticated the accuser, the less people would believe her.

Somewhat worse, he couldn't seem to get out of his own way. I attribute it to something quite beyond his control, at least consciously. His built-in blinders narrowed his depth perception, impeded his peripheral vision. Isikoff had a narrow-minded disdain for anyone he considered unsophisticated. He struck me as someone who considered those less educated, less polished, and less well-spoken than himself the unfortunate "less-thans" who should have known their place in society's hierarchy and didn't. It was through this jaded lens that he appeared to assess their stories, their credibility.

An obvious example would be when he mentions in his book *Uncovering Clinton*, with what amounts to undisguised surprise, that Jones seemed "confident" when he met her. As though someone as unsophisticated as she had no earthly right in the grand scheme of things to go up against a sitting president of the United States. With confidence, no less. What could she have felt confident about?

I believe Isikoff simply can't help the jaded outlook his inherent elitism has created. It is simply an integral part of who he is and the people he wants to be associated with. For perspective, he would happily agree with Hillary's 2016 dismissal with total disdain of the "deplorables" and "irredeemables." Which, of course, means he fits in well with the self-proclaimed liberal elites in the oh-so-sophisticated D.C. establishment.

Isikoff doesn't have much time for those smelly Walmart shoppers among us. It is telling that his contempt for people who work for a living colored his perspective on this story about Jones, the biggest story of his career. It appears to have influenced his attitude throughout his investigative reporting. I believe he looked for reasons to doubt Jones' credibility. This was his almost schizophrenic way of wanting to expose this president while protecting him at the same time.

Now, in 1997, Jones' lawsuit against a sitting president was going forward. Despite the best efforts of the Clinton propaganda machine, Jones was not going to simply fade away. And I had the utmost respect for her lawyers. "Tenacious" does not even come close to describing what they were. Although I had never met her or spoken to her, knowing this president's predatory nature, knowing what was still going on in the White House with Bill being Bill, I knew Paula Jones was being truthful. Isikoff did not.

Isikoff walked into my office at both the best and the worst time. The best had to do with timing; the timing was perfect. I needed an Isikoff yesterday. The worst had to do with the building stress with Monica. I had gotten to the point of no return with her growing hysteria, and it showed. I was constantly on edge, tense, and so tightly wound that I knew I would pop given the slightest provocation. On top of all that, I was fearful for my job, my family and, as unscrupulous as these people were, even my life. All the time. My normally brusque self would have looked positively amiable and downright endearing compared to the person Isikoff met on this spring day.

My natural, if somewhat cynical, pessimism toward reporters notwithstanding, I reluctantly believed he had some credibility. He was with *Newsweek* magazine, which was still a respected media source. I had heard he had been fired by *The Washington Post* some years earlier, although he claimed it had been his choice to leave. Apparently, he had been suspended, which led to a parting of the ways. But I was dealing with one of the kings of spin. And in the spin capital of the world, the truth is whatever you want it to be. I hoped I was doing the right thing by talking with him.

At first, he presented to me as someone who could be an ideal solution, and I was just about ready to jump into this unexpected lifeboat. I was uneasy and hesitant in the beginning, and remained troubled throughout my ten-month contact with him. On the surface, he seemed to want nothing more than to expose the president. So that was good. But I couldn't rid myself of a persistent doubt. I could not shake the sense that the deeper, perhaps conflicting layers of his agenda were known only to him. But I knew with certainty his agenda was not good.

When someone is drowning, a lifeboat represents immediate salvation. The motivation of the rescuer is simply a concern for another day. Michael Isikoff had no intention of rescuing me. In fact, he disdained everything I represented. I desperately needed an investigative reporter affiliated with a legitimate publication. Ultimately, I had nowhere else to go. In the end, we were both using each other to achieve our own ends.

Knowing the liberal bent of the media, including *Newsweek*, I was unconvinced that Isikoff was the right reporter. I wondered if his publication had an agenda that would in some way protect the president, even while exposing him. At the time of his first election, Bill Clinton had been the first Democrat elected to the presidency in twelve years. The media had a vested interested in keeping him.

I also wondered if Isikoff had an interest in all of the Clinton corruption and not just the juicy sexcapades. It quickly became clear that his only interest was in Bill's philandering. This was going to be his own personal Watergate moment, and he had no interest with the "extraneous" issues I considered crucial. That should have warned me about his true idea of what investigative journalism is about.

One thing should be clear, however. If my motivation for talking with him had been a book deal, as the Clinton propaganda smear machine repeatedly claimed later on, dumping the story in the lap of a nationally known investigative reporter would have been counterproductive. Why didn't I simply use my own book as an instrument to get everything out in the public domain? Plus, I didn't make any money off Isikoff. He certainly made money off me when he wrote his book in 1999.

I knew I would be attacked, and when Isikoff's story finally broke, there was a mantra among all the Clinton-covering media, from the Clintonoid defenders and apologists to the talking heads on TV. In a contrived echo chamber, this became written in stone. It was all about a book deal.

The Clintonoids used this line of attack on me because they had no other. After my three years of excellent performance reviews and multiple faster-than-normal pay-grade advances, even they didn't try to smear me as a bad employee. They are not that stupid. They also could not go after me as a disgruntled ex-employee. I was still in the job at the place I wanted. What did they have left to use to attack my credibility? A book deal.

Even that was monumentally stupid. I was going to risk twenty-plus years of pension, my job, my health insurance for my children and myself, literally everything I had worked for, to write a book? A book from which I would have made how much money? A speculative amount, at best. Enough to sacrifice all that I had worked for? Not likely, which is one of the reasons I turned down a proposed book deal. That, and I absolutely did not want to write a book.

Think about this and then consider the intelligence of those in the media who, like chirping birds, swallowed the book-deal idea whole without giving it a thought. These are the people who believe they are the intellectual elites. Should they even be allowed to procreate and pass those genes along?

In fact, I still thought I could preserve my anonymity. I was hopeful that filtering the story through *Newsweek* would do just that. At this point though, I also had a certain level of acceptance. I knew there were going to be serious and ugly ramifications, to which I was not indifferent. Keeping quiet was simply no longer a choice. Interestingly, as conflicted as I remained, there was a sense of liberation as well. It was a "Let the chips fall where they may" feeling, even if I still was not 100 percent sure that talking with Isikoff was the right path to take.

I had reached the point where I firmly, and reluctantly, believed that only I could tell the story as I had watched it unfold. I feared that Isikoff's obvious bias meant that my words would be filtered through his skeptical lens. I questioned whether or not he would get the story right. In the end, he didn't. But for me, he was the only game in town, and I was pretty sure he would get it out in some fashion. That he did.

In the beginning of my dealings with Isikoff, I was treading in dangerous waters. Mostly because I could not trust him, and I knew it. There were others in the *Newsweek* food chain I also had to be concerned with. I did not know if *Newsweek*'s Washington bureau chief or White House correspondent knew what Isikoff was working on. If they did, what was their agenda? Were they working this same angle through other sources at the White House? Most important, if I had learned anything, it was that this White House went ferociously after any threat to its political viability, large or small. Like a heat-seeking missile, the mission was always search and destroy, over and out, leaving nothing but dust in its wake. I knew with whom I was dealing, even if Monica did not: the publicly pleasant, privately bloodthirsty Hillary Clinton.

I didn't know if my name had surfaced in the West Wing as a potential witness to the Kathleen Willey drama. I simply could not be sure. How high up the food chain did Isikoff's story go? Knowing how the White House press corps covered for the Clintons, was *Newsweek*'s White House correspondent leaking to them? I knew if it had gone to that level within the *Newsweek* hierarchy, it was likely that the White House was aware of Isikoff's investigation. Nothing stays secret for long in the swamp that Washington had long since become.

Because of this cozy relationship between those supposedly covering White House corruption for the public and those within the White House, I had a decision to make. Before I could talk to Isikoff, I had to take a significant step in case what I disclosed about the president's predatory behavior did make it back to the Oval Office.

Remember, I was now a presidential appointee at my Pentagon position. I served at the pleasure of the president. Just in case Isikoff's story idea had already surfaced in the White House, I decided to take the bull by the horns and give the White House a heads-up that I would be talking with him. On the chance that his investigation had reached that high, I needed to do the politically correct, "Let's be honest," cover-your-ass thing. I too could don a mask, although I was in no way in the same league as the mask-toting Clintons. Few are.

I had to give the White House a call and get on the record that I tried to warn them. I knew exactly whom to call. I called to notify Bruce Lindsey of an "urgent matter of national media significance." But that is getting ahead of my skis, as they say. An introduction should come first.

Even today, few know much about Bruce Lindsey. He has always flown under the radar. His public presence was virtually nonexistent then and still is now. You would be hard-pressed to find much about him should you be inclined to look. In the power corridors of Washington, D.C., though, Bruce Lindsey was at the pinnacle. And he remained that way for many years, even working with Bill Clinton on the lucrative Clinton access-for-sale slush-fund foundation, continuing his slavish loyalty. He was an anomaly for sure. "First friend" would not begin to cover it. Although precious little has been written about him, Bruce Lindsey was simply the one indispensable Clintonoid.

Everything about him belied his power. Bruce came across as a great guy, impossible not to like. I liked him and also respected him, at least in the beginning. He was mild-mannered, considerate, and always friendly, even sweet. He had an endearing way of constantly peering over his ever-present oversized horn-rimmed glasses.

Nice guy aside, it would have been a serious mistake to underestimate him. There was a reason he escaped the wrath of Hillary all those years, a reason he was entrusted to sit at God's right hand. Quite simply, it was because his loyalty was unmatched, unquestioned, beyond dispute, even though it meant selling his soul—although soul selling was the minimum price of becoming a card-carrying Clintonoid.

Bruce's official title was counselor to the president, indisputably the closest aide to the president. Closer than the chief of staff or anyone else. His desk was never more than mere feet away from the Oval Office. His access was unmatched. He served Bill Clinton as the ultimate fixer and Protector. He was the keeper of the secrets and more.

Bruce was the senior staffer I worked for during the first three months of the administration, in his office mere steps from the Oval Office. He was also the one who blessed my promotion to the Office of Counsel to the President. In the end, it was also Bruce who was behind my removal from the White House.

I placed the cover-your-ass phone call, knowing beyond a shadow of a doubt he would not return the call. That is precisely why I chose him. I had been persona non grata since leaving the White House; the looming Paula Jones lawsuit had tipped the scales for my removal. I knew I had been labeled a malcontent. I was not willing to sell my soul as a tribute to the Clintons. Several people knew it, including the president, Bruce and, most important, Hillary. With the announcement of Jones' lawsuit, I knew my days were numbered.

Interesting that almost four years later, in 1997, my situation was again about Paula Jones. As I expected, Bruce did not call back right away. I was most assuredly not on the team. Not only did I make sure that Monica knew that I had placed the call, but I also made her believe that Bruce's unresponsiveness annoyed me. I made sure she believed that I desperately wanted him to call me back. Had Bruce called back, I would have dutifully warned him of what was to come. Of course, I would have left out my part in seeing that it did.

I did get a call, much later, from Bruce Lindsey. I knew it was a transparent effort to get me back on the reservation, and he strongly urged me to meet with Bill Clinton's attorney, Bob Bennett. This was now concerning the Paula Jones lawsuit, which was moving forward and had become far more than a mere nuisance. Obviously, the Clintons were concerned that I would be a witness for Paula. I told Bruce I would call Bennett, but I never did.

After Isikoff's visit in March and my call to Bruce, I had done my political duty and created my own plausible deniability. Now I could honestly tell Monica about Mike Isikoff and that I had tried to give the White House a heads-up on the brewing Kathleen Willey story. Of course, that was all true. Now the real duplicity could begin.

I left out some truths. I didn't offer that I was contemplating telling Isikoff about Monica's situation, that I was looking for ways to expose the abhorrent behavior of the president. In fact, quite the opposite. I assured Monica I was still a good little foot soldier with an interest in protecting the president. I was now entering major deception territory. It was a one-way path of no return. I didn't know how it would end, but the situation was uncomfortable at best. I had never done anything quite like this before. My lies to Monica then sparked a series of events that reached all the way to the Oval Office.

While I could not predict the path forward or how it might end, I did know that I was shocked. Horrified. Repulsed. In fact, mere words are inadequate to describe what I saw happening to this immature girl. I was becoming increasingly alarmed as Monica mindlessly continued in the irrational pursuit of her objective. She was simply consumed with Bill Clinton, a groupie of the highest order and the most tenacious imaginable. To her, it was simple: she was going back to the Oval Office come hell or high water to resume where she had left off. In a moment of lightheartedness, she claimed that her presidential knee pads were gathering dust. But as the months passed, the moments of lightheartedness were precious few for her. Monica was on a downward spiral at the hands of the president of the United States.

Chapter 16
ISIKOFF: PART TWO

On July 4, 1997, Monica met with Bill Clinton in the Oval Office. It was many months after the election, but she was still hoping she could get back into the White House to have access to her "boyfriend." But on this day, she told him about Michael Isikoff, Kathleen Willey, and me. At that time, she merely referred to me as "a friend" and did not name me. Since he already knew about Isikoff, the existence of the article Isikoff was working on didn't surprise him or seem to faze him.

At about this same time, the Drudge Report announced that *Newsweek* was hot on the trail of yet another one of the president's women on federal property, for a story. I would spend a lot of time worrying about who on earth had leaked this to Drudge. I just could not figure it out. The answer was right in front of me, but it would be a long time before I got it.

Also, about this same time it seemed that everyone was frantically covering themselves. Kathleen Willey called the Oval Office to give them a heads-up about *Newsweek*. The president told Monica about this, and Monica told me. I then told Isikoff about Kathleen's call to the White House. Isikoff promptly called Kathleen to see if she had done this and, if she had, why. Kathleen admitted she had but didn't know why. Then Kathleen asked Isikoff how he could possibly have known she had called Nancy Hernreich, the director of Oval Office Operations. Isikoff tap danced around the question without answering. Then, on the heels of that conversation, Kathleen called Nancy yet again, this time to tell Nancy that somehow Isikoff knew all about Kathleen's previous phone call to the White House. Obviously, the White House had a leak. Since precious few

167

people knew about any of this, it was not difficult for them now to figure out how this was happening. And it was not good.

Ten days later, on July 14, the proverbial shit began to hit the fan. Monica was summoned to the White House late that evening. But this time the president was all business. The White House was starting to take Bill's bimbo problem seriously, and he was getting worried. He wanted to know if the friend she had referred to on July 4 was Linda Tripp. Monica was caught. So was I. She, however, had no idea how dangerous this now was. I did.

Naïve Monica was on a roll. The White House visits that had been virtually impossible to schedule for the past few months were becoming more frequent—except these were not for the reasons she wanted. In fact, after the July 14 meeting, she saw the president on July 24 and again on August 16, ostensibly to exchange birthday gifts. Clinton was laying on his full-court press designed to keep Monica safely on the side of silence at a time of escalating pressure. The Paula Jones case was a huge problem that was not going away. Now he was also in the double-barrel shotgun blast of both Drudge and *Newsweek*.

Monica, without realizing it, posed an enormous threat to Bill, and he knew it. The possibility of her breaking her silence would have been calamitous on a good day, but it would be utterly disastrous during this time.

The president presumed that only a small number of people knew about the warning call from Kathleen Willey to Nancy Hernreich. There was Kathleen, who had placed the call, and Nancy, who had taken the call. Nancy had told the president about the call, and Bill himself had told Monica. I am certain Bruce Lindsey was on the list as well. He usually was. It was likely that Kathleen had told others, but the president couldn't know whom. Since Kathleen was the one raising the red flag, the president and Nancy assumed that the only possible link back to Isikoff was Monica. And they were correct.

During the meeting on July 14, the president told Monica to get me to call Bruce Lindsey. As I've described earlier, Bruce was the presidential fixer in chief. Monica was instructed to notify the president through

Betty Currie that she had done this. Monica assured the president that she trusted me, further assuring him in answer to his pointed question that she had not discussed their "relationship" with me. We were all lying.

Monica did as she was told, but I wasn't eager to do what she asked and did not make the call to Bruce. Monica did not notify Betty of her failed mission, but the president called her personally that evening to get a status report. He was not happy with the outcome. When I learned of Bill's call to Monica, my level of concern skyrocketed. Monica was, and I believe to this day still is, clueless about Bill Clinton. She never understood with whom she was playing. And she did not know Hillary at all. She had no idea the lengths they would go to ensure that none of this saw the light of day. And there was not a chance on the planet to convince Monica of this. Fortunately for her, her naïveté spared her the utter terror I was experiencing during this time.

The behind-the-scenes shenanigans and attempted cover-up exploded onto the public scene two weeks later. On July 29, 1997, the Drudge Report scooped everyone with a screaming headline for its world-exclusive story: "White House Employee Tells Reporter That President Made Sex Pass."

I was floored. I didn't know who had been feeding Drudge, but someone was. I believed it was Isikoff because, although he was scoop sensitive, he was known to find an end run around the cautious hesitance to publish on the part of his editors. Could this be one of those times? It seemed startling to me, but I was certain it was true. Also, at that time, I didn't know of any other person who had Drudge's phone number on speed dial. Eventually, I found out it was someone I knew who did get the story from me.

This leak had resulted in an escalation of events that could not be ignored. Monica was agitated, having already been questioned by the president about this very thing. She had told the president mere days before that she trusted me and hadn't told me anything about their "relationship." She had a vested interest in my appearing to be on the team. To that end, her entire frenzied focus was to get me to call Bruce Lindsey. With the Drudge story's publication, I believed I finally had to call Bruce.

At the president's direction, he took my call this time. I lied to Bruce, removing myself from the equation. I suggested it was Isikoff who had leaked the story to Drudge. Maybe his editors were forcing him to sit on it, and in a fit of pique, he retaliated. I opined he might well have dumped it into the public domain, perhaps to provide his editors with incentive to go forward. Who knew? I had no idea. And for once, this was true. I had no idea at all how Drudge had gotten any of it. At least, not then. While I would put nothing past Michael Isikoff, it is unlikely he would have risked the loss of the almighty scoop.

Regardless of how and by whom the story was leaked to Drudge, the simple truth was that it had been leaked. It was now out in the open. Time to fire up the Clinton spin, lie, and dry machine. Having had much practice over the years, the president and his immediate circle dragged out the reliable script yet again. The bimbo eruptions were commonplace, and they had an efficient method of disposing of all of them. The "nuts and sluts" strategy had gotten them through many of these over the years. All the president's men, so to speak, had long since checked at the door what sense of decency they might have had.

The script called for a very presidential image. The side they presented to the public was every inch presidential, and it was mesmerizing. It became simply unimaginable for anyone to envision this president being the disturbed man "the enemies" would have the public believe. The "vast right-wing conspiracy" was at it again; this president, so devoted to feeling your pain, could not possibly be involved in something this tawdry. There was no one like him. According to Bob Bennett, his famed lawyer, this president had "done more for women than any other president in the history of this country." Knowing what I knew about Bill Clinton, I almost gagged when I heard that line.

Behind the curtain, the Clintonoids knew the unspeakable truth and exerted untold energy and resources to shield it all from view. Ultimately it was just a part of the requirement of resolute loyalty for those in Bill's periphery. The reality was not only disgraceful, it was shocking. This was not a guy "who just liked women," as they claimed, trying to explain his abusive behavior. In fact, in the face of the private and reckless serial addiction he indulged virtually all the time, you might wonder if he liked women at all. Using women and liking them are two very different things.

The Clintonoid enablers also knew that if the full extent of his "liking women problem" ever became known, there would be no surviving it. Even back then, known serial predators were condemned. President Clinton was not simply a husband with a roving eye. This was not just a guy who had serial affairs behind the back of his wife, because while he did have serial affairs, that was child's play compared to the darker side of his compulsive behavior.

The efforts on the part of the president, his wife, his senior aides, and his lawyers, not to mention paid private investigators, were well hidden from view. With Hillary acting as maestro for the Clintonoid orchestra, they worked in concert to identify, juggle, and destroy women. They had perfected their search-and-destroy mission against women like Paula Jones, Kathleen Willey, and even Gennifer Flowers back in 1992. In fact, that it had been used against virtually all the women who had come before was simply left out of the rhetoric. And this mission was coming from people—including Hillary—who would one day brazenly proclaim themselves to be champions of women: "Women must be heard and believed."

That they systematically laid waste to innumerable women was known to all these people within the Clinton tent. They at least were on the inside, having sold their souls. Worse, it was also known to many members of the media. It had been the Clinton tried-and-true modus operandi for as far back as anyone could remember. Somehow it was, for the most part, just accepted as the price of doing business with a rock star such as Bill Clinton. The notable lack of curiosity on the part of the complicit über-liberal media played a pivotal role in perpetuating the behavior.

Along with some friends, my family was at the beach for a week's vacation in early August 1997. I was totally removed from Washington and thoroughly enjoying the mental health break. For the most part, I was able to enjoy a much-needed Monica-free zone and the constant stress her drama entailed.

Then one day I was presented with the latest *Newsweek* issue, in which an article written by Michael Isikoff was brought to my attention. Here was the Kathleen Willey piece he had been working on for months. He quoted me accurately, but for obvious reasons I had not wanted to be quoted by name, which he had agreed with. Yet in the story, he used my name. Worse, Bob Bennett was quoted as saying, "Linda Tripp is not to be believed." It was bad enough that Isikoff had exposed me in a national publication. In the same article, the president's lawyer had called me a liar.

As far as I was concerned, the gloves were now off. Bennett had made the final decision for me. Up until this point, I had still been ambivalent about going after a sitting president for his abusive behavior. Bennett's calling me a liar was the proverbial last straw. I was now determined that his sexual predator client had to be exposed. Lawyers do not always help their clients by running their mouths to the press.

I had agreed just one time to provide a generic comment to Isikoff on the record solely for the purpose of his article. He had led me to believe that I would not be personally named and that I would be quoted as a White House staffer who had witnessed the aftermath of the Kathleen Willey incident—or, at most, a source familiar with the event. With this one exception, all my conversations before this comment and after had been "on background." This was supposed to mean he had no permission to use my name, or to use anything I had given him with attribution.

Other than this single quote, I had never gone "on the record" with Isikoff. With the arrival of his book *Uncovering Clinton* in 1999, it became clear that he had dispensed with that little nuisance. Worse, he had taken violating journalism's rules of attribution a step further by deciding it was open season for his book. He later claimed that since I had testified about much of the story by the time the book came out, he could pull from the public record and use anything and everything he wanted. That was a lame excuse for his lack of ethics. The only place I testified about this was in front of a grand jury, and grand jury testimony is secret. So, my words were not out in the public before Isikoff's writings.

Isikoff violated the journalistic code of ethics with his *Newsweek* article, and in his book went even further. He characterized all of our off-the-record conversations through his own political prism and assigned all manner of motivation to me. He simply painted the picture he chose to paint. If I had doubted his journalistic integrity before, I now knew for sure.

When the *Newsweek* article came out, I swiftly dashed off a letter to the editor, chastising *Newsweek* for the article. I also ran it by Isikoff. He was not pleased, claiming I was attacking him. I was. But more important, I knew one of the White House Clintonoids would see it. I was attempting to go on the record as not having helped Isikoff in his exposé. As it turned out, and as I mentioned earlier, I was not the only one giving the White House a heads-up. Kathleen Willey had called Nancy Hernreich to give her a heads-up about the percolating story. It was a story written by a reporter with whom she had spoken at length off the record. Kathleen had told her story anonymously to Jones' attorneys some time earlier.

While appearing to want to protect the president, she was actively working to undermine him at the same time. How could I blame her? I was trying to do the very same thing. The recklessness and the abuse of power needed to be exposed. Pulling off the Clintons' public masks would prove daunting.

Kathleen and I, miles apart and separately, may well have shared a quiet outrage at Clinton's cavalier abuse of women, but we were neophytes in the Clinton game. We were pretty much helpless, flailing in the wind, not the powerful and connected thugs it would take to even the playing field. And, bottom line, we were both grasping at straws quite independent of each other. Valiant efforts aside, neither of us had a clue as to how to go about exposing this president of the United States for the serial predator he was.

The result was unimpressive, but there is no handbook for how to do this. When you do go up against a reckless president who knows no boundaries and has a wife who is worse than he is, that you will lose is a foregone conclusion. I have always believed that in this case, those of us left standing and yes, breathing, came out better than others in the end.

By the late summer of 1997, I'd had an epiphany of sorts. Now that the White House knew about the Isikoff article and I had been outed, I knew I could not simply keep my personal status quo. I could not do anything about the constant fear I felt concerning possible danger at the hands of the Clintonoids in their quest to protect Bill. But I believed I could do something else to get out from under their thumbs, at least professionally.

I realized I simply wanted out of all of it. I wanted to be free of the Clintons. Regardless of the outcome of my shaky plan to expose not only the Clintons but all the corruption that went along with them, the answer was staring me in the face. I could look for another job at the Pentagon, could revert to career civil service and get out from under the thumb of the president. There was no need to remain a presidential appointee.

I don't know why it had not occurred to me before this, but the escalating saga and the duplicitous role-playing had simply become too much. I was not cut out for this cloak-and-dagger stuff, and I craved above all else normalcy and security. And I still feared what I knew was to come. Although, looking back, I don't know what I was thinking.

In my fog, I did not seem to grasp that since my plan to expose the Clintons was still going to happen, my job was the least of my worries. But at the time, it was something I believed I might be able to control. "Delusional" comes close to describing it.

I quickly began to review any vacancies in the public affairs arena at my grade and, in fact, two grades lower than my GS-15 status. Doing something, being proactive, began to make me feel less like a Clinton victim. I was willing to take a significant pay cut just to get out from under the Clinton machine. I had been at this grade for over three years, so I had already locked in my top three earning years for retirement purposes, and a cut in pay would be well worth the price to have the freedom to say or do whatever I felt was right.

I was determined to shed my status as a political appointment so that at least the job portion of the intimidation would disappear. I don't know what I was thinking. The world's most powerful puppet master and her husband were soon going to unleash Armageddon on me, and I was fighting back by filling out forms. I was smack dab in the middle of the Clintons' radar. It did not occur to me that they were not going to let me escape.

I finally found a job announcement in the late fall for a lateral move at the GS-15 grade, something that seemed to be a good fit. It involved a lengthy application process. I managed by the skin of my teeth to get it finished before the closing date of the announcement. Out of all the applicants, I was ranked one of the top three for consideration for the job. Being in the top three, by civil service hiring practices I was all but guaranteed an interview. Unfortunately, by the time the interviewing process was to take place, the story had hit. It was as far as I ever got.

I applied for a different job, in public affairs at the George C. Marshall Center for European Studies in Garmisch-Partenkirchen, Germany. It was also a GS-15 slot. I believed that in the grand scheme of things, a relatively low-key entity such as this, nestled as it was in the foothills of the German Alps, would be a perfect fit for someone of some notoriety who needed an off-the-beaten-track location to work.

I made the top three again, and I was flown to Munich and escorted to Garmisch-Partenkirchen for the interview. Within what seemed to be five minutes of my landing on German soil, my picture appeared on the cover of the military's paper of record, *Stars and Stripes*, along with an article by someone who seemed to know more details of my visit than I did. When I arrived for my interview, I was presented with the paper and asked to autograph it.

The Office of Public Affairs at the Pentagon—my former employer, the entity that illegally released false, derogatory personal information about me during the height of the Clinton impeachment scandal—owned *Stars and Stripes*. Once again, I had been thwarted by the long reach and the enormous consequence of having gone up against a popular president. The Clintons' political reach is long, and the result of that reach can be debilitating. Remember that when you hear about how the government departments are independent of the White House. Not if the president's wife fills them with her allies. I never applied for a civil service position again. Game. Set. Match.

By this time, I was getting very worried. Clearly the long arm of the vindictive Hillary Clinton was at work here and keeping me under her thumb. As I was a presidential appointee, the Clintons could fire me at any time. I was also, somewhat contradictorily, becoming at least a little apathetic about it. I was more determined than ever to out this predatory president. It was also about now, during the fall of '97, that the media howling about my being in it for a book deal started up again. At first it was coming from the White House, primarily because the Clintonoids could not attack me any other way. Eventually it was taken up from coast to coast.

I must admit that I did reconsider doing a book during this time. For maybe five minutes. Again, it simply was not something I wanted to do. In fact, I had tried to stay under the media's radar. I categorically did not want the notoriety. At no point had I planned to toss everything I had worked for out the window simply to embrace notoriety. The last thing I wanted in life was fifteen minutes of fame. I do understand that there are those who do. I was a behind-the-scenes person. It was what I did well; it was what I enjoyed. It was what I had done for close to thirty years.

I simply did not need or want public attention on any level. I did not seek it. Looking back, that should be obvious even to those who screamed over one another that it was all about a book. With untold opportunities for any of the key players to play a public role, I remain the only one who chose not to. I remained the only one who for twenty-two years never took a cent.

From this point on, virtually everything I said to Monica was either a lie or at least not the total truth. For someone who had spent a lifetime laboring under an oath of office, who took the words "duty," "honor," and "country" so seriously, this was not easy. Remembering this as I write about it today is not much easier. Nevertheless, I saw it as the only way. More than ever it was imperative that Monica believe I was a Clinton loyalist. Not because she held my livelihood and my professional future in her hands; as time went on, those concerns were the least of it. Knowing the Clintons as well as I did, I knew there were far more sinister acts to be concerned with.

After the Drudge Report and Isikoff articles became public, the situation escalated. The stakes grew much higher with the looming Paula Jones case against the president. His future was finally in real jeopardy. Worse, this could easily spill onto Hillary's own chances at the *Resolute* desk in the Oval Office. This could not be tolerated.

I had long since stopped worrying about how I would support my family in the future. Fear of losing my livelihood seemed like a distant indulgence, a luxury of sorts. It paled beside a growing fear that my future at all might be at risk. In case this sounds a little too melodramatic or fanciful, it was not. As an example, one morning in December 1997, I entered my cubicle at the Pentagon and found a sheet of white paper stapled to my chair. On it was written: "The Clinton Death List." I had a little trouble concentrating on my work that day.

Raising Monica's suspicions was dangerous on many levels. For both of us. Along with everything else, she simply could not keep her mouth shut. I knew there were others in whom she confided, and some of them had a direct line to the president. When Monica shared, she totally shared. She generally spared no detail. In her innocence, and in large part because of her crush on the president, she was totally clueless of the risks her sharing might bring about. Blinded by her adoration, she was incapable of seeing the lengths to which the Clintons and their acolytes were willing to go to ensure that his bimbo problem never saw the light of day. I had no such illusions.

I knew I needed real, irrefutable proof of Bill's behavior. You cannot go up against the Clinton machine without it. Your word alone will never be enough. I needed some advice, and I had an idea where I should go to get it: Lucianne Goldberg. She is the literary agent I had talked to in 1995, a year before I met Monica, about a book to expose the Clinton corruption.

I once again contacted Lucianne, this time in September 1997. She was the only person I could think of who might help me get everything out publicly. I just did not trust Isikoff to pull the trigger on everything he had heard from me. I was still convinced that when push came to shove, he would renege on using the information.

Lucianne was good at her job, and she did not suffer fools gladly. I know; I was one of the fools. More important, she was the single human being I knew of who was hooked into a world of extensive connections. She knew lawyers, and these lawyers knew lawyers; she was a product of the New York machine and savvy to say the least. I knew she was somehow hooked into the *New York Post*. And she feared no one. She was the logical choice for me.

Since I had backed out on the previous book we had been discussing, I wasn't sure how receptive she would be to me now. I decided I had to lie to Lucianne when I went back to her for help. I did not like it, I was not proud of it, but I believed it was necessary. I thought if I made her believe I was back on the book bandwagon, she might consider lending a hand. As I said, in the fall of 1997 I found myself reconsidering the project all over again. In the end, neither one of us had the stomach for that whole process.

The more pressing issue became how to most effectively document the proof that would, if not lead to the president's removal from office, then at least to make public his vile predatory sexual actions. I needed proof. I thought if Isikoff had real, solid irrefutable evidence then he would find the balls to run with the whole story. It was Lucianne who guided me at this most critical point in time. It was Lucianne who suggested I start to surreptitiously tape-record my conversations with Monica.

At first, I did not want any part of something that sleazy, but it was not long before I became convinced that it needed to be done. I needed the story in Monica's own words. I was initially concerned about the legality of it. Lucianne innocently and mistakenly assured me that in Maryland, the permission of one of the parties being recorded was all that was needed. Unfortunately, she was wrong, and I almost paid dearly for that later. But I needed real proof, and that could come only from Monica—her voice, her story, her accusations, and the soon-to-be-infamous navy-blue dress.

In any case, Lucianne seemed to be the only person with whom I had any contact at all who believed me and who shared my outrage. She was far ahead of me. She knew I needed proof, that my word alone would be meaningless. That led later to the "documenting of evidence" that was the late in the day taping of phone conversations with Monica. The taping began in October 1997, a year and a half after Monica had begun this saga with me. This meant that everything she had told me before had to be retold. All the conversations from that time forward were a means of getting all the abuse on the record. I have always believed that if I had documented everything from the beginning, the horror of it all as it occurred in real time, the result likely would have been very different.

In November 1997, Monica told me that she had in her possession a blue Gap dress that still bore a semen stain that had resulted from her administering oral sex to President Clinton in February of that year. I called Lucianne Goldberg and told her that in Monica's closet was proof positive that there had been a sexual relationship between Monica and the president. Laughably, we briefly discussed stealing the dress and turning it over to investigators. Later, both *Time* and *Newsweek* reported this as if we had really intended to do it. Lucianne admitted having such a discussion with me, calling it a "Nancy Drew fantasy."

Later in November 1997, Monica admitted she was holding the dress as a souvenir of her love for the big guy. She also told me she was going to have the dress cleaned for a coming family event she wanted to wear it to. Realizing what was on the dress, the president's DNA, I quickly made sure she did not do this. I said, "I would tell my own daughter to save the dress for your own ultimate protection." Monica, still in her fantasy world believing she would have a life with Bill, did not think she would need protection. I knew that sooner or later Hillary and the Clintonoid attack dogs would come after her. They could have their media enablers go after her also, claiming she was lying about the affair with Bill. Monica did not believe me; she could not believe it would ever come to that. I changed tactics and appealed to her vanity. I told her that the dress made her look "really fat." She never brought up the subject of wearing that dress again.

The dark forces of the liberal media made much of Lucianne and me later on. They were ravenous in cloaking us with bile, scorn, and vitriol. We were the nefarious duo who together plotted to take down the president. But that isn't the way it worked. If we were collaborators at all, it was only to the extent that she had ideas as to how I could better do what I had already planned to do.

The portrayal easily sold by the media and the Clintonoid powers at the White House gives us far more credit than either of us deserves. The truth is much more mundane. The fact that Lucianne was receptive to what I had to say about the Clintons didn't indicate her political leaning. The horror she shared with me did not make her a right-wing lunatic. She thought Bill Clinton was unfit for office, no matter how many good things he had done. In fact, I never knew if she was a Republican or a Democrat.

Despite the hue and cry, and clamor to the contrary, my motivation had nothing to do with Bill's politics. The Clintons desperately needed the public to believe it did, that an innocent president—Bill, the poor victim—had been set up by card-carrying members of the omniscient "vast right-wing conspiracy," that Goldberg and Tripp, the evil twins, had plotted his downfall from the beginning. Scores of Clinton apologists and media flakes shouting this from rooftops did not make it so.

No. It. Was. Not. Politics. Ever. It was about a sick, reckless, corrupt president who indulged his predatory needs. It was about a weak man who could not control his base instincts and those who enabled him by lying about his behavior and doing everything possible to cover it up. It was something they had done successfully his entire adult life. I hoped this time he would not be able to pull a rabbit out of a hat.

Of course, I took a massive beating for the lies and the manipulation. Fair enough. It was not nice, but it was necessary. No one was ever able to tell me how else I could have brought the abhorrent abusive behavior out into the open, how else the reckless behavior could have been stopped. I naïvely believed that exposing his sexual abuse was not the bad thing; the behavior itself was. The subterfuge I was forced to use, while unseemly, was also necessary to finally allow me to gather the proof that would expose the president. By January 12, 1998, his behavior could stop. I would finally be able to tell the truth.

Chapter 17

NORMA ASNES AND THE ATTEMPTED SEDUCTION OF LINDA

After I was outed by the *Newsweek* article in early August 1997, my paranoia antennae grew. Not without reason. I had seen enough in the Clinton White House to know what happened to people who were perceived to have crossed them. Toward the end of 1997, before I went to Kenneth Starr's Office of the Independent Counsel (OIC), an event occurred that illustrates my thinking at the time. This event would be what ultimately pushed me to make the final step to go to the OIC. By this point, I would probably have gone anyway, but this made it clear that Hillary had put a target on my back. A little background is called for, the necessity of which will become clear a little later.

The Clintons, with their all-consuming quest for great wealth and increased power, worshipped at the altar of the "really big donor." The really big donors were allowed access everywhere in the White House. Once I left the White House, I was happy that I would no longer hear about or have to see them, unless they were on the news. The courting of these donors was not only about the next election and the one after that—which was going to be Hillary's; it was also about the manipulation of those with deep pockets for the Clintons' own personal gain. Clinton donors were under every single rock, domestic or foreign.

The Clintons positively believed that the White House was their personal and permanent residence. Probably the worst, most disgusting example was their attitude toward the White House as being the donor motel. The Lincoln Bedroom became a revolving door of overnight fat cats. How much more irreverent can they be than to rent out the bedroom of our most revered president for their personal gain? Is nothing sacred to these two or their media toadies? Apparently not. No one seemed to care. It was a blip on the media radar screen, soon disappearing as everything else Clinton-related eventually did.

Between 1993 and Bill Clinton's reelection in 1996, 938 people spent the night at the White House, well over eight hundred of them in the Lincoln Bedroom. The Clintons rented out the Lincoln Bedroom for their personal financial and political benefit to more than eight hundred people. Didn't any of these people see how incredibly disrespectful this was? And we wonder why morals, ethics, and respectful behavior have eroded. With people like the Clintons and their allies setting the example, the wonder is that the erosion hasn't been worse.

The parade of overnight guests broke White House records. This was mostly thanks to the blatant efforts of Virginia's former governor, the ubiquitous Terry McAuliffe. McAuliffe was in charge of Democratic fundraising and Bill and Hillary Clinton's personal finances in general. They were always searching for big money. The White House was quite literally for sale for the first time in our history. There was no shortage of takers, and it was nauseatingly amazing.

For me, it was acutely chilling because I knew that the Lincoln Bedroom had not been used by Lincoln as a bedroom at all. In fact, it is historically much more important. That room served as President Lincoln's cabinet office, an almost sacred piece of American history. Think about it. This is the same room where Abraham Lincoln, his cabinet, and his generals—the men who saved the Union—met to plan how to win the Civil War and save the nation. And the Clintons were treating it like the Princess Suite at a high-end "no-tell motel." Looking back at what is most important to the Clintons, the only thing surprising about it was they did not have hourly rates.

To me, the irreverence seemed sacrilegious, as had the jumping on the Lincoln bed by stalwart Clinton cronies as they rejoiced upon taking the White House in January 1993. Seriously, they did this. But then these were the people who had been those 1960s student radicals who had taken over the dean's office. It was as if they did not know who Abraham Lincoln was and what he did.

One of the 938 overnight guests at the Clinton White House was Norma Ketay Asnes. I met Norma when she was selected to participate in the annual Secretary of Defense–hosted JCOC 58 program. It was May 1995, and I had been at the Pentagon for less than a year. At that time, I was serving as deputy director of the JCOC program. JCOC 59 the following year would be my first as director.

As with almost everyone I met, Norma's political affiliation did not interest me; and at that time, I had no idea she was a close friend of Hillary's. I came to know this much later. She has been identified variously through her enormous contributions to Bill and Hillary Clinton and other Democratic candidates as a philanthropist, producer, self-employed writer, and businesswoman, and then finally as simply retired. At the time, I knew her to be a New York power player, and she typified the JCOC candidate we wanted. She was influential, had a large base, and could easily and effectively share her intimate military experience with a broad audience, many of whom had never had any firsthand experience with the military. On paper, she was an ideal candidate for the JCOC program.

I came to learn that Norma was a really big donor to the Clintons, but despite that, I liked her. She was energetic, gregarious, and a welcome addition to the group. Besides, even though I was sickened by the utter corruption of Bill and Hillary, I recognized that all their donors did not necessarily know them as I did.

Norma was one of the more exuberant JCOC participants. She threw herself heart and soul into the events of the week with a stamina that belied her sixty years. The days of JCOC were long and arduous. The daily events, usually beginning before 6 a.m. and ending late in the evening, were not for the faint of heart. There was a lot of physicality and little opportunity to rest. Norma kept right up. I positively enjoyed meeting her and participating with her in the 1995 JCOC program.

There had been a time shortly after the JCOC program ended when Norma had called around the Pentagon inviting JCOC folks to her big birthday celebration, I believe at her home in Connecticut. Some JCOC staff attended; I politely declined, and she graciously accepted that. Norma occasionally kept in touch following her participation in the JCOC, but it was sporadic and had long since fallen off by the fall of 1997.

In the fall of 1997, the surprising resurfacing of megadonor Norma Ketay Asnes occurred. Several weeks after the *Newsweek* article about Kathleen Willey appeared, Norma called me on my direct line at my desk in the Pentagon. How she got that number, I never found out, but I have a pretty fair idea of who provided it to her.

Norma was calling, she said, to invite me to her country house in Greenwich, Connecticut, for an upcoming weekend. Norma knew I worked at the Pentagon. She was calling the Pentagon, for Pete's sake. She also knew I lived within commuting distance of the Pentagon, not around the corner from her home in Connecticut. I knew she lived on Fifth Avenue in New York, and I also knew she had what she always referred to as her "house in the country" in Greenwich. If you live in Manhattan, apparently Connecticut is the country.

We had a pleasant conversation. If anything, I found the conversation a bit chummier and longer than our previous ones. It was also noteworthy that she seemed adamant and refused to take no for an answer. This was not like the birthday invitation at all, when she seemed fine that I had to regretfully decline. This call left me wondering what the invitation was really about. The timing was naturally suspect, and since I had come to know of her close relationship with Hillary, I knew to at least be on my guard. But my curiosity was aroused.

I had planned to be in New Jersey during that time anyway, so I thought I would see what Norma—and likely Hillary—was up to. Plus, I did have fond memories of Norma, so it might be fun to see her for a brief visit. I decided that weekend to make the short drive from Morris County, New Jersey, to Greenwich, a beautiful drive in the fall. Norma lived on Round Hill, a prominent address in Greenwich, and her lovely home was situated on eleven acres, enormous even by Greenwich standards.

Norma's "country house" was an older, sprawling structure festooned with all sorts of signs of autumn. The property was impeccably maintained, and the clapboard house, while quite large, exuded pure charm. I was greeted at the front door by an artful and colorful bounty of enormous gourds and pumpkins of various pedigrees, flanked by massive bunches of cornstalks. I later learned that everything in this colossal cornucopia had been grown on her property. It could not have been more charming. Nothing ominous here. So far, so good.

Norma welcomed me enthusiastically into her home, a little too enthusiastically considering we had never been close. I know this all sounds a little paranoid, but as the old saying goes, just because you're paranoid doesn't mean they're not out to get you. I decided, just to be safe, to eat or drink only what was served to others as well as me. For those who would find this melodramatic, I can only say we all form our impressions based on our framework of reference. Mine was clearly different than that of most others. I knew what unscrupulousness looked like; I knew what it could do. I lived in a world where quite impossibly I had learned that anything was possible.

I was escorted to the lovely room I had been assigned, and where my overnight bag had magically been deposited. My bag had been unpacked by someone, and I wondered if everyone else's bags were being unpacked for them, too. Whatever the person had been looking for would not have been found in my overnight bag. My oversized purse, on the other hand, was another story. It remained locked in my car all weekend. You cannot be too careful or trusting with these people. I'm not joking.

The weekend was a series of bizarre inner discussions with myself—silent, since I was never alone. It was like a cartoon in which a little devil is whispering in one ear and an angel in the other. The devil was persistently saying, "This is all Hillary and you're in big trouble. This could be your last day on earth, and you did see woods to the rear of the property." The angel was just as persistently arguing, "Don't be ridiculous; it's just Norma being Norma." This is what the Clintons and Clintonoids can do to you: make you more than a little paranoid. Trust me, the paranoia was not as crazy as it seems.

I know now which voice had it right. I might have been pushing up daisies in short order, but at least in a lovely enclave of homes in Connecticut. Of course, there is much to be said about the finality of being hit by a Mack truck, too—and we all encounter those trucks in traffic on a regular basis. I also believe that when my name became a household word twelve weeks later, the Clintonoids suddenly ran out of time and options. I know it sounds nuts, but you were not there.

Instead, this was phase one of what I came to refer to as the Charm Offensive. I'm not a betting person, but if I were, I'd bet Hillary rues the day she went the seductive route instead of the cleaner and quite final route when it came to not just me but Monica, too. It simply never occurred to her avarice-driven self that not everyone is seduced by money and power. That concept remains inconceivable to her.

Norma had arranged a dinner party "in my honor," making me even more curious. It was obvious what was going on. I had not heard from Norma in almost two years. We had hit it off during the JCOC, but as acquaintances, not as friends. Since our time with the JCOC, I had learned a lot more about Norma. She was a big, big FOB (friend of Bill's, or more accurately, friend of Hillary's). Much more so than I had originally realized. Remember, Kenneth Starr was after Bill, since Kathleen Willey had outed him, and Hillary knew that I knew a lot more than she wanted to be made public. On top of all of this, Monica Lewinsky was hovering. The Charm Offensive was all smiles and subtlety.

There were several people around the large table. I am certain I was the only non-card-carrying member of the Democratic Party in the room. To this day, I remember only one of the guests, the very friendly and gregarious Arthur Levitt, the chairman of the Securities and Exchange Commission, seated to my right. He was in fact pleasant company. I remember little else about the dinner, except Norma regaling us with her JCOC adventures as only Norma could. The best part was when she told us about making an arrested landing on an aircraft at sea, and about the catapult takeoff from the ship. That was the highlight of the dinner—or at least the only part of the conversation worth mentioning. Rich people can be as boring as anyone. Likely more boring than most.

Later, before we retired to our rooms, Norma invited me to chat in a cozy sitting room upstairs. While we were going in, the little voice in my head whispered the obvious: "Here it comes."

We started off with a little small talk about the JCOC and then it started, almost casually. Norma tentatively touched on the Clinton "loyalty" issue, and even quietly brought up "women" friends of the president. I listened, saying as little as possible. She spoke of my history with the Clintons, and my future. She reminded me how influential they were, how fortunate I was to have them in my corner.

Then it got a little spooky. Norma brought up my kids, asking how they were doing in college. The only thing is, I had zero recollection of ever having told her I had kids at all, let alone kids in college. Was this Hillary's research team's contribution to the sale in the form of a veiled threat? I convinced myself I was overreacting and hoped my sudden alarm was not showing on my face.

That night I went to bed thinking that if I had doubted there was an agenda before, I was certain now. I was on high alert for the rest of the weekend, but somehow managed to remain composed and seemingly unaffected. I played dumb and gave her no reason to believe her pals the Clintons had anything to worry about from me.

Norma stayed in touch over the next several weeks, just "checking in." Odd, but not really. The picture was becoming clearer and clearer. I had already been more than a little paranoid before the weekend at Norma's. The situation was starting to feel like a spider gathering flies to the web. The flies never know what hits them, and once ensnared, their fate is sealed. I had no doubt what I was.

In these little "Just checking in to see how you're doing" chats, the effort for us to be pals of a sort seemed front and center. She even asked at one point if I was happy where I was, if I was interested in other jobs, other locations, better opportunities. A pot of gold, perhaps? I didn't bite, saying all was good. I wondered if I was not the only one documenting conversations for private reasons.

In late October 1997, Norma called to invite me to an upcoming performance of the Capitol Steps, a political-satire group, at the Arena Stage in Washington, D.C. The performance was scheduled for November 12, and the invitation made me wonder what she was up to. Norma and I traveled in diametrically opposed circles. We were not pals. In fact, we were barely acquaintances. What was with this "Let's be buddies" attitude she had suddenly? Was Hillary pulling all these strings? Wasn't she usually more direct? And deadly efficient? And if Norma and Hillary did not achieve the desired result, what then?

I asked Monica if she would like to go with me to the performance. If she were with me, it would probably tip Norma's hand if in fact she was on a mission. But Monica was too wrapped up with all things Bill and had no interest. I think during this time, or right around this time, she was away on official travel, and in any case, if an event was not Bill-related, she had zero interest.

I went, but not because I had any interest in the production. I kept waiting for the shoe to drop, as I knew sooner or later it would. The event was leading to a climax of sorts, and I found myself once again tempting fate. But still it did not reach a climax. By this time, ample opportunity existed for Norma to show her hand less subtly.

In December, events with Monica, the president, and the Paula Jones lawsuit were starting to heat up. At the same time, the Charm Offensive escalated. Norma invited me to spend New Year's Eve with her at her Fifth Avenue apartment on Manhattan's Upper East Side. This was becoming just plain weird. This time, I graciously declined but thanked her profusely for the invitation. I was polite but firm and now very concerned. There was something wrong with this picture, and I had no doubt that Hillary was behind it.

Except, I made a mistake. I explained to Norma that I was going to be spending much of the week between Christmas and New Year's with my mom in New Jersey. The truth is, I was simply not up for a fun-filled week of escapism while events were heading toward a frightening day of reckoning. Norma persisted: "Well, of course, bring your mother. I would just love to meet her."

Seriously, bring my mother? Why on earth would Norma want my mother there? Where was this leading? My radar was at full attention at this point. Yet, a part of me refused to acknowledge the precarious position I was in. Norma was a great person, but Norma as a double agent seemed a stretch. Even without the fact that I was planning to go to the

OIC, the thought of New Year's Eve in New York with an apartment filled with Clinton supporters was unappealing at best.

But I could not help being curious, and knew there was a Clinton political agenda behind the invitation. I wondered when that agenda might finally show itself. And I was sure it would surface only in person. I also rationalized that my mother would probably enjoy the outing. Mom also has an incredible bullshit barometer. I was eager to hear her observations regarding the agenda lurking beneath the surface.

Mom knew, however, my revulsion toward the Clintons and my horror at what went on in the Clinton White House. She could not help but notice Norma's acute political intensity, and she mentioned that Norma seemed exceedingly politically active and an obviously dedicated Clinton supporter. Later she would say she had wondered why Norma had taken a seemingly sudden intense interest in me during that condensed period. She figured it out.

We arrived at Norma's, the doorman announced us, and up we went. The elevator opened into her beautiful and spacious apartment overlooking Central Park and the Metropolitan Museum of Art. The views were stunning, and Norma was her exuberant self, as gracious as could be and seemingly delighted that we had come. With everything that had been going on with *Newsweek* and the Paula Jones affidavits and Monica, I spent most of the evening anxiously waiting for the shoe to finally drop. And once again, it did not—at least not in any overt way.

Norma had arranged for a light buffet. There was another guest as well, an older woman whose name I can no longer remember. I knew she was not an assassin, but I had no idea how much else she knew or why she was there. The after-dark views out Norma's spectacular windows were beautiful. Lights sparkled like twinkling stars across Central Park. I noted that it did not appear that any of the windows opened, which reassured me as I envisioned the possibility of "accidentally on purpose" falling out of one.

I know, I understand; it all sounds a little too over the top. You had to be there knowing what I was about to do and what was already coming down on the Clintons. Involved in something like this with Hillary knowing I knew Monica and what was going on there, Hillary would have wanted to make sure I stayed out of it and kept my mouth shut. A little paranoia is not always a bad thing.

It was a lovely, quiet evening. We enjoyed nice conversation and a few drinks. It was a relaxed and quite comfortable time. Occasionally the conversation veered in questionable directions, such as when Norma started asking about my vision for my professional future and if New York appealed in that regard, or when she mentioned that the sky is the limit for someone like me. Friends in high places and so forth.

I was just beginning to believe this talk was as blatant as Norma's approach was going to get, when I went down a hallway in search of a powder room. Along the way I saw an open door leading to a room that was absolutely covered with all things Hillary. It showed the many faces of Hillary over the years, morphing from one iteration to the next—ever changing on the outside, with only the inside unfortunately remaining the same. On the walls and across every surface were images of Hillary, often with the seemingly never-changing Norma herself: framed and unframed photos, magazines and memorabilia. It was a veritable shrine to Hillary the brand, the first lady in name only, the future candidate in the making. To me, it was all too creepy, and I did not enter the room. It was all there to see right from the hallway. You simply could not miss it; this glance into the inner world of Norma was chilling. Was I supposed to see this? All the other doors were closed.

When I reflect on the time between October and the end of December 1997, I am convinced that Norma had been warned about me and had been tasked to fact-find. If she had a more specific mission, I am not exactly sure what it was. I am certain that starting up a pajama-party, girl-girl friendship was not the purpose.

The only thing I can come up with is perhaps Hillary thought I would "talk" to Norma and she could then report to Hillary. By then they all knew that I was up to no good. If they knew nothing else, they knew I had been quoted in *Newsweek* about Kathleen Willey. They also knew I was a friend of Monica's. That would have been enough for Hillary to dispatch

Norma to determine how dangerous I was going to be. She could then determine what needed to be done. Overly melodramatic? Again, if you believe that, you simply do not know these people.

In the end, I never gave Norma even the slightest hint of my intentions, so any reports back to Hillary would have been rather benign. When news of these visits hit the media, I was supposed to be seduced by this *Lifestyles of the Rich and Famous*–style full-court press. I suppose it is anyone's guess what the true motivation might have been. There were no overt suggestions of bribery. There were no obvious attempts to seduce me with material wealth on any level. I can see that as being beneath Norma's dignity. If a seduction was taking place, it was subtle—the suggestion that I would have support in any endeavor I might wish to pursue in or out of government. Even if there had been overt attempts to bribe me, my trust in the Clintons had long since fallen below zero. If the Clintons are anything, they are users who think nothing of tossing people to the curb once you have given them what they want.

Twelve days later, I would meet with the Office of the Independent Counsel for the first time. This was Kenneth Starr's investigation. Nine days after that, the shit would hit the fan when what I had done went public. I never heard from Norma again. Was Norma surprised on January 21, 1998, when my involvement in the Monica Lewinsky story hit the news? I rather doubt it.

Bruce Lindsey was Hillary's fixer in chief in addition to Bill's. When I first went to work in the Clinton White House, I worked for Bruce. He and Vince Foster were the two fixers Hillary most trusted. Bruce was the yin to Hillary's yang. Unlike Hillary, with her icy demeanor and frightening behavior, Bruce was hard not to like. He was soft-spoken and earnest, and had a disarming smile. They were polar opposites with the same goal, different yet complementary and both just as ruthless. I got along with Bruce quite well.

Just before being banished from the White House, I made a huge mistake. I met with Bruce to express my serious concerns about events in this White House. In retrospect, I don't know what I was thinking.

Approaching Bruce with my concerns about the Clintons was like going to a prison guard to complain about the room service. This dumb move marked the real beginning of my end. He listened at the time with an expressionless gaze. Looking back, I am convinced that Bruce was a good person, one who was as appalled as I was when I presented him with my concerns.

I ignored the fact that Bruce was first and foremost a Clinton operative—in fact *the* in-house operative. I chose not to believe this very nice guy was as dirty as the Clintons themselves. But nice guy Bruce was in on all of his bosses' dealings and had long since become a tenacious fixer who would do anything for them. He knew where all the bodies were buried, so to speak, and worked full-time in keeping them six feet under. It was a massive undertaking. He had long since abandoned a conscience in favor of the "Any means to an end" mentality. So, he eagerly lowered the boom on perceived Clinton enemies, with an "aw, shucks" smile. Always.

Looking back, I think Bruce believed I could be seduced into staying "on the reservation" with just a little effort. It was his idea to find someone close to me who could be used to keep me in line. After my *Newsweek* quote, Norma would have told Hillary all about me. I imagine that Bruce and Hillary together needed a hook, a person who could pull this off. Norma might well have been that person. This is speculation, but it makes sense.

If this sounds a little self-aggrandizing, understand something: nothing is too trivial to Hillary when it concerns covering up her and Bill's sleazy and often criminal actions. This is even truer concerning Bill's dangerous addiction. His sickness was the granddaddy of all scandals. His recklessness and his lack of concern for his position or his surroundings simply could not be allowed to surface. Nothing, no one, was too small or too insignificant to handle to ensure that none of his behavior saw the light of day in the public arena.

His behavior could easily have sunk not just his ship but, more important, Hillary's presidential aspirations; that simply could not be allowed to happen. This was always the one issue they could not sweep under the rug. Evidence of his sexual addiction had to be buried, and they absolutely had to find a way to win. Hillary always knew that if any issue was going to endanger their political viability, it was this one. As I've said, it was not a question of "Boys will be boys" or even just marital infidelity. It was a sickness, one so reckless as to jeopardize virtually everything.

I believe Norma's attempts were a soft-shoe effort to pull me back into the wonders of the Clinton administration. They were clumsy attempts to keep me in line, to keep a lid on me and make sure I kept my mouth shut. However, I believe there would not have been anything soft about what would surely have followed had I not become a household word days later. For those who would hoot in laughter, I would remind them that their personal interaction with the Clintons probably is nonexistent. Be thankful. I was not so fortunate.

Chapter 18

OFFICE OF THE
INDEPENDENT COUNSEL

I had made up my mind and set a date to go to the Office of the Independent Counsel. This was the office behind the investigation headed up by Kenneth Starr, popularly known as the Starr investigation, originally sanctioned to independently investigate the Whitewater land acquisition by the Clintons and two of their friends. As the investigation peeled off the layers of corruption surrounding the Clintons in Arkansas, however, the investigation grew.

I had struggled for months with how best to go public with the president's predatory sexual behavior. As I mentioned, during the fall of 1997 I realized that it had to be done. When I came to this conclusion it was like lifting a boulder off my shoulders. I felt a significant sense of relief. Making the decision and following through on it are two very different things.

After being hustled on New Year's Eve by Norma Asnes on behalf of Hillary, I set my date for Monday, January 12, 1998. Carved in stone, that was my D-Day. I set it almost two weeks in the future to give myself a little time to psychologically prepare. And I did.

On the Saturday and Sunday before January 12, I began to get cold feet. I knew the media would rip me to shreds. Do not let anyone kid you; facing that is not a pleasant experience. I also knew the Clinton slander machine was going to go full blast at me as well.

Monday came, and I was back to being absolutely determined. Or so I thought. I put in my normal day at work, then decided the best thing to do was call the OIC. At 9 p.m., I called and spoke to a prosecutor named Jackie Bennett. I was still a little nervous about what I was doing and at first refused to give my name.

I told him I had tape recordings of phone calls from a woman who'd had an affair with the president. I went on to tell him that this same woman lied about it in the Paula Jones case and was trying to get me to lie also. I further went on to say that there were people trying to get her a job to buy her silence. One of these people was the extremely well-known and politically powerful D.C. lawyer Vernon Jordan.

Bennett asked me a few questions, then I revealed who I was. I said something like, "You probably know me. This is Linda Tripp. I was a witness in the Vince Foster case."

I could feel the anxiety, excitement, and elevated enthusiasm over the phone. We talked for a few more minutes, and he asked me a few questions to verify who I was. I then agreed that someone from the OIC could come to my house that night to interview me.

When I hung up the phone, I thought I might melt into the floor. The relief, the release of tension and stress, was almost instantaneous. After all these many months, years even, I had found my outlet: powerful people who I just knew were going to believe me and bring the Clintons to account.

Around 11:30 p.m. or so, a van arrived in front of my house. Four men scrambled out and hurried up to my door. I wrote down their names. They were Jackie Bennett, the lawyer on the phone; Stephen (Steve) Binhak and Solomon (Sol) Wisenberg, two more lawyers with the OIC; and an FBI agent, Steve Irons.

The five of us talked for over two hours. Each of them politely and professionally questioned me, covering the same ground several times. I knew exactly what they were doing: objectively assessing my credibility. Any investigation of this kind of notoriety will receive dozens, if not hundreds, of crank calls from people claiming to have information. When you are dealing with potential criminal wrongdoing by a president, you'd better be careful.

They thanked me and left around 2 a.m. Being the experienced professionals that they were, I had no idea if they believed me. Before they left, we set up an opportunity to record Monica.

Monica and I had made a date to get together later that same day, January 13. We were to meet at the Ritz-Carlton in the afternoon for coffee.

I had intended to use my own recording equipment to record our conversation. Instead, FBI agents outfitted me with their equipment. This consisted of a microphone and high-tech recorder. The microphone would enable the FBI to listen in real time while we talked.

Monica and I met at the restaurant and found a table. She was more talkative than normal, which is saying something. On a good day, I could barely get a word in.

She started in right away coaching me on how to lie. Her lawyer—she told me this—had explained to her how to do it: just say things like "Not that I recall" and "Not that I remember"—lies that are almost impossible to prove.

Monica was doing this to get me to submit an affidavit to Paula Jones' lawyers. She wanted me to change my story about what had happened to Kathleen Willey.

By this time, I was starting to believe that Kathleen was telling the truth and that Bill Clinton had not just sexually harassed her but had criminally sexually assaulted her. Monica wanted me to commit perjury to protect him. While listening to her prattle on, knowing the FBI was listening in, I almost felt sorry for her. Her naïveté was about to catch up with her.

Unknown to me, while she was telling me these things, the microphone I was wearing malfunctioned. The agents who were listening could no longer hear us. Unaware of the problem, I saw two agents come into the restaurant and sit down at a nearby table.

Monica continued to explain to me what to put on an affidavit to provide cover for Bill Clinton. This subornation of perjury is a felony. It was also standard operating procedure in the Clinton White House. Of course, not being a lawyer, I did not realize that inducing someone, a subordinate, into committing perjury is at least as criminal as committing perjury yourself.

Toward the end of the perjury-coaching session, she even tried to tell me that the president did not consider falsifying a sworn statement as lying. To the best of my recollection, she said, "He thinks of it as simply being safe. Being smart and good for everybody."

I was almost sick to my stomach. Bill Clinton had so used, abused, and screwed up this immature girl, she was convinced that lying was not lying. It was simply being smart and safe. What she was admitting, and the tape was recording, was implicating him in a conspiracy to commit a felony. And, as an officer of the court, which Clinton was, he was conspiring to perpetrate a fraud on the court.

Monica left, and the two agents and I did also. They told me what had happened with the microphone and were enormously relieved to find that the tape recorder had gotten every word.

The next day, January 14, Monica brought to the Pentagon office further incriminating evidence. This time it was written evidence. She gave me a three-page document with more detailed points to make in an affidavit. This had to have been written by a lawyer, although I never found out which one. It was far too detailed and professional for flaky Monica to have produced.

Apparently, the lawyers were particularly concerned about what I had to say about Kathleen Willey. They told me to include statements such as "I never saw her go into or come out of the Oval Office," "I never saw the president behaving inappropriately with anyone," and "I now believe Mrs. Willey messed up her lipstick, hair, and blouse herself"—things like that to refute my earlier statements.

Oddly, despite the taping of my conversation with Monica and the affidavit bullet points, the OIC lawyers were still skeptical. They wanted something more solid, stronger proof that Monica had been sexually involved with Bill—that she was not indulging herself with a schoolgirl fantasy.

Monica and I had planned another get-together for lunch on Friday, January 15, at the Ritz-Carlton. The OIC named this Operation Prom Night.

My role was to get Monica there, and get her relaxed and talking. Considering I could almost never get her to shut up, mine was the easy part. We were in the lobby chatting for a short while when, suddenly, several FBI agents swept in. You can imagine the scene this made in the lobby of a five-star luxury hotel. The other people must have thought we were terrorists of some sort.

They hustled us up to the tenth floor, where OIC lawyers had two adjacent rooms. As soon as we arrived on the tenth floor, Monica flew into a rage directed at me. She realized she had been set up.

Steve Binhak took me alone into one room while Monica was taken into another. Binhak interviewed me until around 4 p.m. During those hours, I felt no elation whatsoever. I had just trapped a young girl who looked up to me. It sickened me. I also realized it had to be done. Possibly the most corrupt president in our history, a man who to this day should be a registered sex offender, had to be held to account, as did his enabling wife. But I also felt no pride in what I had done and the part I had played. In fact, I felt like I needed a shower.

EPILOGUE

by Dennis Carstens

Linda Tripp's input regarding her time working in the Clinton White House sadly must end here. *A Basket of Deplorables* is entirely based on what she personally saw and did, and her involvement with the disgraceful legacy of the Clintons. As she mentioned, this book came from a journal she was writing for her children and grandchildren. It is a look at the behind-the-scenes Clintons by someone who was there and had no interest in protecting them.

Linda's firsthand account ends here because, sadly, she passed away on April 8, 2020. Her death was sudden and surprising. She had been diagnosed with cancer on April 2, hospitalized the next day, and passed a few days later.

Unfortunately, she had been unable to finish her story. Although her role in the investigation was mostly complete when she went to the OIC, she would continue her involvement by appearing before a grand jury, giving depositions, and presenting affidavits. To stay out of prison, Monica would become the star witness of the OIC. What you have read to this point pretty much covers Linda's story.

Much of the rest of the story I have gleaned from Ken Starr's excellent, very readable book entitled *Contempt: A Memoir of the Clinton Investigation*. If you have not read this book, I strongly recommend that you do so. Unlike most books written by academics and journalists, Starr's account is well written and an easy read. To attempt reading almost every other book on this subject is like wading through molasses up to your waist.

Even worse, almost all of them are attempts to vindicate the Clintons and portray "poor Bill" as a victim.

When Monica was presented with the evidence of Bill Clinton's crimes and her involvement, she wisely insisted on having an attorney of her own. However, Monica's father, a successful surgeon in Los Angeles, foolishly sent a private attorney to Washington to represent her. He was a lawyer who primarily did medical malpractice lawsuits, not criminal defense. At the time, I was a practicing attorney myself, and I remember much of what happened and how this man embarrassed himself and the bar.

The medical malpractice lawyer was in ten feet over his head representing Monica. For the next several weeks, he managed to avoid a perfectly good immunity deal for his client while making a fool of himself. This seemed to be primarily so he could spend a lot of time in front of the TV cameras. This is a textbook case of how not to represent your client. He became a national joke among members of the criminal defense bar. Eventually he was fired, and the case proceeded.

Predictably, the Clintons, being who they are, and the media, being what they are, made Starr the focus. He was portrayed as a Republican hit man out to get poor little Bill Clinton. Judge Starr was a sanctimonious Bible thumper who was stuck in the sexual Stone Age, that he must be a Puritan for whom using the word "gosh" would be a mortal sin. You get the picture.

Unfortunately for the Clintons, this time their lies did not work. The Clinton cover-up machine was thrown into disarray by two occurrences. First, Bill was forced to give a deposition in the Paula Jones lawsuit against him. A deposition is testimony given that is sworn to under oath exactly as if someone is sitting in a witness chair in a courtroom. Being true to himself, Bill lied several times during his deposition, which is perjury—a crime punishable by prison. He denied ever having had any sexual relations with Monica. He even emphatically denied it on film, which was later shown many times on TV.

Second, in late July 1998, Monica, after signing an immunity agreement, turned over to Starr's investigators the infamous blue dress with the semen stain on it. A blood sample was taken from Bill Clinton on

August 3, and on August 17, the FBI reported its scientific conclusion: Bill Clinton was the source of the semen on the dress "to a reasonable degree of scientific certainty." DNA had finally caught the Clintons and their enablers in a web of perjury and subornation of perjury.

To their everlasting credit, Starr and his team of unbiased professionals in the OIC persevered. On September 9, 1998, the OIC delivered a 445-page referral—the Starr Report—to the House of Representatives' sergeant at arms. In it, the OIC detailed an eleven-count impeachment referral, which included ten counts of perjury and obstruction of justice. Count eleven was a detailed, fact-based list of the many times Bill Clinton had clearly abused the power of his office.

Two days later, an unredacted version was released on the internet. To make the report as factually based as possible, the OIC had included detailed accounts of the sex acts between Bill Clinton and Monica Lewinsky. This, of course, created a storm of protest among those who had spent months calling Starr a sanctimonious prude. The Democrats should rename themselves the Democratic Hypocrisy Party.

The House would vote two articles of impeachment to the Senate: one count of lying to a grand jury and one count of obstruction of justice. Fortunately for Bill Clinton, the Senate Democrats decided that perjury and obstruction of justice were not crimes when one of theirs commits them. Of course, they swiftly changed their minds when they impeached Donald Trump for acts that did not rise to the level of a crime. Bill's lawyers managed to make the trial about sex and marital infidelity and not criminal behavior. The Democrats jumped on this, and Bill Clinton, the second president in history to be impeached, was acquitted on February 12, 1999. Despite his clear and beyond-a-reasonable-doubt guilt, "Slick Willy" walked again. Poor little Billy. Once again, the victim.

LINDA'S LAST WORD

I should have known in the end that Bill Clinton would get away with it. I had held a ringside seat in the White House as the Clintons turned all that was good and decent into so much rubble. I saw firsthand how they operated, how "the politics of personal destruction" was orchestrated by the masters. I watched them destroy decent people simply for their own pleasure.

I should have known that even an impeachment could not bring him down. The Democrats willingly sold their souls by covering up for him: "Call it a personal marital problem." Apparently, none of them had ever read the articles of impeachment. He was not impeached for adultery. He was impeached for multiple felonies: perjury, suborning perjury, and actual obstruction of justice. These are real high crimes of which he was clearly guilty.

I should have known that there would be an unprecedented pardoning frenzy in the last moments of Bill's presidency, and particularly about the stunning caliber of those he pardoned and the money that changed hands. Among those pardoned was Marc Rich, the number-one tax cheat in the nation's history, who openly bribed the Clintons for a pardon; Rich had been on the FBI's Ten Most Wanted Fugitives List for years.

I should have known that White House heirlooms would walk out the door with the Clintons. The Clintons infamously, but of course "mistakenly," took $190,000 worth of White House items with them when they left. Things they didn't realize were not theirs—like furniture, tableware, silverware, expensive china, rugs, and a variety items of other items—managed to find their way into the moving vans "by mistake." And, once again, the Clintons' excellent legal talent allowed them to keep all but $120,000 of the items.

I should have known that Hillary would put up a "registry" of pricey gifts she needed her wealthy donors to pony up for as she temporarily exited the White House.

I should have known she would whine about being broke and practically impoverished when they left the White House, unable to pay all the mortgages on their various homes. They somehow had to get by on just $20 million for book deals. Poor Bill and Hillary. She got an astronomical advance for a book deal accepted minutes before she was sworn in as a newly minted senator. Doesn't your heart just bleed for them?

I should have known all along that virtually nothing could or would ever touch either one of them. It makes me very sad for all of us. Are we ever going to have real, equal justice in this country?

As author and commentator Dick Morris has so pithily put it, there were a "Saturday-Night Bill" and a "Sunday-Morning Bill." Sunday-Morning Bill knew the ludicrousness and the recklessness of his alter ego's choices. He, more than anyone, understood that he and Hillary would never survive politically if the unvarnished truth of Saturday-Night Bill's dark well of injudiciousness was ever to see the light of day. His political career and his presidency would be in jeopardy. More important, Hillary's political future would be dead in the water. The truth would never be allowed to surface—and in the end, quite luckily for both Saturday-Night and Sunday-Morning Bill and, of course, Hillary, it never did. They, along with Monica, were united in their talk of an "affair." Monica let Bill use her one last time, and she saved him in the end.

This misconception, and one that Andrew Morton perpetuated in his book about Monica, was the exact premise for the masterful spin that ultimately resulted in Bill Clinton's acquittal in the Senate. "It was an affair; everyone does it; it's no big deal; and it's between Clinton and his wife"— all statements having nothing to do with the unbearably harsh reality. To this day, the myth continues. It is still referred to as "The Lewinsky Affair" and likely always will be.

With a coordinated plan of lies, with false sworn affidavits, with everyone involved developing a curious case of mass amnesia, many were participating in what appeared to me to be a massive cover-up. And this includes Monica's mother, who knew it all, each excruciating detail, but inexplicably morphed into someone else entirely. Seemingly overnight, she became a fragile, confused, and severely befuddled damsel in distress when she appeared before the grand jury. The media ate it up. Starr was once again the bad guy. Now he was no longer just the sex police; he was also the bully. The portrayal worked. Starr had no choice but to prove that the under-oath statements in his report were lies. His report contained distasteful facts, absolutely none of which would have been necessary absent the campaign of lies orchestrated by the president and the first lady themselves.

There is no doubt in my mind that a lot of this offended Starr's personal sensibilities, as it might well have for any reasoning person. Somehow the perception of him, not the content of what transpired, became the most offensive. It should have offended all of us.

But his investigation was never about his personal sensibilities or even his personal value system. It was always about the rule of law. Now, twenty-two years later and with the benefit of twenty-twenty hindsight, I can see that a lot of Bill's behavior might have been received differently if the case were happening today. This is particularly so given the startling revelation regarding the former president recently: that Bill Clinton was happily aboard convicted sex offender Jeffrey Epstein's "Lolita Express" plane twenty-six times. And the Clintons, true to form, lied about this. It is possible that many are finally seeing the depravity for which Bill and Hillary Clinton have always been known by the people behind closed doors who gave their souls to protect them.

The worst of it all is that Bill Clinton's pattern has not changed. In 2020, it might be difficult to envision how someone in the public arena could bob and weave so effectively with those sorts of accusations surfacing. But as I've said, he has always been protected, first by those around him, including his wife, then by a compliant media who trivialized and made fun of the accusers, attacking their credibility and ultimately dismissing them as kooks or worse.

This is what we get when the media chooses to believe accusations aimed only at those of one political party. Now that 90 percent of the media has dropped all pretense of being objective, professionals have become unindicted coconspirators in endless cover-ups of politicians they prefer. The "women must be believed" pendulum has already swung back to provide cover for liberal Democrats.

That is why if Bill Clinton were confronted with the same sort of accusations today, the media would have a way of "not believing" once again. And that is the power of the Clinton machine.

That he did survive in 1998, and in spectacular fashion, is due to the transformative illusion the smoke and mirrors created. The Clintons achieved overwhelming success by couching "The Lewinsky Affair" as a matter of marital infidelity, a subject between a husband and a wife, having nothing to do with his position as president, and the business of no one other than the two of them. And above all, by saying that evil enemies in the "vast right-wing conspiracy" were behind all of it. This was the biggest magic act of all time, and Bill's reckless behavior was, once again, hidden from public view. At least most of it.

Sadly, in the end, this magic act meant that Bill's behavior would continue, and I am certain nothing much has changed all these years later. When his name was linked with the late and notorious Epstein's, regarding multiple jaunts to Epstein's "sex island," I just sighed. It was so eerily reminiscent of all those years ago, as the denials took wing and saved Bill from any real accountability or consequence. There he was, now claiming that his relationship with Epstein was aboveboard. That he was always surrounded by Secret Service, totally innocent of participation in Epstein's house of horrors. There was no guilt by association there. Nothing to see here, folks. Let's move on, again.

It was all so disgustingly familiar. Bill was always surrounded by Secret Service at the White House, too. It certainly never stopped him then. I can say without reservation that there are scores of women out there who could attest to this, and that sad situation continues because he has never been identified as the sexual predator he is. He is so far surviving this latest scandal with bells on, ever strengthening his feeling of omnipotence. I believe he himself is shocked at how wildly successful he has been. His success has to have exceeded even his expectations.

The intensity surrounding every cover-up was always a team effort— led by the chief protector, Hillary. It allowed him to continue to indulge his uncontrollable impulses and prey on a multitude of women, then go on to appear publicly as being selfless, dedicated, and steadfastly committed to the cause of women in general. The irony is rich but unknown to most people.

Back in the summer of 1997, Bill's team did what they had always done and effectively spun the ugliness away. When Bob Bennett, zealous if somewhat foolish advocate for his number-one client, brazenly uttered those richly ironic words, "Bill Clinton has done more for women than any other president in the history of this country," there was much he left out.